T0245645

MODERN NEW ZEALAND CRICKET GREATS

MODERN NEW ZEALAND CRICKET GREATS

From Stephen Fleming to Kane Williamson

BY DYLAN CLEAVER

mower

A catalogue record for this book is available from the National Library of New Zealand.

ISBN 978-1-77694-019-6

A Mower Book
Published in 2023 by Upstart Press Ltd
26 Greenpark Road
Penrose
Auckland 1061, New Zealand

Text © Dylan Cleaver 2023
The moral right of the author has been asserted.
Design and format © Upstart Press Ltd 2023

All rights reserved. No part of this publication may be reproduced or transmitted in any form or by any means, electronic or mechanical, including photocopying, recording, or any information storage and retrieval system, without permission in writing from the publisher.

Cover and text designed by CVD Ltd
Printed in China by Everbest Printing Ltd

To all those cricketers past and present whose skills have given me endless hours of watching pleasure, and to all those who have indulged my passion, especially Michelle, Liam and Olivia.

CONTENTS

CHAPTER 1

THE GOLDEN GENERATION

New Zealanders have just lived through the country's greatest era of cricket.

That's not a sentence that many brought up with a love of the great game in the 1990s thought they would read. In that decade, the national side took the gains made in the 1980s — primarily through the deeds of the great Sir Richard Hadlee and the burgeoning talent of Martin Crowe — and flubbed them away in a fog of amateur attitudes while the rest of the world, led by our neighbours across the Tasman Sea, took a more rigidly professional approach.

The green shoots of a recovery started to emerge under the increasingly sophisticated leadership of Stephen Fleming and, despite a significant dip as the 2000s gave way to the 2010s, truly took flight when Brendon McCullum and coach Mike Hesson created an environment where failure was accepted as long as it came with grass stains and skinned elbows. New Zealand started playing with a fearlessness combined with fun that we had never seen before on our cricket fields, particularly not in tests.

Four ICC tournament finals later, including a heartbreaking tie in the 2019 one-day final which was determined in England's favour by the short-lived boundary countback rule and a win in the inaugural World Test Championship, have surely cemented this era as New Zealand's greatest. Using test cricket as the most convenient yardstick, New Zealand's ascension to the inaugural World Test Championship would have seemed inconceivable to our grandparents and those before them.

It took New Zealand 45 tests to record their first victory, a 190-run win against the Everton Weekes-inspired West Indies at Eden Park in 1956. That happened to be the year the mighty Springboks toured New Zealand and the All Blacks ran out 3–1 winners, the first time the men from South Africa had been beaten in a test series since the 1890s. That series, played out in front of packed stadia and followed intently by a febrile public, gave the All Blacks a type of unofficial world championship status. It also ensured that our cricketers, despite that breakthrough victory, remained very much on the bottom bunk of the country's sporting affections.

New Zealanders loved their cricket but never developed a proficiency for it as they did with rugby. The reasons for this are many and varied, but some are more obvious than others.

New Zealand's wet springs and short summers, combined with the fact most of the grounds were dual-purpose rugby and cricket, meant ground conditions, and specifically pitch conditions, were rarely ideal. With a few outstanding exceptions such as Stewie Dempster, Martin Donnelly and Bert Sutcliffe, none of whom played in a New Zealand test win, we tended to produce batters who were high on grit and low on polish. Our seamers needed only to be naggingly accurate to be successful in domestic cricket, so bowlers with real pace, like Jack Cowie, were rarities.

There was no professional framework in the New Zealand game, as opposed to England's historic county championship, and although Australia's path to full professionalism was more potholed (Kerry Packer would reflect that cricket was the easiest sport to take from the establishment because 'nobody bothered to pay the players what they were worth'), their cricketers were better looked after on their long absences from work than New Zealand's ever were. That made it extremely difficult to keep good players in the summer sport.

In a similar vein, New Zealand's early- to mid-twentieth-century population was skewed rural, and it was much easier for farming folk to carve out time for rugby than it was for cricket.

All these factors gave rugby its pre-eminence and pushed cricket to the margins. This was true in a literal sense as well, with arenas that began as cricket grounds, such as Eden Park and Lancaster Park, becoming very much a rugby stadium first and a cricket ground second. (This is evident to this day with postage-stamp-sized straight boundaries at Eden Park provoking a mixture of mirth and disdain when games are broadcast around the world.)

New Zealand had just seven wins from the first 100 tests they played, the century coming up during a dull 0–0 drawn series in the West Indies in 1972. Well, to qualify that, the West Indies players and supporters found the series dreary; New Zealanders had a far more positive view of it from a distance thanks to the reports and subsequent tour book, *Caribbean Crusade*, penned by the country's most recognised cricket scribe, Don Cameron. He wrote:

'For 90 days the New Zealanders had battled through the heat and turmoil of what must be physically the hardest cricket tour in the world. They had started as nervously as any tyro putting his first tentative foot on a tightrope.

'There were several times when they teetered on the brink of collapse and fewer times when they marched sure-footedly onward. Yet they did not fall, they did not fail and the mere fact that they reached the end of the tour unbeaten was more a triumph than the record books could ever indicate.'

Cameron noted that 12 matches and 12 draws were hardly figures that suggest triumph, 'let alone moderate success'.

'Yet . . . it was a triumph for the New Zealanders — victory over their own failings, over hard and often harsh conditions, over the excruciatingly bad luck of losing all five test tosses, over all the ingredients that make a tour of the West Indies a physical and mental ordeal. A triumph gained simply because they, perhaps more than West Indies, [had] that one priceless thing that will never find a place in Wisden's records. Guts, spirit, morale, *esprit de corps* — call it what you will. The New Zealanders had it in ample measure.'

The New Zealanders had not given up, even when the odds appeared impossible. 'By refusing to yield they survived, sometimes bloodied, but never bowed. A triumph, yes. Modest by the standards of the harsh, hard world of international cricket, but still a victory that must hold a place of pride in a New Zealand cricket history that has not always been a saga of success in terms of tests won.'

There, in the opening pages of Cameron's account — the tour book was a vital connection between team and follower in the days before live broadcasts — the word 'triumph' is used five times to describe a tour in which they drew all five tests and the seven first-class matches. This is not to belittle the achievement, or Cameron's relentlessly positive framing of the expedition, but it does show how steeply expectations have risen in recent years, to the point where 2022's 0–0 draw in a two-test series in Pakistan, a notoriously difficult place to tour, was viewed as a minor disappointment.

The 1970s was a seminal decade for cricket, with the inaugural World Cup — still played in daylight with a red ball, whites and each innings lasting 60 overs — and Packer's rebellious coloured-clothing revolution, but pace of change in New Zealand was slower and more incremental. There were maiden test wins against a disbelieving Australia at Lancaster Park, thanks to twin centuries by Glenn Turner, and against England at the Basin Reserve, which owed much to the fast bowling of the two Richards, Collinge and Hadlee, combined with a substandard wicket. However, the most significant happening was the relaxation of residential rules for county cricket in 1968. The likes of Turner, Hadlee, Geoff Howarth, John Wright, John Parker and David O'Sullivan all took advantage of the rules around overseas players and enjoyed stints on the county circuit. They brought back to New Zealand domestic cricket some of the more professional attitudes and approaches to the game.

New Zealand's credibility took a great leap forward in the 1980s. This author was at the ground for the final day of the second test win of that decade, against India at the Basin Reserve. Although I'd been dragged along as an infant to matches before, this was the first test I can recall, with the four-pronged pace attack of Hadlee, Lance Cairns, Martin Snedden and Gary Troup defending 253 against a batting line-up that featured the great Sunil Gavaskar, Dilip Vengsarkar, Gundappa Viswanath, Kapil Dev and an 18-year-old Ravi Shastri who was batting No. 10. I can't recall a lot about the day except how crisp and magnificent the newly redeveloped Basin Reserve looked, how the crowd seemed momentarily lost for voice when a Snedden delivery tore the great Gavaskar's stumps asunder, and how a man in front of us kept informing one and all that the 'Indians are going to cruise this' even when they were eight down and 100 runs from victory.

I also remember the rift it caused between my late mother and Ngaio Primary School, which I attended for about 18 months. I'd either been spotted in the crowd by the TV cameras or one of my 'mates' had dobbed me in, but regardless of how I'd been rumbled, my teacher was not happy. I'm pleased to report that when Mrs Tarrant expressed her displeasure about my unscheduled day off, she was given a fearful upbraiding by my mother who reminded her that the school had recently organised a school-day outing for pupils who wanted to attend a Royal New Zealand Ballet performance of *The Nutcracker*. Attending a test-match thriller was, to her mind, just as valuable a 'cultural' experience. Well played!

Test victories throughout the decade were becoming more

regular, but they were still something to be cherished. That Basin day was New Zealand's 12th in 143 attempts. By the end of the decade, it had reached 27, with notable home-and-away series victories against the two countries we took most of our cricket cues from, England and Australia. The decade had also started with a bang, with a series victory over the mighty West Indies, but the umpiring controversies and subsequent churlish behaviour from the tourists had cast a shadow over that 'triumph'.

The 80s starred the aforementioned Hadlee and Crowe, but also a number of role players who could elevate their games to go toe to toe with the best, including openers Bruce Edgar and particularly Wright, middle-order stalwarts Jeff Crowe and Jeremy Coney, outstanding wicketkeeper and back-foot dasher Ian Smith, medium-pacers Lance Cairns and Ewen Chatfield, and spinners Stephen Boock and John Bracewell, the latter who played with a maniacal fast-bowler's edge.

The man who has rarely been given enough credit for New Zealand's evolution from minnow to respected opponent was Howarth, who captained the side from 1980 through to 1985. The Aucklander who would move to Northern Districts to advance his career was a fine strokeplayer whose form fell away alarmingly while he was in charge, but his captaincy remained top notch right until an end that he did not see coming. Howarth had played many seasons of county cricket for Surrey and instilled in the team the sense that they didn't have to take a backward step against anybody.

Writing in his book *Victorious 80s: A Celebration of New Zealand Cricket 1980–87*, journalist Peter Devlin had the following to say about Howarth, 'the player and captain who made that victory ride through the early eighties'.

'Howarth was just short of 29 years old when he first took up the reins, and he immediately instilled in his players that little extra: the determination to make the most of their talents.'

Devlin quoted Howarth's vice-captain, John Wright . . .

'From my point of view and since I started playing, Howarth was the first guy to work out how we should play the game. He had that little bit of arrogance and got through to the players that they were good enough as a team to compete on an equal level with any other test side.

'On the field he was tactically excellent, he knew his cricket. He got us so much better organised on tour, and although a lot of us had our own self-motivation, he was the one who saw that it was applied in the right way. I rate Geoffrey, and Hadlee, as the two who gave us the edge in so many of our matches.

'I don't think New Zealand or New Zealanders realised just how good Howarth was or the extent of his contribution to our standing on the test scene. He took us into a new world.'

Devlin regards Wright's comments as fulsome praise from 'a player who should know'.

'And he's right that Howarth's contributions were not saluted with much significance by leading administrators. He was allowed to slip out of sight and out of mind, even if in the end he had lost batting form, had eyesight problems, and difficulties with his county, Surrey. Compare, say, the exit of Greg Chappell, Dennis Lillee and Rod Marsh from the Australian team, the adulation, the exposure in their last test, and Howarth's departure was a miserable affair.'

New Zealand's fortunes didn't collapse with the departure of Howarth. Coney was an able replacement, but by the time the 90s picked up speed he too was gone, Hadlee was soon to retire and Martin Crowe, by far and away the best batter in the country, was struggling with injuries and, when available, seemed to be at constant war with the administrators and, by his own admission, himself.

Despite a rollicking ride to the semi-finals of the 1992 World Cup, jointly staged by Australia and New Zealand, the decade is regarded as a bleak one. Our neighbours to the west, flush with broadcasting cash, started to pull away from the rest of the world in terms of talent development, as their first-class competition, the Sheffield Shield, was regarded as vastly superior to all other domestic offerings, even the County Championship. Still, the sheer number of games being played now meant New Zealand kept picking up wins, often against more modest opposition as Sri Lanka (1982), Zimbabwe (1992) and Bangladesh (2000) had been awarded full-member nation status by the International Cricket Council, with varying degrees of success.

In 2002, in their 296th test, New Zealand raised a metaphorical bat for 50 test wins. Just 168 tests later, after beating Sri Lanka 2–0 at the end of the 2022–23 season, New Zealand has rocketed past the century and now has 112 wins after 464 tests.

Again, leaving out the short formats and using only the greatest form of the game as the yardstick, New Zealand had won 17 per cent of their tests up to 2002. In the past 20 years or so, New Zealand, now styled as the Black Caps, have won 36 per cent of their tests.

It would be clumsy, even deceptive mathematics, to call this twenty-first-century age of New Zealand cricket twice as good as all those who have come before, but a Golden Era? You bet it was, but don't be fooled into thinking the rise in fortunes has been linear.

In the period between Fleming and McCullum there were dark times. Coaches came and went; New Zealand Cricket toyed with Australian 'change-agents' to lead high-performance strategies and programmes; there was a poorly mishandled change of captaincy from Ross Taylor to McCullum that served to drive a wedge not only between two of New Zealand's best players but also encouraged ex-players, many of them carrying chips on their shoulder, to vent about New Zealand Cricket incompetencies.

It was an ugly time, and I had a ringside seat for it, at one stage being one of three bylines on a *New Zealand Herald* series of articles titled 'The Shame Game'.

It was really only the Black Caps' stunning, unbeaten run to the World Cup final in 2015 — highlighted by Grant Elliott hitting a six off the penultimate ball to beat his native South Africa in a semi-final at Eden Park — that rinsed away the angst and anger from that period.

While test matches are still considered by purists to be the yardstick by which a country's cricket health is measured and its gold standard, you cannot ignore the white-ball exploits, particularly as the new format on the block is now the most significant financial driver of the global player market.

At the time of writing, New Zealand had a positive winning record in T20 internationals and in 2021 made their first T20 World final, losing to Australia despite a brilliant 48-ball 85 from Kane Williamson. New Zealand has been at the vanguard of T20 innovation, with Brendon McCullum's astonishing 158 in the first Indian Premier League game setting that tournament alight and helping establish it almost instantly as one of the world's richest and most widely followed professional leagues in any sport.

The influx of money brought into the sport has been, on the whole, a positive, but it has also put New Zealand, with its tight player pool and small market, in a precarious position. NZC cannot compete with the bigger member boards in terms of what they can pay their players, so it has had to tread a fine line with the players' union — the New Zealand Cricket Players' Association — to create an environment where it can centrally contract its best players, while allowing them leave to pursue opportunities in franchise T20 leagues, particularly the monolithic IPL. It doesn't always work, and Trent Boult's recent rejection of his NZC contract has caused some consternation as he was still seen as a player with much to offer the international game. By and large, though, NZC's flexibility and cooperative relationship with the union has allowed it to maintain its best talent in the game for longer and enabled it to not just compete but thrive in an era where the Big Three — India, England and Australia — have got bigger and richer.

While the future of test cricket has been a regular topic of conversation for decades — in the digital era anybody would be laughed out of a room if they proposed a game that lasted five hours let alone days — the true pinch-point might be in one-day international cricket. Bilateral and tri-series ODIs used to work the financial levers of the sport, but they have become less and less attractive. Nevertheless, they still occupy an important part of the content churn, even if they're less likely to be remembered than tests and tournaments. New Zealand have been ever so slightly on the wrong side of the one-day international ledger after 804 games (to the end of the 2023 away series in Pakistan), winning 369 out of 804 matches, but the team is a regular presence at the back end of the ICC's showpiece World Cup, having made the semi-finals in 2007 and 2011 and the 2015 and 2019 finals. They were denied the 2019 final in excruciating circumstances when the game was tied after both the 50th over and the Super Over. Having conceded the trophy to England on boundary countback, the Gary Stead-coached side won global plaudits for the way they conducted themselves.

That has been part of the universal appeal of New Zealand cricket over the past decade: the sides are widely regarded to have gone about their cricket in the 'right way'. That's a nebulous concept, but following a morale-sapping innings defeat to South Africa in 2013, the first test after the controversial change in captaincy from Taylor to McCullum, the Black Caps' hierarchy gathered in a Cape Town hotel room to address the public's perception of the team. It was agreed that even if it wasn't for the fact they had been skittled for 45 after winning the toss and electing to bat, the New Zealand public no longer saw them as representative of the nation's best ideals. In fact, they saw them as overpaid, underperforming prima donnas.

Coach Hesson, McCullum and influential manager Mike Sandle determined that although their results might take some time to improve, there were immediate steps they could take to improve their image and processes. Immediately thrown out was sledging, the practice of trying to intimidate the opposition verbally, and over-the-top celebrations of wickets and milestones would also be tamped down. In the field, they would chase every ball to and beyond the boundary if necessary. They would remain uniformly positive and try to regain the childlike sense of joy that accompanied the pulling back of the curtains on a Saturday morning to be greeted by sunshine. Off the field, the task was even simpler: they would prepare well, be polite and approachable and wouldn't do anything to jeopardise the team's reputation or performance.

If you weren't prepared to buy into this ethos, you were gone.

The results gradually improved, but the on-field characteristics of the team were further streamlined in horrible circumstances during a test versus Pakistan in Sharjah, UAE, in late 2014. After the first day's play, which Pakistan dominated to the tune of 281 for 3, news filtered through that Australia opener Phillip Hughes had died. He had been on life support, having been felled by a bouncer in a freak incident during a Sheffield Shield game. The second day was called off and when play resumed on the third day, the appetite for competition between the two teams was minimal. Hesson read from a statement following the day's play.

'Today wasn't about cricket. Today was about supporting one of our fellow players and the players really struggled. There is no doubt about that. I think the key for us was just helping the individuals in the group.

'We were just trying to get through the day, to be fair. Just trying to get through the first session and helping each other get through it. And then we just moved on to the next one. We didn't think too far ahead. We weren't really conscious of performance today. We just were worried about looking after each other.'

What Hesson didn't mention was that they'd just about played the perfect day's cricket and would continue to do so throughout the test, turning it into an innings victory. A dark time provided a lightbulb moment. What Hesson and McCullum discovered was that if you played without the burden of consequence, if you stripped away the fear of failure, it enabled the team to play with free minds. All that nagging doubt that cricketers tend to take with them onto the field — 'a failure with the bat here and I could be gone'; 'a poor spell here and I might not get another bowl' — was lifted. The results were spectacular.

While the circumstances around that Sharjah test could never be replicated — nor would you ever want them to be — some of the principles learned could be baked into their style, like playing for the sake of playing, not for any predetermined outcomes.

McCullum's thoughts around on-field behaviour also crystallised in Sharjah, particularly around the issues of sledging and confrontation. There were no celebrations of batting milestones or wickets, no bowlers getting in the face of batsmen, no displays of petulance. They were just 11 cricketers trying to enjoy the sport for what it was — a game.

In an interview with the *New Zealand Herald* when he was announced as New Zealander of the Year for 2014, McCullum described the approach like this.

'We wanted to be known as a team that no matter what situation we were in, we were going to make it bloody tough for the opposition to beat us. They might beat us, and if they outplay us that's fine, but we're going to make it hard.'

He said they intended to play an attacking style of cricket: ' . . . in the field we're going to chase the ball to the boundary as hard as we can; you're going to see a team that works incredibly hard off the field; and you're going to see a team that's respectful and even-keeled in their emotions. You see that now with the way Kane Williamson and Ross Taylor celebrate hundreds compared to other teams around the world. Very rarely do we get into confrontations on the field. We want to be known as a team that respects the game, works hard and plays attacking and innovative cricket.'

The other element that fed into this rise in fortunes was an obvious one, but one that often goes wrong: picking the right players and giving them a fair opportunity. You can only play without fear, after all, if you are safe in the knowledge that a couple of failures won't see you expelled.

The last decade has seen New Zealand pick settled sides, often to the frustration of the public and media who want to see the next big thing given a chance, or an underperforming regular jettisoned. Some 39 players, from Shane Thomson (test number 169) to Mathew Sinclair (208) made their debuts in the grim 1990s. In the 10-plus years since the start of 2013, just 28 players have made their debut, and that is in a player environment made increasingly volatile by the lure of franchise T20 tournaments.

This stability has allowed players to flourish in the knowledge a singular failure will not be a final failure. Players have been given licence to display their myriad skills rather than focus on job security, which can lead to selfish, numbers-based decisions.

The team that made the World Test Championship final against India at Southampton in June 2021 was a great example of a team comfortable in their skins and full of trust in each other.

The eleven selected had, at the time, 610 caps between them, an average of 55.5 tests per player. Just 24 players in the history of New Zealand cricket had amassed 50 caps or more by 2021 and seven of them — Tom Latham, Ross Taylor, Williamson, BJ Watling, Tim Southee, Neil Wagner and Trent Boult — took the field at Hampshire's Rose Bowl. (This ground was chosen by the ICC because the world was still in the grips of the Covid-19 pandemic and the ground had a hotel on site, reducing the potential contact between players and infected members of the public.) Only Devon Conway in his third test and Kyle Jamieson in his eighth had fewer than 10 tests, but both had enjoyed spectacular starts to their career after long apprenticeships at first-class level.

This was a team that knew exactly how they wanted to play and had the utmost faith in each other to carry out their respective tasks. It was in all respects the crowning glory, the fruits of the labours of all who had contributed to this era of unprecedented success.

It was Taylor who hit the winning runs (read Chapter 9, Glory at the Rose Bowl, for more details) with a flinch down the wicket and a flick over square leg after getting the signal from his captain and non-striker Williamson that it was time to end it. Even accounting for the fact there was an element of predetermination about the shot — no matter where Mohammed Shami bowled it, Taylor was going to try to hit it for four — it was glorious, but it was what happened next that will be immortalised. These two brilliant, undemonstrative batters, numbers one and two in New Zealand's test run-scoring charts, stopped in mid-pitch for a hug, before walking off, arms around each other's shoulders.

If you want an illustration of New Zealand's greatest period of cricket in a single frame, that is your picture.

Now, on to the players who made it happen more than any others.

CHAPTER 2
MAKING THE CUT

The primary role of this book is to highlight the players who had contributed the most to New Zealand's rise and rise to something approaching powerhouse status.

The first job in preparation was to determine what constituted modern. I consider Shane Bond (2001–10) a modern player, for example, but my teenage son has no recollection of him playing for New Zealand — though he does have a couple of his playing shirts, gifted to me after I ghosted his autobiography.

The first decision was that it should be restricted to those who had played the bulk, if not all, of their international careers this century. The term 'the bulk' needed to be formalised, so I settled on this: they had to have debuted in the past 30 years, so 1993 was the debut cut-off; and the year 2000, Y2K, the twenty-first century, had to be closer to the start of their career than the end.

It's not perfect. Time is an abstract concept, but I'm comfortable with the idea that playing the bulk of your career in the newish millennium constitutes 'modern'. As it turned out, two players who played plenty of cricket in both the 90s and noughties made the cut, though the closest to miss out due to the 'bulk of' cut-off line, Nathan Astle, made it in by virtue of playing 774 more days in the 2000s than he did in the 1990s.

Whenever you come up with an arbitrary line, there will be fine players who fall just on the wrong side. There was a big part of me that considered shifting it just so I could fudge the numbers and consider including Dion Nash (1992–2002). Having said that, doing anything with numbers would be missing the point when it comes to Nash, whose importance to the Black Caps during a fallow part of their history was not measured by runs and wickets as much as it was by attitude: convincing those around him who might have had more natural talent — another abstract concept — that they were capable of mixing it with the best. In all likelihood, Nash would have missed the final cut anyway, because his body could only rarely keep pace with his mind, and he just didn't play enough cricket.

A more persuasive case could be made for Chris Cairns (1989– 2006). He made his debut in a different era, but his peak years, when he was by common consent the finest fast-bowling all-rounder in the world, coincided with the start, albeit faltering, of New Zealand's rise. You can't help but think that if his debut had occurred four or five years later, both he and the Black Caps would have benefited in the long run, but such was his prodigious talent he was thrust in, like Martin Crowe before him, when his mental faculties had not yet caught up with his preternatural physical gifts. Early Cairns showed flashes of the brilliance that would later become commonplace, but he lacked the mental strength to deal with the fluctuations of the international game. There is, however, a soap-opera element to Cairns' life that would have made for a compelling chapter. With his famous dad, the tragic death of his sister, his rebellious early years and contentious relationships with authority, failed marriages, allegations of match fixing and a subsequent successful defamation claim and perjury trial, Cairns was a headline generator. Even today, as a middle-aged man, he is still creating compelling copy as he recovers from a near-death brush with an aortic dissection, a spinal stroke and bowel cancer.

It was tempting to change my definition of 'modern' to squeeze the all-rounder in, but a debut in the 80s, no matter how misguided that initial selection might have been, stretches the word 'modern' beyond any credible start point.

Now that the publishers and I had settled on the timeframe, there were myriad complicating factors, most notably that in 2005 another international format, twenty20 internationals, joined tests and one-day internationals as part of the landscape, quickly morphing from a purist-prodding novelty to the automatic teller machine of cricket.

How, then, do you rate the exploits of those who played a limited or no role in this branch of cricket? The short answer is you can't penalise somebody for not playing a form of cricket that barely existed during their careers. You can, however, reward those who did play it very well. To put this in human terms, Astle is not penalised for playing just four T20Is, but Martin Guptill's record in the format gives his case more weight.

T20 has complicated matters, though. There's no doubt about that, and not just because some players in this book played far more of it than others. There's also the fact that traditional metrics, like averages and aggregates, don't translate very well to the format. T20 is a game dominated by key moments. It is not a sport that lends itself well to consistent narrative arcs but instead is marked by dramatic spikes. It is the only format where a quick-fire 14 off four deliveries might be more valuable than 60 off 50, for example, or where two dot balls delivered towards the end of the innings might have far more bearing on the result than a couple of wickets taken in the powerplay. Every time there is a player auction for the Indian Premier League there is always at least a couple of players who are bought for amounts that don't seem to reflect their ESPNcricinfo Statsguru pages, but that tournament is a data-rich environment, and owners and team managers are always looking for an edge and looking for those players that might not produce high volumes of runs or wickets but who generate match-altering plays.

Without access to that data, we, the public, still tend to view T20 through a traditional prism: who's scoring the most runs and who's taking wickets at a good economy rate? These are the players who we see as the most valuable, but Stephen Fleming, the outstandingly successful coach of the Chennai Super Kings, might have a completely different view.

The evolution of the shorter format continues apace, and while its importance is acknowledged and even celebrated, when assessing the players to come, it definitely takes up far less space and weight than the other two formats.

Speaking of weighting, tests still reign supreme to the author's eyes, and success in the five-day game means more than success in the white-ball formats. Everybody who made this imaginary 12-man squad played and enjoyed at least a modicum of success in test cricket, while one player did not play a single white-ball international. In other words, you could qualify as a one-format great as long as that format was test cricket. Maybe if somebody drags this book off some dusty bookshelf in the year 2080, that qualifier might seem counterintuitive — even a little bizarre. It is not beyond the realms of possibility that in a generation or two's time, test cricket and those who play it well might seem like a novelty.

Even now, the weighting of test cricket is based on old-world and intrinsic values; the extrinsic certainly favours the shortest format, which has had a massive impact in the new world.

And what of one-day cricket? Media mogul Kerry Packer supercharged the format with coloured clothing, white balls and matches played under lights as the grey 70s turned into the vivid 80s, but less than 50 years later the format is being written off in some quarters as tired and boring. Increasingly, it is being seen as the odd format out as the purists demand that the sanctity of tests stays intact, while franchise T20 tournaments continue to proliferate.

This book reflects the importance of 50-over cricket through this era and, indeed, New Zealand's cricket history. You can make an argument that the most important day in this country's cricket story came on 1 February 1981, when Greg Chappell instructed his younger brother Trevor to bowl the last ball of a tri-series one-day final to Brian McKechnie, the only ball he'd face in the match, underarm. That 'low' act, designed to deny McKechnie the opportunity to hit an improbable six to tie the match, ignited and re-engaged a latent fanbase that had become disillusioned with the boring test cricket played in this era. While one-day cricket's global pre-eminence is being tested, the format continues to have a special place in the hearts of New Zealanders.

White-ball cricket, particularly T20, has accelerated the development of new trends. For example, being a metronomically accurate bowler was once the gold standard of limited-overs bowling, but with batters more adept at accessing all parts of the ground and being more fearless in doing so, being able to mix and disguise different types of deliveries has become critical.

Strike rates have ballooned as batters become more focused on run rate than wicket preservation. This has even bled into red-ball cricket. It feels like it has reached its apotheosis with Bazball, the ultra-attacking test cricket played by England under Brendon McCullum, but who knows where the game will head — switch-hitting batters seems fanciful as we watch the game now, but in a few short years they might be commonplace. I can also see a day where bowlers, no matter how far down the order they bat, are expected to be proficient batters. The days of out-and-out rabbits à la Chris Martin seem numbered.

It feels important to mention that because it is possible to read some of the numbers beside these players and wonder what all the fuss is about. Nathan Astle springs immediately to mind. That ODI strike rate of 72.6 is nothing special, right? I mean Kane Williamson, not a noted power hitter, strikes at 81.

All I can say in response is that one-day cricket was different back then. It was really only the late-90s when scoring quickly in the power-play — the first 15 overs in those days — became commonplace, as strategy was typically loaded towards preserving wickets for hitting out in the death overs. Astle was a very, very good one-day player — a great in fact.

If you compare someone like Tim Southee's one-day economy rates to a Hadlee or Ewen Chatfield, they look garish by comparison, but again, a radically different game. Southee could actually be a glutton for punishment, with his role being to bowl in the overs where the batters are most likely to be attacking.

It's not to say Chatfield and particularly Hadlee couldn't have succeeded in the modern game. They most certainly could have, but they would have required a vastly different approach.

There were other questions to ponder.

How many should make the cut? Once the cut-off period was determined, my longlist stretched to 24, with eight 'definites', nine 'maybes' and seven 'long shots'. I considered an XI, a XII, a top 15 and even a top 20. Twelve seemed the most logical because of the cricketing connection to a team selection, which then led me to questioning whether it should be a genuine squad, with the right mix of batters, bowlers, all-rounders and a wicketkeeper, or just pick the best XII and be damned. As it was, the 'squad' is quite well balanced, though if it ever played, somebody who would be more comfortable in the middle order would probably be required to open.

There were other questions that hovered but were resolved.

With the increasing exposure of women's cricket, should I include some of New Zealand's most dominant female players, such as Sophie Devine or Suzy Bates? After considerable thought, the greats of the women's game feels like its own project, not an adjunct to this one.

Should players require a certain level of longevity?

This is one of the toughest things to consider, but in the end we decided that if they were considered great then they likely played enough, even injury-prone athletes like Bond.

Should performances below international level be considered, such as Andre Adams and Jeetan Patel, who have taken just short of 1400 wickets between them, most of them in county cricket?

No.

Is there room for those with 'one-off' moments of extreme heroism, like Grant Elliott in the semi-final of the 2015 World Cup, or Ajaz Patel who took 10 wickets at Wankhede Stadium, the beating heart of Mumbai, the city in which he was born and from where his family immigrated to New Zealand when he was eight years old?

They were lovely stories, both, but again it was a hard no.

Finally, and more trickily, how do you assess current potential for greatness? In four years' time, are readers going to be astonished not to find Kyle Jamieson, Devon Conway, Daryl Mitchell and Tom Blundell on the pages?

Possibly, but they haven't qualified as greats yet, so just like Cairns and Nash were cursed by starting a little early, they are cursed by starting a little late.

You might ask, is this all one man's opinion? The answer to that is no. The longlist was put in front of people whose opinion I value, including statistician extraordinaire Francis Payne. In the end there was broad consensus of all those I canvassed on 10 names, with the final two places fought out between Neil Wagner, Martin Guptill, Mark Richardson and Tom Latham.

Payne fought hard for Wagner and Richardson. While I agreed with the former, I couldn't elevate Richardson ahead of the other two. While I loved his rare qualities as a stubborn, skilful and wonderfully neurotic opener, with a relatively slim body of work nearly all confined to one format, his numbers had to explode off the page à la Bond, but they didn't quite do so.

The toughest decision came down to Guptill versus Latham.

As late as March 2023, I was having second thoughts, at one point emailing the publisher suggesting an 11th-hour switch-out. It just didn't make any sense to omit Guptill, who was a consistent match-winner in T20 and one-day sides during this period. I mean, he scored 547 runs at the 2015 World Cup, more than any other player. That doesn't happen by fluke. Latham, while a top-quality test opener and one-day keeper-batter, was more of a stabilising presence than dynamic, but as I continued to work my way through the players, it became more and more obvious there needed to be some compromise.

There was one other player who didn't generate as much buzz around my cricket 'advisers' as I thought was warranted. Kyle Mills played 231 times for New Zealand from 2001 to 2015 and took 327 all-format wickets. For context, that is more matches and wickets than either Bond or Wagner — in fact, he played well over three times as many matches for his country than the latter. Although Mills never quite cracked the test format — mainly because there were better options rather than any poor run of form on his part — he was a bona fide one-day great. Only Daniel Vettori has taken more than his 240 wickets in ODIs for New Zealand, yet he rarely, if ever, gets the plaudits he has earned. Why? The only argument that makes any sense was that he lacked a bit of 'X factor', a notoriously unreliable indicator of quality.

This feeds into a broader debate about what makes a great. As mentioned before when discussing Nash's charms, it can't just be determined on the strength of your Statsguru page, but you do need numbers that indicate proficiency.

In test cricket, average runs scored per innings and average runs conceded per wicket are the most-turned-to statistics, yet in white-ball cricket the value of 'averages' is being increasingly challenged. To that point, 'playing for your average' has become a modern cricket pejorative as it implies self above team. Strike rates — runs scored per 100 balls and balls bowled per wicket — are more valued, but even that is a simplistic representation of a player's worth. The data available to team analysts in this digital world is almost infinite. When an IPL franchise is considering spending millions of rupees on a player for a single tournament, they want to know everything, from information as basic as whether they prefer slow or quick pitches to as detailed as how quickly they score against right-arm around-the-wicket orthodox spinners.

We are not going to get that granular here, other than to say numbers have played a role in selection.

Ideally, you want a player with good numbers, who was or is a proven match-winner, who played a decent volume of matches, who is influential beyond his batting or bowling and who passes the eye test, the last being a notoriously fickle exam that differs from person to person.

Upon writing the player chapters, I noticed a few curiosities. Cricket in New Zealand has been an overwhelmingly white, middle-class sport, particularly in the big cities, though that is changing. Players like Dipak Patel, Jeetan Patel, Roneel Hira, Tarun Nethula, Jeet Raval, Ish Sodhi, Ajaz Patel and Rachin Ravindra — some born in India, some in New Zealand and one in Kenya — have all represented the Black Caps and there will no doubt be many more to come. In these pages there are two players who have proud connections to iwi (Shane Bond who is Ngāi Tahu, and Trent Boult who is affiliated to Ngāi Tahu, Ngāti Porou and Ngāi Te Rangi), and Luteru Ross Poutoa Lote Taylor, who is Samoan. BJ Watling and Neil Wagner were born in South Africa, the former in coastal Durban and the latter on the highveld of Pretoria. The faces of New Zealand cricket, small 'c', are changing.

In these pages there are players who were raised by single mums. One grew up on a farm. Just two went to private schools and even then, Tim Southee started at Whangarei Boys' High before taking a scholarship to King's College in Auckland. The biggest chunk went to single-sex state schools but four — Guptill, Bond, Fleming and Trent Boult — went to state co-educational high schools.

It was a timely reminder that no matter how far you think school and youth sport in this country is tilting towards the elite, money can't make you great. That requires something internal. Something impossible to buy.

In these pages, regardless of creed or class, are 12 modern New Zealand cricket greats. They are, in order of debut: Stephen Fleming, Nathan Astle, Daniel Vettori, Shane Bond, Brendon McCullum, Ross Taylor, Tim Southee, Martin Guptill, BJ Watling, Kane Williamson, Trent Boult and Neil Wagner. There's also Tom Latham, a 13th man if you like.

CHAPTER 3
STEPHEN FLEMING
(ONZM)

Debut: 1994							Last match: 2008
	Matches	Runs	Ave	S/R	100s	50s	Catches
Test:	111	7172	40.06	45.82	9	46	171
ODI:	280	8037	32.4	71.49	8	49	133
T20I:	5	110	22.0	129.41	-	-	2

Wins as captain: Tests 28 (win % 35), ODIs 98 (win % 44), T20Is 2 (win % 40)

Cards on the table. There was a point at the start of this project where I considered choosing only from players who debuted from 31 March 1998 onwards. In other words, they had to have debuted in the past 25 years. In some ways it might have tied a neater bow on it, but the more I thought about it, the more I came to realise that the key word in the title, the key word in the concept no less, was 'greats'. The word 'modern' was important but slightly more nebulous. I knew I had to find a place for Fleming because, to my mind, he was the starting point, the catalyst for this modern era. If winning the World Test Championship was Point B, you don't get there without starting somewhere, and the elegant left-hander was Point A. He was by no means a perfect cricketer, but he was the perfect man to lead New Zealand into a 'modern' era, a better era and, eventually, the greatest era.

Elegant and urbane, Stephen Fleming overcame a rocky start to his career to become one of the most respected captains of his generation.

By shortly after the turn of the new millennium — the Y2K one, not the technically correct one — Fleming was already New Zealand's most successful test captain. He didn't just represent the green shoots of recovery after the indignities of the early- to mid-1990s, but he was the root and stem for everything that came after.

Yet when it comes to assessing Fleming's career, there is an undeniable sense of something not quite finished; not so much underachievement as hard-to-define achievement. He was the almost-accidental captain who became an astute and sometimes brilliant leader, and the can't-miss batting prodigy, Martin Crowe's heir apparent no less, who never quite lived up to his promise. He was a giant of the New Zealand game, yet he has already in some respects become a footnote on the bold-type pages written by Brendon McCullum and Kane Williamson.

Is that last point unfair?

Absolutely.

One of the first things to know about Fleming is that he was raised by a single mum, Pauline, in the working-class suburbs of Christchurch. It is not important in any prurient sense, although there was still a stigma in polite society about solo motherhood when Fleming was born in 1973, but because it shaped a sense of responsibility that framed much of his career.

It first emerged in a cricketing sense when Fleming received and then turned down a Lord's scholarship in 1992, choosing instead to take up a hard-won position at teachers' college. That's not a decision most sports-mad teens make, but he'd seen his mum struggle in unfulfilling jobs to make a good life for him and wanted the security of a profession behind him should his cricket dream fail to materialise.

It also emerged from a puff of smoke in Paarl, South Africa in 1994 and the rubble of Karachi in 2002. There was a need to do the right thing, even if the right thing wasn't always the easiest thing.

It might have even been there in the 80s when, despite the overtures of powerhouse sports school Christchurch Boys' High, Fleming chose to stay local and attend Cashmere High, a state co-ed school that treated sport as part of the social fabric of the school more than a high-performance pathway. Fleming waltzed straight into the 1st XI in his third form, Year 9, and remained there, finding it no impediment to making Canterbury rep teams, his languid talent often seeing him play up an age group.

He slotted with similar ease into the Sydenham premiers as a 17-year-old. The club, which Fleming had belonged to since he was knee high to a grasshopper, had a reputation in Christchurch as being a tough team but not necessarily the most talented. When it could call upon the likes of Blair Hartland, Darrin Murray, Richard Petrie and Lee Germon, who would all play for their country, it was stretching things to call them a team of plucky scrappers.

As is so often the case with the ultra-talented, Fleming's club apprenticeship was short. He was instead playing and leading New Zealand youth teams and in the new year of 1992, when he was just 18, he made his first-class debut for Canterbury against Northern Districts in the pleasant surrounds of Seddon Park.

He made 0.

* * * * * * * *

Fleming finished that debut season with just 46 runs and an average of 11.5, which didn't scream 'future international'. There was something about him, though, that had been recognised early and never left him: time.

His technique was good. As a right-handed left-hander, he could veer towards the slightly loose and at times technically lazy, but

35

under the tutelage of Sydenham mentor Bob Carter, the principles of a solid defensive game were lurking in the background. Despite being tall for his age, Fleming never looked awkward at the crease and would use his height and long levers to play an expansive driving game. When his timing was on point, he made batting look so easy and effortless there were shades of a taller David Gower at work.

The following first-class season provided more evidence that it was just a matter of time before Fleming donned senior national colours. He scored 94 against Otago before Christmas, demonstrating an aversion for centuries he only rarely conquered, 73 against ND and a breakthrough century (118) against Wellington at Lancaster Park. He did that in front of New Zealand's brilliant Nos 3–4 combination Andrew Jones, who scored a match double of 77 and 86 not out, and Martin Crowe, who went even better and scored 152 and 137 not out. Fleming had just been appointed New Zealand Youth captain and it was already written that it wouldn't be long before he climbed into the senior ranks.

In winter 1993 he spent some months in the Northamptonshire academy set-up under the guidance of Carter and returned to New Zealand with mixed results. There was, however, another century, this one against ND, and with two three-figure scores behind him and a number of pleasant cameos, Fleming, a fortnight shy of his twenty-first birthday, was drafted into the New Zealand team to play India at Seddon Park. Fleming scored 16 in New Zealand's substandard first innings of 187, but facing a significant deficit and under pressure in the second, he batted with tremendous poise to put New Zealand in a position where it could not lose. A debut century seemed all but a formality until he pushed a little loosely at off-spinner Rajesh Chauhan and was caught at slip for 92. The man of the match award he picked up would have at least provided a little consolation.

(It is a purely hypothetical exercise, but you can speculate that if Fleming had crossed the 100 threshold in his first test, that may have become more habitual throughout his career. It is also worth noting that while New Zealand was rightly celebrating the emergence of its first bona fide young batting prodigy since Crowe, India's Sachin Tendulkar passed 2000 test runs in the same test and he is three weeks younger than Fleming.)

Two days later, in Napier, Fleming scored 90 on one-day international debut, sacrificing his wicket with a run-out in the final over. He became the first New Zealander to score a half-century on debut for New Zealand in an ODI since Vic Pollard in 1973. It was a heady start to his New Zealand career, one that guaranteed he would not only be selected for the tour to England in the winter but would be watched closely.

As it was, he flattered to deceive a little, being troubled by England's bevy of right-arm seamers coming around the wicket to him. He looked the part in scoring 54 at Trent Bridge and a nice double of 41 and 39 at Lord's without offering anything of real substance. That would come from Crowe who, on his final tour to England and nursing a chronic knee injury that severely limited his mobility, scored a brilliant century at the home of cricket and an even better one in tough conditions at Old Trafford.

New Zealand's next test assignment was their first to South Africa since the end of Apartheid and the republic's reintegration into the global sporting scene. It was a keenly awaited, long assignment that involved a three-test series split by a one-day tournament involving the hosts and New Zealand, Pakistan and Sri Lanka. The tour started brilliantly, with a convincing win in the first test at Wanderers, with Fleming scoring 48 in the first innings and his New Zealand Youth teammate Matthew Hart starring with a five-wicket haul as South Africa collapsed for 189 while chasing 327 to win.

It was to be the high point of the tour — well, on the field anyway.

This was a team in the midst of a long and ugly transition period. Barring Crowe, the stars of the 80s like Richard Hadlee, John Wright and Ian Smith had gone, while popular coach Warren Lees had been let go after an administrative bungle saw the team continue a tour to Sri Lanka despite being close to a deadly suicide bomb attack. Four players and the coach had returned home, and the team was split, in every sense. Geoff Howarth had been appointed coach in Lees' wake and Ken Rutherford was captain, a bold move considering the antipathy Crowe, their best player, had towards both. Right from the start there were whispered concerns about the rather laissez-faire approach to team and personal discipline.

Add to that the truth that a couple of the players seemed more interested in the social side of touring than the cricket and it was a powder keg waiting to explode, which it did rather spectacularly in the pleasant surrounds of Paarl.

Having lost all of their completed matches in the one-day tournament, New Zealand faced a Boland side in a warm-up match before the second test at Durban, but the conditions were so dangerous — future international umpire Marais Erasmus took 6 for 22 off his nine overs — that the match was abandoned after one day.

With free days in the offing and wives and partners arriving on tour, there was a party atmosphere that extended to a lunch gathering with the Boland players at a winery on what would have been day two. The party carried on back at the team hotel, and at various points in the day and night some players smoked marijuana. In the annals of 'Players Behaving Badly', this was silly rather than seditious, but there had already been concerns voiced about the slipping standards on the tour — according to Rutherford, manager Mike Sandlant had already called a team meeting to address these worries in no uncertain terms two days earlier — so it was clear there would be, at the very least, internal repercussions once word started filtering through the camp about what had taken place.

In *Balance of Power*, Fleming recalled the day after, where rain had forced the cancellation of practice and a team meeting was called instead.

'As it happened, [Dion] Nash was the first in, I was next and Matt Hart was the third to be interviewed. Nashy came back and said, "It's sweet, I've taken the rap, just deny everything," and I said, "Nah, you can't do that — we'll all stick together."

'So I went in and Mike Sandlant asked me if there was some marijuana smoked at the hotel. That was his next shock — he didn't know there had been some smoked earlier. I said, "Well, I didn't smoke at the hotel but I did at the winery, so yeah, I guess I was involved." He said he was disappointed but thanked me for being up front and said we'd talk later. Harty knew that Dion and I had both admitted it, so he went in there and put his hand up too.'

Three players — the youngest trio — had been in, and three players had admitted involvement. The 'investigators' broke for lunch. Following the adjournment, all the other players denied any involvement. Fleming, Nash and Hart were called back into a room and told they were being fined $250. Sandlant said he knew they weren't the only ones and that he appreciated their honesty, but there had to be a price to pay.

The tour continued and New Zealand kept playing poorly, although Fleming signed off the tests with a strong double of 79 and 53 in Cape Town. If he felt any sense of satisfaction about putting together his third and fourth test half-centuries, that dissipated quickly when he discovered that New Zealand Cricket, by now apprised of the Paarl incident, was launching its own kangaroo court. In what was a fairly shameful episode in the organisation's history, despite knowing that the group of 'perpetrators' went far wider than those who had owned up, NZC chose to suspend only Fleming, Hart and Nash, all of whom were seriously worried that their careers were over, and subject them to the usual talkback opprobrium.

In an unplanned and unscripted PR coup, however, Hart's mum Dot appeared on radio with the intention of defending her son and his two mates, but in the process informed the wider public that far more players were involved, as was at least one partner. In the space of one well-meaning call from a protective mother, the public mood changed. Fleming, Hart and Nash were by no means heroes, but curiously they were now seen as the only members of that touring squad to come out with their reputations enhanced. The jury remained out on the quality of their cricket, but at least they were honest!

Wrote Ken Rutherford in *A Hell of a Way to Make a Living*: 'In the end the three honest players were left high and dry by their teammates . . . to me the tour was irretrievable from that point. Fleming, Hart and Nash became very inward and although Nash flew home injured shortly afterward the other two almost totally ceased to contribute to the team. It certainly seemed they had lost respect for the other offenders and felt isolated.'

Fleming conceded that the incident changed him, and not necessarily for the better. An idealistic view of the world of professional sport was ushered out, and in its place pragmatism stepped in.

'I just knew that the Stephen Fleming standing there in Christchurch wasn't the same person as the one who left the dressing room after the third test at Cape Town,' he would write. 'I was hardened and I was more independent, realising that I had to look after number one. I became a lot more selfish about what I wanted to do, and it was almost, "The rest of you be damned." It was all about me for a while there. There was no team as such, and that was an indication of where the side was at during those years. It was full of individuals, so there was no such thing as a team culture.'

It would eventually be Fleming and a garrulous and dog-eared Australian coach called Steve Rixon who would start to chisel away at that era of selfishness, but it would get worse before it got better.

With Howarth, Sandlant and Rutherford all removed from their respective positions following the South African travesty, NZC appointed John F. Reid as caretaker coach during the ill-fated 1994–95 centenary season, then started afresh with Glenn Turner as coach and Gren Alabaster, a schoolteacher, as manager. One of Turner's first moves was to appoint Lee Germon, Fleming's Sydenham clubmate, as captain, despite him having never played a test. It was obvious and perhaps even understandable that they would try to inject some discipline into what had become a bit of a rabble, but all three possessed what might be described as a puritanical approach to cricket, and almost immediately some players began to chafe at the new strictures.

In tests, Fleming returned from his suspension and notched another half-century against the West Indies, and he finished the tumultuous 1994–95 summer with 66 against Sri Lanka in Dunedin. A monsoon-season tour to India was not fruitful, and neither was a one-off test at home against Pakistan to start the 95–96 summer. When Fleming ran himself out in laughable circumstances for 49 to start the series against Zimbabwe, it felt like he was determined to get in his own way of success — not even 84 in the next test could dampen that sense of underachievement. During the two-test tour to the West Indies, a tour marred by player unrest and the early departures of Chris Cairns and Adam Parore, he did manage an unbeaten half-century but could only watch on as his great mate Nathan Astle came into the side and did what he couldn't, scoring centuries in back-to-back tests. In Lahore, under new management, Fleming may well have reached a long-awaited century, but ran out of partners on 92 during a stunning win, and he could be forgiven for thinking something similar was on the cards when he was eighth man out for 67 at Rawalpindi.

In one-dayers it was a remarkably similar story, though he achieved a breakthrough of sorts on that awkward Caribbean tour, scoring an unbeaten 106 in a win at Port of Spain's bubbling Queen's Park Oval.

Still, when England arrived in the summer of 1996–97, despite his undeniable talent, Fleming was 23, had played 22 tests and 55 ODIs and had exactly one international century. He wasn't failing

41

by any stretch as he was averaging 36.8 in tests and 32 in ODIs, but his inability to play an innings of substance and genuine heft was becoming a talking point that he couldn't help but hear.

One test later he had his cherished ton, a cultured first-innings 129 in a test remembered for Astle and Danny Morrison's final-day rearguard. Two tests later, despite a double of 1 and 0 in an innings defeat at Wellington, he was captain.

Initially, it was through an injury picked up by Germon at the Basin Reserve, but word was already leaking that Rixon's lens was focused on the long term when he chose Fleming as his replacement for the final test, a four-wicket loss at Christchurch where the 23-year-old skipper did his best to marshal an attack spearheaded by an 18-year-old spinner called Daniel Vettori.

On the Sunday of the test, the tabloid *Sunday News*, working with a single-source tip-off and placing as much faith in a hunch as hard information, led the back page with a photo of the injured Germon visiting the players' dugout at Lancaster Park with the headline 'STUMPED!' It informed its readers that Adam Parore would almost certainly be reinstated as the test keeper and Fleming would continue as test captain in future series.

While Germon did return for the ODIs against England that followed, they were the final matches of his international career, as the Fleming–Rixon axis, complemented by former All Blacks captain and noted educator John Graham as manager, set about working to restore the country's lost cricketing lustre.

The cards almost immediately started falling in Fleming's favour, some through luck, some through good management. There was the emergence of Vettori, a world-class spinner, for one, as well as Astle, who might not have been the most cultured middle-order batter but was a tremendous athlete and possessed the right stuff between his ears to maximise his potential.

They were followed soon after by another Shirley product, Craig

McMillan, whose burgeoning talent was accompanied by the sort of braggadocio appreciated by Rixon.

Perhaps more than any other factor, however, was the reignition of Chris Cairns' career, although it was not without a false start or two. It was difficult to fathom, but Cairns had debuted in tests in the 80s — the 'Greatbatch' test at the WACA in 1989 — and in ODIs 18 months later, but a combination of injuries, turbulence in his off-field life and attitude had prevented him coming close to tapping out his extraordinary all-round talent.

Turner, who had clashed with Cairns regularly and intransigently, wrote scathingly of the player in *Lifting the Covers*, perhaps the most vituperative of that curiously bitter genre of New Zealand literature — the cricket biography.

'For Chris to face up to the stresses and strains of international cricket,' wrote Turner, 'is like asking an alcoholic to work in a [pub].' He noted that Cairns was rude and obnoxious, poorly organised and required anger management.

When Cairns caught a taxi home in a clearly inebriated state at 4 am in the middle of the innings defeat to England at the Basin Reserve, it was a crossroads. The official response was muddied and NZC, and Graham in particular, was left embarrassed. Cairns would be given no more chances and rather than sulk, it kick-started the best years of his career and provided a tremendous fillip for Fleming's nascent captaincy.

The other thing that helped tremendously was that Fleming started scoring consistently, if still a little frustratingly. He scored 50s in the first six tests of which he was in charge, the highest being 91 in the first innings against Australia at Brisbane. It wasn't the start of something big. Instead, he scored a duck in the second, failed twice at Perth and bagged a pair in Hobart. A one-off test against Zimbabwe at Auckland did not bring about a return to form, but a tour to Sri Lanka did, with a double of 78 and 174 not out in the first test at Colombo providing him with his second test century and first as skipper.

It took another 46 innings before he scored another, when he was one of four New Zealanders — Lou Vincent on debut, Astle and Parore were the others — to score a century at the WACA in Perth, with New Zealand almost pulling off a stunning series robbery of Australia, and probably would have with competent umpiring, after the first two tests were drawn.

Fleming would never have to wait for a century for as long again. At Kensington Oval, Barbados, he scored 130 to lead New Zealand to a test win that would turn into a first series win in the Caribbean. Back in Sri Lanka, he would defy Muttiah Muralitharan for a few minutes shy of eight hours on his way to an unbeaten 274 (following up with 69 not out in the second innings for a match aggregate of 343 without being dismissed). Pakistan were taken for 192 at Seddon Park in 2003, and the following year he put aside the disappointment of 97 at Headingley with 117 at Trent Bridge, a ground where he would later play three happy seasons for Nottinghamshire. Before the clock had ticked over to 2005, he had his second test double, a five-hour 202 in an innings victory in Chittagong, Bangladesh, passing Crowe's New Zealand record for test runs in the process.

Fleming had to wait a wee while for his ninth and final test century, a wait that included surgery to remove a benign tumour on his face, but it was worth it — a mammoth 262 on a flat deck at Newlands, Cape Town, not far from the place where he feared he had committed an act that had ended his career before it had really started.

* * * * * * * *

Batting was only ever part of the equation in the Fleming package. His pre-eminence owed more to his captaincy than prolific run-making. It might be a semantic exercise, but it actually owed more to his leadership than it did to his captaincy.

He led the team through some of the most volatile times in the country's cricket history. There was the debris and rancour left behind from the Howarth and Turner coaching eras, and the reimagining of how New Zealand should play (after decades of taking their lead from the English professional game, they adopted a far harder, Australian-type edge under Fleming and Rixon).

There was also volatility off the field, with the bomb blast of Karachi and the unrelated players' strike that followed closely on its heels.

Fleming was an experienced captain by the time he led his players to Pakistan in 2002, even if he was still in his twenties. Created by a bloody partition from India at the end of the British Raj in 1947, there was a frisson to touring Pakistan that couldn't be replicated elsewhere in the cricket-playing world.

New Zealand had been scheduled to tour for a three-test series in 2001, but it was cancelled due to security fears following the 9/11 terrorist attacks on the World Trade Center and Pentagon. As a replacement, a three-ODI, two-test tour was rearranged for the following year.

Under tight security, the three ODIs passed off without incident, unless you call stifling summer heat and an illness ravaging the camp — pretty much par for the course with subcontinental tours in those days — incidents. Pakistan won the three ODIs and the first test in Lahore was a bit of a joke, with Inzamam-ul-Haq's mammoth 329 bettering by 10 New Zealand's aggregate across two innings. The innings and 324-run margin, New Zealand's worst loss and the fifth-worst in history by any team, did not flatter the hosts.

On the morning of the second test in Karachi, a suicide bomber had targeted a bus that was full of French and German naval engineers working on two submarines. Some 14 people died, including 11 French.

Across the road at the Pearl Continental Hotel, the New Zealanders were getting ready to leave for the ground. They didn't know who the bomb was targeting or where it emanated from, they just knew that most of the windows from the front of their hotel had been blasted out and that there was carnage on the ground floor, with smoke, rubble and blood all featuring. Fleming, on the second and later of two buses to leave for the ground, was about to have breakfast when it hit. In the chaos and confusion, he feared it had been the New Zealanders' early bus that had been targeted. Reg Dickason, the team's security consultant, was urging everyone to 'get the f*** outside'. His very real fear, conditioned through experience, was the detonation of a follow-up device.

New Zealand Press Association's Mark Geenty, a long-time and very fine cricket writer, was on the tour. He recalled the scenes in a piece for Stuff.

'Players gathered by the pool, calling their loved ones in New Zealand. Sirens blared, amid chaotic scenes by the wreckage just around the corner, out of sight. One or two curious players took a peek but most stayed well away, avoiding any sights that might later haunt them. Everyone was safe but wanted out and manager Jeff Crowe, a good man for a crisis, soon confirmed the 7 pm flight to Singapore was booked. Tour over.

'I returned to my windowless room, crunched over the broken glass to the desk in the corner, got a dial-up connection with that melodic screech and filed some words. One preview of a career as a war correspondent was enough.

'Hours later, hundreds of armed police and soldiers lined the route to the airport as the bus completed an uneventful journey and delivered its shaken passengers. Watching some ashen-faced players swigging from a bottle of Montana's finest was one abiding memory of that journey.'

For Fleming, the trauma cut deep. For a few horrible minutes, he thought he had lost half 'his' squad. Out of curiosity, he had gone for a quick look to survey the damage and almost immediately wished he hadn't. It was no surprise, then, that he broke down in front of the media upon arrival back to New Zealand.

The players' strike was a very different sort of breakdown. It would take a book in itself to detail all the twists and turns, but the gist of it was that the players were right to demand a better and more coherent system of payment from a national body that was seeing more and more revenue through television and licensing deals. Where they were wrong was that their PR strategy of 'say nothing and let NZC come to us' gave the floor to NZC and alienated the players from the public, many of whom were still of the school who believed that pride in the silver fern on the chest was the only payment you needed to play for your country. With an effective front man in chief executive Martin Snedden, a former international himself, and communications professionals at his side, NZC worked the information vacuum extremely well, and public sentiment fell well and truly on the side of the establishment rather than the uprisers.

In hindsight, that's an overly simplistic and facile way of looking at it. The formation and early actions of the New Zealand Cricket Players' Association is one of the most important junctures not just in cricket's history here, but in the history of sport in New Zealand. It nevertheless took a toll on Fleming, whose staunch backing of the players' association despite being New Zealand's shop-window cricket-statesman got him offside with many of the game's leading administrators and public figures.

It was timely, then, that a few months later he was erasing memories of 'insubordination' with the innings of a lifetime.

* * * * * * * *

With many of the players in this book, the tendency is to brush over the relative flippancy of the white-ball formats.

With Fleming, you can't. He was a brilliant strategist in both long- and short-form cricket, but tactically, he may have been at his best leading in ODIs. Seldom did he get a big decision wrong.

In the foreword to Fleming's biography, Shane Warne, who

remained a good friend until his untimely death in Thailand aged just 52, wrote that 'he has the capacity both on the field and in the changing room to inspire his group of men with an astute cricketing brain in a way that is very refreshing.

'As an opponent, he has countless qualities, but most noticeable are his calmness, his ability to read a situation and his analysis of a player's strengths and weaknesses.'

Much like his test record, his eight ODI centuries against 49 half-centuries is kind of nuts and in no way indicative of just how good a batter he was, but let's face it, 57 plus-50 scores represents a hell of a career.

At his first World Cup on the subcontinent in 1996, he enjoyed a steady if not spectacular tournament, much like three years later in 1999 in the United Kingdom, his first as skipper. He marshalled an attack containing leading wicket-taker Geoff Allott superbly over those months but got it wrong at the toss in the semi-final. Choosing to bat, New Zealand posted a seemingly competitive 241 for 7 at Old Trafford, but the pitch flattened out into a perfect batting strip and Pakistan lost just the one wicket in chasing it down with time to spare. He did, however, have the consolation of remaining in England at the conclusion of the World Cup to lead New Zealand to a historic 2–1 test series win, still the only tour to see New Zealand win two tests in a series in the Mother Country.

The following year, New Zealand won its first and only major white-ball tournament, with Fleming, despite a modest output with the bat, hoisting the ICC Champions Trophy in Kenya thanks to a brilliant Cairns century in the final against India.

Three years later, back in Africa for the World Cup, Fleming scored 321 runs at an average of 45.9, the showpiece being a brilliant 134 not out to see his side past co-hosts South Africa at a fiery Wanderers Stadium. Batting with stunning control and no shortage of venom, he made a reworked target of 226 off just 39 overs seem like child's play, at one point hitting brilliant and bullish all-rounder Jacques Kallis for four boundaries in four balls. Bad luck, bad circumstance (New Zealand forfeited their game against eventual semi-finalists Kenya in Nairobi) and bad batting prevented them moving beyond the Super Six stage, but Fleming's century against the co-hosts remains a totemic reminder of the skipper's ability.

* * * * * * * *

Fleming's final test series as skipper was a drawn home series against Sri Lanka, the first-test victory marked by a minor controversy when the New Zealanders ran out Muralitharan as he went to congratulate Kumar Sangakkara on reaching a back-to-the-wall century. It was silly cricket by such an experienced player, but there was a level of cynicism to New Zealand's approach that was distasteful, with Brendon McCullum, later to be managed by Fleming, conceding later that he regretted taking the bails off and appealing. It did reflect a hard-headedness on Fleming's part, a willingness to push the imaginary 'line' that other New Zealanders might have backed away from. In a one-day series in Australia he copped a lot of criticism for gifting South Africa a bonus point in a tri-series by instructing his players to go slow when a victory was out of the question — a point that would help lock Australia out of their own finals.

In another incident, he blatantly targeted young and emotional South Africa captain Graeme Smith with a prolonged and manufactured verbal attack before the start of their innings during an otherwise unremembered bilateral ODI at Eden Park, calling him a time waster and a 'f***ing disgrace'. It seemed to work, however, as Smith fell for an unconvincing 15 off 33 balls and South Africa fell short of a revised target of 178 off 29 overs by three runs.

If there was a criticism of Fleming's reign, it's that in a bid to throw off the tag of passivity, they'd gone too far down the road of on-field aggression, which had also spilled into the domestic game with some unseemly results. Fleming's teams might not have gone down the route of 'mental disintegration' that Steve Waugh's Australians proudly did, but there was no question that they weren't interested in pursuing any Corinthian ideals either.

Even with the media, who mostly enjoyed Fleming's considered responses to enquiries, he could occasionally be prickly. Certainly, he was not averse to challenging those he disagreed with, something that most of those who have followed him would have their media minders do.

The end of Fleming's career wasn't as he had scripted.

He led the team to the World Cup in the Caribbean, his fourth tournament, with high expectations. Fleming batted well, scoring half-centuries in the elongated and atmosphere-free 'carnival' against Kenya, Canada and South Africa, an unbeaten ton against Bangladesh and a useful 45 against the hosts.

The semi-final, against Sri Lanka at Sabina Park, unfortunately came down to the toss. Sri Lanka won and batted on a flat pitch under blue skies. The cloud cover rolled in for the afternoon and New Zealand stood little chance, even less when their best player was dismissed for 1, trapped in front by a Lasith Malinga thunderbolt.

That was Fleming's last ODI. He had decided to quit the format, hand it over to Vettori, to prolong his career in tests. He wanted to keep leading in the five-day format, but the selectors decided a clean captaincy break was needed.

Without the captaincy, the drive quickly dissipated. He played on under Vettori for a year, but rather than draw the curtains after the 2008 tour to England as most expected, with the final test on his adopted home ground at Trent Bridge, he announced the 2007–08 home summer, which ended with a series against England, would be his swansong.

There was something beautifully apt about his final test. In the utilitarian environment of McLean Park, Napier, Fleming finished with 59 and 66, his final half-century — the 46th of his career —

and pushed his career average above 40 by the barest of margins. It dropped his conversion rate from 50s to 100s to 16 per cent. Of those who have scored 5000 test runs, only Arjuna Ranatunga and Mark Boucher have failed to turn 50s into 100s at a greater rate.

These were all things that mattered more to statisticians than the man himself.

Fleming had seen the emergence of a new form of the game and recognised quickly the potential it held. Captaining New Zealand in its first T20I against Australia at Eden Park, he went along for the festival and instead saw the future.

'What made me raise my eyebrows was how the crowd treated the game,' he said in Brendon McCullum's *Inside Twenty20*. 'They were into it and desperately wanted us to win. It was not a situation where you could slack off and say, "Well it's only Twenty20."

'That might have come as a surprise to a few of us.'

What shouldn't have come as a surprise is that Fleming got deep into the weeds of the format earlier than most. His playing days might have come too late to sustain a long career as a franchise player, but he quickly established himself as one of the most successful and sought-after coaches in the game, with his Chennai Super Kings having won the Indian Premier League four times.

His cricket story is still being written.

CHAPTER 4
NATHAN ASTLE
(MNZM)

Debit: 1995							Last match: 2007
BATTING	Matches	Runs	Ave	S/R	100s	50s	Catches
Test:	81	4702	37.02	49.6	11	24	70
ODI:	223	7090	34.92	72.6	16	41	83
T20I:	4	74	24.66	110.4	-	-	3

BOWLING	Matches	Wickets	Ave	Economy	5w
Test:	81	51	42.01	2.26	-
ODI:	223	99	38.47	4.71	-
T20I:	4	4	12.5	7.31	-

Former England opener, coach, commentator and raconteur David Lloyd was once chewing the fat with a few of his reporting compatriots when the name Nathan Astle came up. Legend has it that he muttered words to the effect that if Astle was an international cricketer, then 'my arse is a fire engine'.

Turns out that Lloyd, known as Bumble and a beloved if occasionally hapless figure in cricket circles, was in this case as good a judge of a cricketer as Dick Rowe, the man who turned down the Beatles, was of popular music.

Astle wasn't just an international cricketer, but he was arguably the first great New Zealand cricketer identified with the twenty-first century. While his great friend and former housemate Stephen Fleming might have something to say about that, Astle's game reached a higher platform, particularly in test cricket, a little more rapidly than Fleming's, even if he did come onto the scene later and with far less fanfare.

In fact, Astle owed his selection in large part to his fellow Cantabrian. Were it not for Fleming's honesty over his injudicious use of pot on the ill-fated tour to South Africa in 1994, Astle might not have got an opportunity so soon. Once he did get his chance, he took it as if he was born onto the big stage, which runs counter to his personality in most respects.

Astle once played an innings of such incandescent brilliance that they turned it into a DVD — *Kiwi Master Blaster*. And if a DVD sounds like a piece of old-school technology, it fits, because Astle is an old-school sort of guy.

The batting all-rounder liked to play cricket, but he never did like to talk about it all that much.

'Nath would never offer advice. But if you approached him he was happy to share his thoughts and they were usually very sound . . . [he] was one of those guys who would hardly say anything but when he did everyone stopped in their tracks, jaws dropping, and waited to hear every word that came out,' his long-time teammate Daniel Vettori would write.

Astle seemed embarrassed by the trappings that came with being an international sportsman. Allergic to the spotlight, he has also become something of an enigma, eschewing the usual broadcast and punditry trappings of a post-playing existence to settle into family life in his hometown of Christchurch.

It's almost like he wants to be forgotten, which is difficult when he provided the public with so many memorable moments.

* * * * * * * *

The best place to start an essay about Nathan John Astle is at the end; the end of his international cricket days, at least. It's not because it's a huge hornet's nest of controversy that requires forensic re-examination. It doesn't fit into the tabloid mantra of 'if it bleeds, it leads', though it was a surprise to learn that Astle had emotions like the rest of us.

The end is the best place to start because it opened a previously shut window and allowed us to learn a lot about the way Astle operated, about what drove him to success and, eventually, what drove him from the game.

Coach at the time John Bracewell was conveniently cast as the villain in the Astle endgame, and while there are no doubt things he could have and possibly should have done differently to keep one of his most important pieces through to at least the 2007 World Cup, there was something more elemental than a coach and player not being on the same page. It was a simple equation really: when it started to become unclear to Astle if his game was what the selectors were looking for, it was time for him to leave.

In *Nathan Astle*, a book that eschews the traditional pun-heavy title, the eponymous subject wrote: 'You don't make a decision lightly to give up something that has been your work, your life, and your passion for more than a decade. My decision to retire from international cricket after our one-day win over England in Adelaide in January [2007], all started, I believe, 15 months earlier, when I was dropped from the Black Caps.

'From then on — from when I got back into the team permanently against the West Indies in February 2006 — for some reason the enjoyment just wasn't there, even though we were doing well and I was scoring runs.

'I just couldn't find the satisfaction that had always been there in the past when the team was doing well and I was doing well. That was when I started to think, "Hang on, this is not quite right".'

That feeling became more acute to the point where in the middle of an ODI series, and although it became public in the immediate aftermath of a Jacob Oram-inspired win against England, Astle had decided a couple of days before that match that he would suit up one last time and catch the next plane back to Christchurch.

He hadn't been batting particularly well. He scored 1 in his final knock in Adelaide and in four of his previous six ODI innings he'd failed to leave a single scratch on his scoresheet. Astle could have these little streaks of futility — he scored 19 ducks in his ODI career alone, so he wasn't immune to falling to a good one early — but he always came out the other side. He no doubt would have this time too, but he'd made up his mind.

'When Nathan said, "Mate I'm done", to even say, "Are you sure?" would be almost a slap in the face for a guy who is so sincere,' Fleming said at the time. 'To me, he was gone . . . He's not the sort of person who was looking for a pat on the back, to be told, "Come on mate, we'll get through this week first", or stuff like that. It's not what makes him tick.'

Remember, this was also World Cup year, and that tournament was one that New Zealand Cricket under Bracewell had earmarked as one they could give a really good shake. Astle was a big part of those plans, so there were discussions as to what they could do to keep him around. The team by now had moved to Perth to prepare for their next game and overtures were made to try to convince him to stay on, including letting him leave the tour and return home to clear his head before coming back for the Chappell–Hadlee series at home later in the summer and a final World Cup tilt.

Astle appreciated the effort and the sentiment, but his internal pros list was far too short and his cons far too long. By that stage he resented having to go to team meetings and couldn't rustle up the motivation to train or practise in a manner befitting his status as one of the best ODI players in the world, so he rejected all the schemes.

That he didn't buckle and stay on for an extra few months didn't surprise anybody who knew him well.

Astle wasn't one for turning.

* * * * * * * *

Astle was born in Christchurch in September 1971, and he was no ordinary child, having been born with an extra thumb on his right hand. The one closest to his index finger was removed and the remaining one only moves from the base. Given that Astle is right-handed, you might think it would be an impediment to a life in sports that require a lot of handling, but the minor deformity didn't get in the way of his table tennis, football or cricket, the three sports for which he showed the most aptitude. The Astles were a sporting family, with sister Lisa playing for the White Ferns in 1993 and brother Daniel representing New Zealand at table tennis.

Astle probably showed more promise as an attacking midfielder on the football fields of Christchurch when he was at primary and intermediate school, but although he was not the prettiest cricketer at the crease, his incredible eye–hand coordination soon saw him recognised in the cricket circles as one to keep a watching brief on.

There's an old line about New Zealand's three biggest cities that has enough truth about it to stand the test of time. It goes something like: In Auckland they ask you where you live, in Wellington they ask you where you work and in Christchurch they ask you where you went to school.

Curious then that of the five major cricketers to emerge out of Christchurch in this era, none went to what you might describe as the major cricket schools. Shane Bond and Andrew Caddick, who would take 234 test wickets for England, went to Papanui High School, Stephen Fleming to Cashmere High and Craig McMillan and Astle went to Shirley Boys' High.

At Shirley BHS, Astle made the 1st XI in his first year and he and future Black Cap and national coach Gary Stead formed a potent top-order duo. They were playing senior cricket while they were still at school. Astle's approach to batting as a youth player was not dissimilar to how he would bat for the rest of his life. If asked to explain it, he'd eschew the subtleties of the coaching manual and opt for: 'See the ball, hit the ball.'

He scored a truckload of runs and in youth cricket had the useful habit of turning starts into centuries. There might have been more effortlessly talented players than him on the age-group scene — look no further than Fleming — but none that appeared to be as relentlessly capable of scoring centuries. He was rumoured to have racked up 25 three-figure scores across school and rep cricket before he had turned 20, maybe not in the Kane Williamson class, who was said to have accumulated 40 by the time he left school, but pretty impressive nonetheless.

By the 1991–92 season Astle had progressed from his East Christchurch-Shirley club into the Canterbury senior set-up, but runs did not come easily in his first few first-class campaigns. If anything, he was earning a reputation more for his miserly performances with the ball, particularly in one-day cricket. After 15 matches and three first-class campaigns, Astle had not yet scored a century and had passed 50 only twice.

The concerns some coaches in the youth and national set-up had about some technical shortcomings Astle possessed seemed to be manifesting in domestic cricket, but in the 1994–95 season, the right-hander's fortunes changed — and changed in a hurry. He went quickly from being viewed as a more-than-handy domestic journeyman to a Black Cap.

He started that season's campaign with 96 and 24 against Auckland, followed it up with a duck, three wickets and 175 against Northern Districts, and scored an unbeaten 59 for the unfortunately named Sir Ron Brierley XI against the touring West Indians. Next thing you knew — thanks in large part to Fleming, Matthew Hart and Dion Nash being unavailable through suspension — he was playing for New Zealand in a rain-affected one-dayer against the same team at Eden Park. Batting at No. 6, Astle scored a handy 25 from 23 balls, and bowled three expensive overs against a rampant Brian Lara.

In his fourth ODI, against Sri Lanka at Seddon Park, 'fortuitous' circumstances saw Astle promoted to opener. Mark Greatbatch had suffered a back injury after the first ODI and Astle, who was in the squad but had not played that game, came in as a direct replacement, so as not to disrupt the rest of the order.

He scored 95. Greatbatch came back for the third ODI and Astle went to No. 3. Despite having to that point never occupied a top-order role for Canterbury, with a few exceptions he batted in the top three for the remainder of his career, the vast majority of those as an opener who specialised in bludgeoning the new ball, then picking off the ones and twos when the field dispersed.

In his ninth match he scored 114 against India at Nagpur. It would be the first of 16 ODI tons, a then-record for New Zealand.

* * * * * * * *

Astle's test debut came a year after his ODI bow.

In a low-key, frustratingly dull 0–0 home series against a competitive, but limited, Zimbabwe, Astle made a couple of minor contributions. On his first test tour, however, a 0–1 loss in the West Indies, he announced himself with back-to-back centuries. The first, 125, came after a first-innings 54 at historic Kensington Oval in Bridgetown, Barbados. It came in a heavy defeat and started another type of trend: Astle would in some ways be New Zealand's patron saint of lost test causes over the next decade.

In his next innings he scored 103 at the Antigua Recreation Ground in St John's — a patch of grass famously next to a prison that was renowned for high-volume run-scoring, with Brian Lara having totted up world-record scores of 375 and 400 not out at the ground, and the mercurial Chris Gayle also scored a triple there. While he fell well short of these marks on what was, behind the scenes, a desperately unhappy tour — more colourful reports painted a picture of near-mutiny against the leadership of coach Glenn Turner, manager Gren Alabaster and captain Lee Germon — Astle had locked down his place as a middle-order linchpin for the foreseeable future.

Following a fruitless tour to Pakistan, where he picked up the first of his 51 test wickets but few runs, England arrived in the summer of 1996–97, and in the first test Astle pulled off one of the great lost-cause escapes in history.

Having watched Fleming finally get off his test-century *schneid* in the first innings at Eden Park, New Zealand was still staring down the barrel having conceded a lead of 131 and finding themselves inexplicably at 105 for 8 at lunch on the final day, with Astle on 7 and Simon Doull yet to score. There were only a couple of thousand people lolling around in the sweltering stands in that concrete jungle on that Tuesday, there to witness what the *New Zealand Herald* hyperbolically described as 'suicide disguised as cricket'. It wasn't hara-kiri, but it was truly awful, best exemplified by Adam Parore, a wicketkeeper batting at No. 3 to accommodate another wicketkeeper as captain, first running his skipper out in brazen fashion and then getting himself stumped as lunch approached. No wonder, when the camera later panned to Germon, the skipper, he looked to be caught somewhere between anger, confusion and emptiness.

Doull hit away merrily for 26 when play resumed after the luncheon adjournment, but when he departed there was the best part of three and a half hours left, a lead of 11 and just Astle and, less convincingly, No. 11 Danny Morrison between the home side and ignominy. By tea, with Morrison defying expectations and limiting his usual expansive but hapless repertoire to the forward defence and the nudge, they were 76 ahead. With Eden Park's short boundaries and England's line-up containing powerful hitters like Alec Stewart,

Nick Knight and Craig White, New Zealand was still close to an hour from safety, but there was at least some hope.

Over by over they crawled to safety and when Astle drove powerfully through the covers to bring up his third test century, stumps were drawn. It was masterful defiance, though Morrison, probably rightly, got most of the headlines. 'I rate myself as an underachiever with the bat,' Morrison said in the wash-up, 'and here was my chance to bore the tits off everyone.'

He would not get another chance. He was dropped before the second test — the improbable 10th-wicket partnership and subsequent escape his unlikely coda to international cricket. Astle, on the other hand, would get plenty more opportunities.

He was a constant presence in the middle order and scored spectacularly but not always consistently. He batted well in partnership with McMillan (the pair from the same school would become brothers-in-law when they married twins) to score a ton at Old Trafford on the successful 1999 tour to England and recorded another couple of centuries against Zimbabwe — New Zealand played a lot of cricket against Zimbabwe in the 90s — but it was his seventh and eighth three-figure scores that captured significant attention.

Century number seven came on a fearsomely quick WACA wicket at Perth in a test New Zealand came close to winning. Only four Kiwis reached double figures in the first innings, but all went on to notch centuries, including one on debut for Lou Vincent, one to Fleming and another to Parore.

Astle's unbeaten 156 was, however, the best of the lot, punctuated by booming cover drives and savage hooks and pulls. Glenn McGrath might have set the record for the most disgruntled teapots in an innings as he tried and failed to dislodge Astle.

Two tests later, as 2001 ticked over to 2002, New Zealand was being horribly thumped by England at Lancaster Park, Astle's home ground.

* * * * * * *

Few people remember that England won the first test of that series by a whopping 98 runs. Even fewer people remember that it was Graham Thorpe who would take out man of the match honours for a double century (dropped second ball in the slips by . . . Astle!); or that Nasser Hussain's first-innings century might just have been the most skilful display of green-wicket batting seen that summer; or that Matthew Hoggard took seven wickets in the hosts' pitiful first innings as England used only three bowlers; or that Andrew Flintoff blasted his maiden test century.

It is remembered as Astle's test — as it should be.

'Wow! That's one of the most ripping displays of power batting you could ever hope to see,' Mark Nicholas gushed when Astle went to 150 just 22 balls after he had reached 100.

He wasn't done.

The sound of the ball cracking off willow was like nothing you'll hear again in these days of dehydrated bats with fat, fat edges. Martin Crowe described it as the sound of a shotgun, but this time he didn't have the imagery quite right: it was more like the crack of a hunter's rifle resounding across the Mackenzie Country as Astle kept pinging the quick bowlers into the stands.

This, however, he got right, after Astle deposited a Caddick delivery over the commentary box and onto the roof of the stand: 'It is just the most pure, perfect exhibition of hitting of all time.'

Asked about it years later, Astle would tell *Cricket Monthly*: 'It just kind of happened. There was no point where I really thought I should have a go. It was one of those days that everything I was hitting was coming out the middle of the bat. People ask me a lot about it, but the only thing I can say was that it even amazed me because usually you go through patches in an innings where you hit it well and then struggle a bit, but for some reason, everything hit came out of the middle. It was the best I'd hit it. I never repeated it. I seemed to be in the right position at the right time and things happened in slow motion. There's one I hit off Caddick that actually went over Grandstand No. 1, over the roof and down the road. To be fair, all of them were pretty decent hits and would have cleared the boundary on most grounds.'

That innings is, in many ways, Astle's legacy, but how much did it mean to the man himself? Quite a bit as it turns out. He's not by any stretch a keeper of mementoes, but he still has the Kookaburra bat from that innings, which remains, at 153 balls, the fastest test double century.

* * * * * * *

It would be wrong to say the rest of Astle's test career was a disappointment because the numbers don't bear it out. When he retired, he had 11 test centuries. At the time that placed him third on New Zealand's all-time list behind just Crowe and John Wright. He has since been passed by Kane Williamson, Ross Taylor, Tom Latham and Brendon McCullum, but he remains seventh on the centuries list (Henry Nicholls and Fleming are next with nine), and eighth on the run-scorers chart.

His 51 wickets put him at number 38, but his value as a bowler was to dry an end up, something he did with a minimum of fuss and remarkable efficiency.

As a fielder, he is right there in the top echelon, either in the cordon or the outfield. If you were to carve out a Mount Rushmore of modern New Zealand fielders, Astle would be a strong contender alongside the likes of Chris Harris and Martin Guptill.

Astle was a New Zealand test great, but it was as a one-day player where he did his finest work.

His 16 centuries were a record at the time and although he has since been passed by Taylor and Guptill, he will likely sit inside the top five for a long time to come and possibly forever as bilateral ODI series become increasingly squeezed from an overflowing calendar. Williamson (13) might get there, but it's hard to see another player getting past him for a generation or two.

His 99 wickets put him at number 18 on the New Zealand charts and his 83 catches, many of them absolute specials, place him firmly inside the top 10.

He scored his first century against India at Nagpur in 1995 and his first World Cup century a year later in Ahmedabad during New Zealand's opening match against England. Bizarrely, he failed to reach double figures in his nine subsequent bats at World Cup tournaments — five in the 1996 India and Pakistan event and four to start the 1999 England-hosted event. He finally broke that dreadful string with 11 against Scotland at Edinburgh, but he never came close to doing his talent justice at the format's showpiece event, with more ducks (5) than centuries (2) or 50s (1) combined. His World Cup average of a tick over 20 and a strike rate of 70.5 was a poor return against his overall numbers.

Astle was a rarity among New Zealand batters in that he performed very well in Asia, with six of his centuries and nine 50s coming on the subcontinent.

Strike rates were different back then, when 300-plus totals were still a rarity. Astle was a noted hard-hitting opener, but it was debate around his strike rate that saw him dropped in late 2005 and started the process towards what many considered his premature retirement.

Since scoring an unbeaten hundred against India in a tri-series final victory in Harare, Astle had struggled for runs and for tempo in subsequent one-day series against South Africa away and in a home Chappell–Hadlee series.

'With hindsight, the way I'd been approaching my batting in the few months before I was dropped hadn't been how I usually played the game,' Astle wrote in his autobiography. 'It was a bit more circumspect.'

Bracewell, who magnanimously contributed quite heavily to the book even in the face of criticism of his treatment of the player, said the dropping was twofold: to increase depth in the squad ahead of the World Cup and to reignite Astle's approach, as he felt 'he was taking fewer risks than he once had [and] was becoming a little more conservative'.

Specifically, what the selectors believed was that Astle wasn't pushing the pace enough through the middle overs. That he started quickly, then went static. It was a message he would have accepted to a degree and worked on, but it got lost among the other discussions around blooding players and giving him a kick up the butt. There was a more insidious criticism, too, that Astle could get preoccupied by landmark scores, the anti-Williamson in effect, but the numbers also don't bear this out, with Astle having nine scores in the 90s in ODI cricket, which does not indicate a player obsessed by raising his bat.

All the hullabaloo, whether justified or not, had the effect of wearing down Astle and his love of the game. It sent his mind in the direction of retirement.

* * * * * * *

In *Turning Point*, Vettori cursed the fact that Astle had retired before he took the captaincy, believing he would have been the ideal teammate to lean upon for behind-the-scenes advice.

'Nathan was stability personified. He never really wavered throughout his career and because of that he was a tremendous mentor and example for the new guys in the team. Nath was a constant: the same person at the start as he was at the end. He just got on with his game and tried to ignore all the bull. I loved him for that . . .

'It's not that he wasn't worried about everyone else's performance. Nath was just Nath. He stuck to himself, worked hard, kept his nose clean and, if someone came to him for advice he was always willing to help and was without exception level-headed . . . He's an insular person: his own man. But he was one of the main reasons our team succeeded, just purely from his performance and composure.'

When Astle retired, he joined the ill-fated and short-lived Indian Cricket League, captaining the Mumbai Champs.

If there's one regret Astle might carry from his playing days — and it might be difficult to get him to ever admit this — it's that Twenty20 cricket didn't come along a few years earlier. As it was, he only played four T20Is before he quit.

He was an outstanding test cricketer and a fantastic one-day player. At his considerable peak, he would have been a brilliant and highly sought-after (read, high-priced) T20 player.

Regardless of format, he was always his own man — something that has never changed.

CHAPTER 5
DANIEL VETTORI
(ONZM)

Debut: 1997						Last match: 2015
BATTING	Matches	Runs	Ave	100s	50s	Catches
Test:	113	4531	30.0	6	23	58
ODI:	295	2253	17.33	-	4	88
T20I:	34	205	12.81	-	-	9
BOWLING	Matches	Wickets	Ave	5w (10w)	Economy	S/R
Test:	113	362	34.36	20 (3)	2.59	79.5
ODI:	295	305	31.71	2	4.12	46.0
T20I:	34	38	19.68	-	5.70	20.7

Wins as captain: Tests 6 (win % 19), ODIs 41 (win % 50), T20Is 13 (win % 46)

It was difficult to reconcile that the man who played his last match at the World Cup final at the Melbourne Cricket Ground in 2015 was the same person as the boy who made his debut 18 years earlier at the Basin Reserve.

The boy was fresh-faced behind the spectacles, his hair as bouncy as his run-up, his action long and loose; the man was grizzled behind the glasses, capable of growing a full beard in a single morning and with perfectly grooved, yet somewhat mechanical, action honed from bowling 43,665 deliveries on the international stage.

Vettori was a cricketers' cricketer, hugely admired by all those he played with and against. He was also damned unlucky in that his peak coincided with New Zealand cricket's least successful years in the twenty-first century. He captained between the tail end of Fleming's successful reign and before Brendon McCullum set about reshaping both the fortunes and the ethos of the Black Caps. In that regard, Vettori's interregnum years tend to be overlooked and mostly forgotten, but it is through no fault of the man himself, who often played like a giant in a team of Lilliputians.

Vettori was a master craftsman with the ball and something else entirely with the bat, yet he fashioned himself into one of the greatest all-rounders New Zealand has produced. You could make an argument, indeed, that if Vettori's unorthodoxy with the bat had been immediately recognised as an advantage rather than an impediment, he could have finished with more than six test centuries and an average of 30. As it was, that was a fantastic return for a batter whose main claim to fame was being able to access the same third-man boundary with a thousand different shots.

With the ball, it is true that Vettori's test numbers, although very, very good, do not quite do him justice. He would have pushed past 400 test wickets and averaged closer to 30 than the 34.36 he ended up with if he hadn't been pressed so regularly into a holding role on unresponsive wickets. Indeed, if Vettori had played half his tests on the subcontinent rather than the pitches of New Zealand that rarely, even on the last afternoon of a five-day test, turned off the straight, he would likely have been talked about among the finest spin bowlers to have ever played the game.

Ever resourceful, Vettori honed a game to suit home conditions, relying more on guile, drift, dip and unerring accuracy than high revolutions and side spin. In doing so, he became the perfect New Zealand spin bowler and one of the vanguard that proved that spin was not only employable in cricket's newest, splashiest format but potentially more effective than pace.

He became captain of New Zealand for all three formats and was a sought-after coach in his post-playing career. He did this all while remaining one of the most impenetrable cricketers this country has produced.

'He was a hard individual to get to know — he didn't let his guard down very often — but he was always respectful,' wrote Ross Taylor in his autobiography.

Alternative Commentary Collective co-founder Mike Lane, who played cricket with Vettori at school and has remained a friend, said it wasn't a protective shield he put up to deal with the trappings of fame. Even as a kid Vettori would tell you what he thought you needed to know and nothing more.

'He knew he had some talent and was happy to let that do the talking for him,' Lane said. 'It's not an act. We all thought he was a great guy, but he genuinely didn't think his life outside of cricket was interesting enough to bang on about, so he kept it to himself.'

Thankfully his life in cricket was worth banging on about.

*   *   *   *   *   *   *   *

The grandson of Italian immigrants, Daniel Luca Vettori's story as such is that he arrived pretty much fully formed as a spinner of prodigious talent when England toured New Zealand in the summer of 1996–97. The weird thing is, if you're to isolate the spin-bowling part of his story, it's pretty much true.

In one of those curiosities that life in a small country throws up, one of Vettori's schoolboy cricket friends was a guy who made his name in satirical television shows such as *Eating Media Lunch* and *Seven Sharp*.

Jeremy Wells even wrote a tongue-in-cheek foreword to Vettori's typically noncommittal attempt at an autobiography, *Turning Point*. 'Even at the tender age of 15, Daniel Vettori had an innate ability to make a cricket ball dip, bounce and turn. He was devastatingly accurate, rarely bowled a bad ball and had the talent to get wickets against players who went after him. He bowled long spells and once he had the ball it was hard to get it back off him. Amazingly, this young exponent of spin had only been tweaking his craft for a year when I played with him. Previously he had bowled left-arm medium pace, and friends who faced him in those pre-spin years likened him to a blond Wasim Akram . . . It's futile to speculate on what his career may have been like as a left-arm medium slow bowler, but it's fair to say that his conversion to left-arm orthodox spin in 1993 was inspired.'

You have to dig fairly deep to learn more about his pre-spin days.

Vettori's father, Renzo, was the son of an Italian concrete worker who hailed from Roncone, a small village in the Dolomites (on the drive from Milan to Venice, turn left at Brescia and if you hit the Austrian border, you've gone too far).

Vettori was born in Auckland and took up cricket when he was six and the family was living in Sydney. Renzo, who works in the dairy industry, and Robyn, a nurse, settled in Hamilton, and Vettori went to the Catholic primary school, Marian, before attending the independent Anglican school St Paul's, an institution most noted for sending its Year 10 boys off to live in the bush for six months at Tīhoi, a fairly inhospitable piece of country sandwiched between Lake Taupō and the Pureora Forest.

The other life-changing event that took place during Vettori's school days was a minibus crash on the way back from a football tournament in New Plymouth in 1994. The vehicle veered off the road and flipped down a bank, leaving Vettori with a fractured vertebra in his lower spine. He still managed to scramble up the bank to wave down some help, but he ended up in hospital for several weeks, and sport played no part in his life for the remainder of that year until he regained strength in his back.

Whether it was while digging himself a latrine in Tīhoi, or

scrambling up the bank on the way back from New Plymouth, or a former principal that suggested the future was spin that provided Vettori with the epiphany that would see him permanently ditch left-arm swing for left-arm orthodox, it was a decision that was to have enormously positive results for New Zealand over the next two decades.

* * * * * * * *

If that was an extremely short, potted rehash of his childhood, his elevation to the New Zealand team was even shorter — two first-class games long, in fact.

Vettori had enjoyed smooth progress through the Northern Districts age-group system and had toured England in 1996 with the New Zealand Under-19 team under the tutelage of John Bracewell — a team that also included Jacob Oram, Craig McMillan, Matthew Bell, Matthew Walker, David Sewell and Gareth Hopkins, all of whom would go on to play for the senior side. The England team was made up of a lot of players who became county journeymen, but captain Gareth Batty, the late Ben Hollioake, Jimmy Ormond, Ed Smith, Matthew Hoggard, Usman Afzaal and Owais Shah would all play for England, while David Sales had a long first-class career that involved a stint at Wellington. New Zealand won the three-test series 1–0, with Vettori taking 12 wickets for 289 across the matches, while displaying the sort of parsimony — just 2.3 runs per over — that was to become his hallmark.

His performances on tour caught the eye of the Northern Districts selectors, who immediately drafted him into the senior squad at the start of the 1996–97 season, but just as a reminder of how young he was, his mum didn't let him play because she insisted he studied properly for his bursary exams with a view to a health sciences degree at Waikato University, which was to be his portal to a future in pharmacy.

In January 1997, however, he was let loose, first playing the touring English at Seddon Park, capturing the wicket of future captain Nasser Hussain (who was also to become his first test wicket, on both occasions being caught by Bryan Young at slip).

That was just the entrée before a stunning Plunket Shield entrance. At Nelson's Trafalgar Park, Vettori took his first five-wicket bag. His victims — Glen Sulzberger, Mark Greatbatch, Mathew Sinclair, Greg Loveridge and Andrew Penn — all internationals. In the second innings he added three more to finish with a match haul of 8 for 142.

It was assumed that Vettori was now on a fast track to the Black Caps, but few realised quite how fast, given he had turned 18 while in Nelson with ND.

'I was selected out of the blue in the [second] test squad to play England,' Vettori recalled in *Turning Point*. 'Convenor of selectors Ross Dykes rang Chris Kuggeleijn to run the decision past him, and to ask his thoughts. Something along the lines of, "Can this kid handle it? Will he be overawed?" Kuggs vouched for me and said I'd be fine and the next thing you know Dyksey was on the phone to my mum. She was a bit apprehensive, it's fair to say. She thought I was a bit young. She was concerned I'd miss out on my youth, but I think in the end she was pretty stoked for me.

'She rang to tell me to phone Ross Dykes. When I did he told me the news and ran through a few details. I don't think I heard him say anything after he told me I was in the team. I was stunned: pretty happy, for sure, but shocked really.'

So was much of the cricket-following public. While ball-by-ball commentary of first-class cricket meant it had more exposure and cachet than it does now, it was still a fairly fringe pursuit. Who was this kid with the Pantene hair and exotic-sounding surname?

It was a question Paul Holmes, the host of the high-rating current affairs show *Holmes*, tried to answer on the eve of Vettori's debut. The eponymous host, in that high-velocity, inimitable style of his, rattled off an introduction for his viewers.

'It's being rated by those who write about these matters, who pontificate about these matters, it is rated as a really bold move; a young man straight out of school, straight into the New Zealand cricket team for the second test against England,' Holmes blurted.

'The Pakistanis have got Shahid Afridi, the bulky batsman-bowler who recently smashed the world's best around the park, he's 16, but now Mr Steve Rixon and the New Zealand selectors have got Daniel Vettori.'

What the hundreds of thousands of viewers saw staring back at them was an almost impossibly young, relatively guileless kid who looked about as ready for the toughest test that cricket can provide as a sumo wrestler would look on the 3-metre springboard at the Olympics.

'I was very young when I started. I was very light and I had a lot of hair — there are many photos out there that I deeply regret,' he would tell the *New Zealand Herald* in 2010.

Looks can be deceiving, however. Vettori kept his answers short, not giving himself the opportunity to say anything he'd regret later, and even corrected Holmes when he referred to Shane Warne as another left-arm spinner. He was savvy enough to come through his first real media test unscathed.

He repeated that and then some in his two proper on-field tests.

* * * * * * * *

If you watch footage from Vettori's early days you will see an unusually long, loping run-up, a busy front arm and a lot of boyish enthusiasm. Up until his delivery stride he didn't necessarily look like an international cricketer, but the results at the other end suggested he was born for it. In his first test he remained undefeated with the bat at No. 11 and took 2 for 98 as a fairly wretched New Zealand side — Lee Germon was keeper-captain while Adam Parore was shoehorned into a No. 3 position he was clearly unsuited to — was defeated by an innings at the Basin Reserve.

When Germon was injured ahead of the final test, Stephen Fleming stepped in to begin what would be the longest reign of any New Zealand test skipper. A rejuvenated side appeared to have England on the ropes, but a poor second innings with the bat meant England were chasing 305 to win. At 118 for 2 the test was delicately poised going into the final day, but Mike Atherton's experience and Fleming and Vettori's lack of it was the difference in the four-wicket loss. Even so, the spinner's return of 4 for 97 off a whopping 57 overs — too many of them delivered over the wicket to right-handers, looking to leverage the rough, but which Atherton happily kicked away for hours upon end — provided a window to a brighter future.

Vettori's first couple of years were a whirlwind. The test programme was busy, and he was young and naive enough to bowl all day every day if that's what was required. He took his first bag, a five-for, in his fourth test and his first on the home soil of Hamilton's Seddon Park. Vettori never did make it through the gates for his first day at Waikato University, but the next season started in Zimbabwe, still a decent team at that stage in their history, and came back through Australia, before Zimbabwe were hosted. As autumn fell, New Zealand was off to Sri Lanka for the three-test series that they lost despite winning the first test, and despite Vettori's 6 for 64 leaving his team with a target of 296 in the third. A fairly useful spinner, Muttiah Muralitharan, made sure New Zealand got nowhere near that.

The Indians' skill at playing spin and South Africa's all-round skill made for a lean home summer in 1998–99, though Vettori did winkle out four Proteas batters at the Basin Reserve in a marathon innings that saw him bowl 54 overs. He bowled well on New Zealand's successful tour to England, the crowning glory for the departing coach Steve 'Stumper' Rixon, as New Zealand triumphed 2–1, the wins coming at the iconic London venues Lord's and The Oval, the latter coming in the decider when Chris Cairns turned the match on its head with a brutal display of hitting. Vettori's input into that test is often overlooked, but it shouldn't be. He made a dashing 51 in the first innings at No. 10, coming in to join Fleming (66 not out) at 157 for 8 and departing at 235. He took three first-innings wickets as England folded for 153 and 2 for 36 from 16 quality overs as the hosts buckled for 162, chasing 246 to win.

The first tour under David Trist was to India, where Vettori starred in a loss at Kanpur, taking 6 for 127, including the wickets of Sachin Tendulkar, Rahul Dravid and Sourav Ganguly — a trio that would end up with a mere 103 test centuries between them.

The West Indies were dispatched as the entrée of the 1999–2000 season before the main course arrived — the all-conquering Australians. Vettori was just 21, had taken 91 test wickets and after the first test at Eden Park he had become the second-youngest player to reach 100 test wickets behind Kapil Dev after a double of 5 for 62 and 7 for 87. Vettori's match analysis, in a loss it has to be noted, was the second best for a New Zealander behind Sir Richard Hadlee's famous 15 for 123 at the Gabba, though it has since been passed by another left-arm spinner, Ajaz Patel. At 21 years and 46 days, Vettori had become the fastest spinner to 100 wickets.

It had all seemingly come so easy. Maybe not the batting — at that point he had scraped together four half-centuries but had accumulated just 618 runs at an unflattering average of a tick over 17 — but we'll get to that later.

One test later, the wheels fell off. Unbelievably, given that Vettori had been complaining about a sore back and a loss of feeling in his legs during another loss to Australia, this time in Wellington, management still felt it appropriate for Vettori to bat the second innings with a runner and to bowl eight second-innings overs in a match that was a lost cause.

Vettori missed the third test, but his injury coincided with the first decent break the national side had faced in a long time. That was the good news. The bad: he broke down again in the first test upon his return, against Zimbabwe in Bulawayo. It provoked a few recriminations in the high-performance set-up.

'One of the least tasteful aspects of that experience was being accused by NZC later of not following the fitness programme that was set down for me, and having to face suggestions that I had shirked my responsibilities and didn't take the rehabilitation more seriously,' he wrote. 'I was annoyed because the claims were misplaced.'

It was the first significant setback of his international career. He wouldn't return until the November 2001 tour to Australia, where he took a six-wicket bag in Perth to put New Zealand on the cusp of an improbable series victory, but it wouldn't be his last.

* * * * * * *

If you extrapolated the first three years of Vettori's test career and took into account his capacity for improvement, it seemed a given he would go on to break many New Zealand records, including Hadlee's test tally of 431 wickets.

But this country has always maintained a complicated relationship with spin bowlers.

'I'm not sure whether the spin bowler is properly understood or appreciated in New Zealand. This is mainly because our conditions are so seamer-friendly that most sides — apart from the international ones — don't see a big need for our services,' wrote Vettori in *Turning Point*.

In the early 2000s, despite having one of the best in the business in Vettori, they realised they were better off effectively neutering him in a bid to win more test matches. The thing is, it worked.

India brought a high-powered batting and spin-bowling unit to tour here in the summer of 2002–03. The pitches were so green it made a mockery of the concept of a fair contest between bat and ball, in much the same way sides now complain when they tour the subcontinent and find balls turning square and going through the top in the first hour.

The conditions were so alien to India they totalled 535 runs across the four innings in the two-test series, and their highest total was 161, scored in the first innings of the first test at the Basin Reserve. VVS Laxman averaged 6.75 for the series; Ganguly 7.25; Sehwag 10. Daryl Tuffey and Jacob Oram, decent bowlers but neither would get to 100 wickets in their careers, took 24 wickets between them at a cost of around 10.

'Despite playing in both tests at Wellington and Hamilton — I didn't get to bowl an over,' Vettori would recall. 'It was much the same when we won the first test against Sri Lanka in 2006: another seamer's paradise. I think I received two overs.'

Vettori wouldn't have thought, he would have known. One of his greatest strengths, according to teammates, was his ability to recite lines of numbers as if straight from the *New Zealand Cricket Almanack*.

'He's a statistics freak,' wrote Craig McMillan in *Out of the Park*. 'Not quite in Richard Hadlee's class, but not far behind! [He] knows not only his own stats but everyone else's. He's our "Mr Cricket" if you like and he's the only guy I know who travels with the *Almanack* in his cricket coffin. Any cricket-question game played during the day's play is usually dominated by Dan.'

New Zealand coach from 2003 to 2008, the hyper-aggressive off-spinner John Bracewell, would regale Vettori with tales of his own playing days, and how he would deliberately hide from chairman of selectors Frank Cameron when he knew he was looking for him to tell him he would again be 12th man.

Bracewell was a wicket-taking spinner and a handy lower-middle-order player who once scored a test century that played a massive role in a first series win in England, yet he still spent 15 tests carrying the drinks for lesser-qualified seam bowlers.

Spin bowling might have been a flummoxing art to many a

selector, but it didn't mean they weren't occasionally seduced by the idea of a left-arm twirler.

Hedley Howarth, older brother of Geoff, was a fine operator who was turned into a bowling machine by captains who were more interested in drying up an end than letting him develop his craft. On the famous 0–0 tour to the West Indies in 1971–72, Howarth was bowled into the ground on unresponsive pitches. His 338 overs included a remarkable 100 maidens and although he took just 14 wickets across the four tests, Garry Sobers said: 'We saw a lot of Howarth's bowling and we never really figured him out.' Neither did his skippers and Howarth was never really the same after the Caribbean tour, drifting instead into the family fish wholesalers business as Central Districts slow left-armer David O'Sullivan was often preferred.

It's fair to say New Zealand's adventures in left-arm orthodox in the post-Howarth, pre-Vettori era were scattergun. Stephen Boock was the most reliable, but despite a career spanning 11 years, he played just 30 tests and none between February 1980 and 1984. Others tried were Evan Gray (10 tests), Mark Haslam (4), Mark Priest (3) and Matthew Hart (14).

The post-Vettori left-arm landscape has been just as fickle, with Bruce Martin (5 tests), Mitchell Santner (24), Ajaz Patel (14) and Rachin Ravindra (3) all given opportunities without quite grasping it. Ravindra's time will come again, but most likely as a top-order batter who can bowl a bit, rather than a frontline spinner.

'In contrast, I was lucky that someone took a punt on me, and that I came into a team that was probably crying out for a spinner. I received good opportunities, performed reasonably tidily and my early form carried me through some later periods when I wasn't bowling as well. It's certainly a tough job in New Zealand because of the conditions,' Vettori wrote.

* * * * * * *

Vettori had advantages that others who came before him didn't. The most obvious one, the fundamental one, was that he was a better bowler.

Another was that he could toggle brilliantly between test-match lines and strategies and the more prosaic demands of limited-overs spin bowling. For the bulk of his career, if he was fit and available, he played every format.

He was a sound fielder with a good set of hands (though towards the end of his career he could make chasing a ball to the boundary look as if he was running the 42nd and final kilometre of a marathon into a Wellington southerly).

He was a marvellously effective batter and at one point the undisputed best No. 8 in the world. His 2227 runs, scored at an average of 39, are still the most at No. 8, as are his four centuries at that position.

You could write a chapter on the quirky excellence of Vettori's batting alone. While he played some important cameos in white-ball cricket, it was in tests where he and his Gray-Nicolls flourished. He would readily admit to being embarrassed where his batting stood when he broke his back, believing it didn't do his talent justice, something his school teammates would have agreed with, having seen him score hundreds while batting up the order for his 1st XI.

The post-stress fracture Vettori was far more diligent. By the end of the 2003–04 summer he had raised his test average into the 20s and marked his newfound confidence with a century, 137 not out versus Pakistan at Seddon Park, sharing a big partnership with Fleming (192). By the end of his career, he had totted up six tons and was unlucky not to have had more, being dismissed for 99 against Pakistan at University Oval and for 96 against Australia at the Gabba, the last of his 23 half-centuries.

Even today he sits in the top 10 of New Zealand test run-scorers and while it might be a slightly manufactured club, only Kapil Dev and Ian Botham can say they belong in his club of 4000 test runs and 300 wickets (though Stuart Broad may soon join them).

The other advantage Vettori had over his predecessors was that he was a leader.

All his skills and acumen were to be consolidated in 2007 when he was announced, somewhat controversially (though not as controversially as a future leadership change), as 'captain of every-thing', the phrase he regrettably used to his wife Mary when he got off the phone from Bracewell.

Stephen Fleming had stepped down as one-day captain after the 2007 World Cup but had indicated a desire to continue as test captain through to the 2008 tour to England, the likely end point for his international career. Bracewell and selector Hadlee, however, thought a clean break was the most beneficial way forward, and Vettori got the job of tossing the coin for all three formats. Fleming would continue to play through to the end of the 2007–08 season, which was a shame in many ways, because his experience could have been critical on the disappointing tour to England.

It is fiendishly difficult to assess Vettori's captaincy.

McMillan put it bluntly when he said Vettori had received a 'hospital pass', given all the retirements — Fleming, McMillan, Astle, Cairns — in the years immediately before he took the reins.

Certainly, his record in tests was not good, but then again, neither were the XIs he often took to the field with. To compensate for the lack of out-and-out talent, Vettori and Bracewell came up with a theory that if you could take the game into the last day then anything could happen. More often than not, it didn't.

Being one of the early adopters of the Indian Premier League, Vettori's leadership took a serious hammering from former England captain Michael Atherton when he was one of a tranche of Black Caps to turn up 'late' for the 2008 tour to England, missing the warm-up games to maximise their earning with their new franchises.

In the form of an open letter to Vettori, Atherton wrote in *The Times*:

'The captaincy of your country is like a nice cake, don't you think? There are trimmings and the icing on top — the fat contracts, the acclaim, the public profile — but there is a lot of effort that is needed to make it work. While everyone else can just turn up and enjoy the finished product, the chef is responsible for making it edible. Responsibility. It is a key word, wouldn't you say? All that extra time in the kitchen that no one else sees.

'Like most people in the game, I am delighted that cricketers are finally getting well paid. But invalidating [touring] contracts and ignoring agreements are among the less edifying sights of this rupee-fuelled frenzy. You did not have to accept the captaincy of your country, just as New Zealand did not have to accept playing four warm-up matches. But to accept and then turn up with just over half a team is downright rude. Clearly, in this new world, old-fashioned manners count for little.'

It feels like a quaint take now on what is a vastly different landscape from the days when Atherton played, but at the time it stung. Atherton's words were widely picked up and redistributed around the world to a generation who mostly nodded in agreement with him. Even more awkwardly, he was presenting the toss for the first test at Lord's, which started the day after his column appeared.

Vettori's captaincy came under further scrutiny when New Zealand lost a test from a seemingly impossible position in Manchester, but the real drama lay in the one-day series to follow. Finely poised at 1–1, there was drama in the fourth match at The Oval (one game had been rained out) when Grant Elliott was run out late in the chase after colliding with bowler Ryan Sidebottom. Stand-in England skipper Paul Collingwood refused to rescind the appeal and the New Zealanders, including the mild-mannered Vettori, were seen to be apoplectic on the players' balcony. Following the match, which the Black Caps won by one wicket, they refused to shake hands with their counterparts. It was juicy stuff. New Zealand would end up winning the series 3–1, but there were mixed reviews as to whether New Zealand had shown the necessary gumption in the wake of a clear breach of the unwritten rules of cricket, or whether they had acted boorishly. Vettori's response was beautifully equivocal.

'I was incensed with what happened and the whole group of players were. We couldn't understand it, sitting up there on the balcony. . . But Paul has come and spoken to us, apologised and acted in a contrite way. We'll move on from the situation and hopefully it doesn't happen again. . . That match was as tense as it gets and we were apologetic for maybe the way we acted on the balcony.'

Vettori was not a fire-and-brimstone leader, however, tending towards the analytical. A huge fan of baseball, he liked to know the percentages when he made decisions. Unquestionably, his strength as a captain and probably the strength of his game by this stage was in the white-ball formats. Under his watch, Vettori's sides made the semi-finals of the World T20 in 2007, his 4 for 20 pivotal in an upset win over India in the Super Eight stage, and of the 2011 World Cup in India. In the latter he won enormous credit for marshalling his attack to defend 221 in the quarter-final against red-hot favourites South Africa. He opened with himself and off-spinner Nathan McCullum and utilised just 18 overs of seam in the match, with Tim Southee bowling a high percentage of off-cutters for nine of those.

In 2009, his side made the final of the now-defunct Champions Trophy in South Africa. Although they lost comfortably to Australia in the showpiece finale (sound familiar?), the semi-final against nemesis Pakistan was a personal triumph for the skipper, who took 3 for 43 and then scored 41 off 42 balls in New Zealand's nervy but successful pursuit of 234.

It was around this point where Vettori's omnipotence started to create headlines. Bracewell had left in 2008 and filling his shoes had not proven easy.

Wrote Taylor: 'I don't know whether Dan set out to accumulate power — he doesn't come across as that sort of person — or it just happened that way. The instability in the coaching set-up created a vacuum that he filled. Dan's an intelligent guy. He probably took the view that it was his head on the chopping block so he should be in control. The problem was that some players didn't feel comfortable talking to him. You're probably not going to share your fears and insecurities with the captain under a conventional structure; when the captain is also the coach and selector, you're even less likely to do so.'

It was joked that Vettori wasn't just captain, acting coach and selector, he was also the coach driver, the physio and treasurer.

The circumstances arose when Bracewell was replaced by affable Englishman Andy Moles, who had impressed at Northern Districts where he devolved a lot of responsibility to his trusted senior players. However, he struggled to replicate that success with New Zealand, who, under Bracewell, had been used to the coach doing a lot of the heavy lifting. Matters had evidently come to a head on a tour to Sri Lanka, just prior to the Champions Trophy campaign, where Moles had struggled physically in the sweltering conditions.

When the team returned to New Zealand, information leaked that Moles had reviewed particularly poorly and the team was agitating for a change, which many pundits and punters saw as a gross abuse of player power. However, writing in the *Dominion Post*, Jonathan Millmow said the concerns were justified.

'The affable Englishman has struggled with the transition from taking a first-class side to an international one and patience has run out.

'This is not player power; it is a plea for help.

'Daniel Vettori's men are not angels, but neither are they backstabbers. They have voiced their concerns through the correct channels and were not the leak.

'This team wants to do better but the consensus is it can no longer carry Moles and his sidekick, Mark O'Donnell, along for the ride.

'The players' reviews claim Moles has offered little of substance technically or tactically since replacing John Bracewell 12 months ago.

'Bad habits have also been allowed to go unpunished and Vettori has been forced to take up the slack. Vettori is not Superman. Next he'll be driving the team bus.'

Once the reviews of Moles' stewardship had gotten into the public domain, his continuing in the role was untenable. He was replaced in the interim by Mark Greatbatch, whose up-and-down personality also rubbed some of the senior players the wrong way, and then on a full-time basis by John Wright.

Vettori had always stated that he didn't want to skipper the team for as long as Fleming and stayed true to his word, relinquishing the captaincy after the 2011 World Cup and semi-retiring from one-day cricket, though he would be brought back for the 2013 Champions Trophy and, most famously, the 2015 World Cup campaign.

Despite having seemingly played his last test against the West Indies in Antigua as Vettori was finding it hard enough on his creaking back to walk upright let alone play five-day cricket, he was drafted into the team for the final test of the series against Pakistan in the UAE in 2014 — the match interrupted for a day by the death in Australia of Phillip Hughes. He played as the third of three spinners behind Mark Craig and Ish Sodhi and his final statistical check mark in the game was his 362nd wicket, a dubious leg-before decision to remove tailender Mohammad Talha.

On the same tour he was drafted in for his final T20I, scoring a duck and again being used as the third spinner, this time behind Anton Devcich and Nathan McCullum. He bowled opener Ahmed Shehzad for his 38th and final wicket in that international format.

At the 2015 World Cup, he was a key on-field sounding board for Brendon McCullum as New Zealand played a high-octane game right through to that disappointing final at the Melbourne Cricket Ground. Never less than metronomically consistent at the bowling crease, his tournament will be more remembered for an act in the field in the quarter-final and with the bat in the semi-final.

At Wellington Stadium, he leapt improbably high on the third-man boundary to catch Marlon Samuels, before casually returning to terra firma and tossing the ball nonchalantly in the air as if to say, 'Nothing special.' The sight of 10 grown men charging down to the edge of the ground to mob their sheepish veteran is one of the great vignettes in New Zealand cricket history, while the catch itself launched a series of Air Vettori memes.

A few days later his intervention was even more pivotal. Batting with Elliott in the final over of a piano-wire-tight semi-final against South Africa, he somehow dropped a horizontal bat onto a near-perfect Dale Steyn yorker and rocketed the ball for a boundary to the left of Morné Morkel, who had been crabbing to his right pre-delivery to try to protect the very short fine boundaries. It's not a shot you'll see in any manual and while it was only the entrée to Elliott's match-winning six two balls later, it was every bit as skilful a piece of batting.

Vettori's final match in national colours came in the MCG final. He knew it, his teammates knew it, but there was to be no fanfare. Vettori just got ready for the match. He did so perhaps a little too willingly, pulling a leg muscle in the warm-ups and only just getting through the game. While Michael Clarke got a guard of honour from the New Zealanders as he headed into bat before shuffling off into retirement, Vettori just got sledged from the field.

And that was it. Vettori slunk off quietly into a coaching career without any tribute videos or tearful press conferences. It was all very typical of Vettori.

Why, he would have thought, would anybody be interested in me banging on about my career?

CHAPTER 6
SHANE BOND

Debut: 2001						Last match: 2010
BOWLING	Matches	Wickets	Ave	5w (10w)	Economy	S/R
Test:	18	87	22.09	5 (1)	3.21	38.7
ODI:	82	147	20.88	4	4.28	29.2
T20I:	20	25	21.72	0	7.0	18.6

It is the great pity of Shane Bond that he doesn't just stand as one of the greatest fast bowlers New Zealand has ever produced, but also one of this country's greatest what-if stories.

Bond was an electrifying presence with ball in hand, but a litany of serious back injuries and badly timed minor ailments restricted his appearances for his country to 120 matches across all formats. Rarely, if ever, did he turn in a poor performance across the nine years he played, and it was a measure of the regard he was held in that he was widely considered the finest fast bowler the country had produced outside of Sir Richard Hadlee, though that mantle might have been challenged of late thanks to the class and, yes, longevity of Tim Southee and Trent Boult.

In full flight, Bond was a sight to behold. He could touch 150 kph and combine that with a late in-ducker that was attracted to the stumps like iron to a magnet. He also possessed a leg-cutter and, towards the end of his career, an out-swinger. He holds a remarkable record in that he never bowled in a test innings, even a truncated one, where he didn't take a wicket. Of those who have played at least 15 tests, his strike rate of a wicket every 38.7 balls puts him third in the all-time list behind South Africa's Duanne Olivier and England's George Lohmann, a handsome man who was unplayable on uncovered wickets, played his last test in 1896 and took his last breath at the age of 36, having contracted tuberculosis nine years previously.

Unlike many of his contemporaries, Bond didn't reserve his fiercest spells for the test format either. He loved one-day cricket, and one-day cricket loved him back. If he'd started his career a little later, he might have been remembered as the first truly great T20I bowler as he defied convention in maintaining express pace and an excellent economy rate.

Bond's international career could have ended on a sour note, as he signed for the 'rebel' Indian Cricket League, making himself persona non grata with Indian cricket's governing body the BCCI, who used their muscle to leverage the ICC and ensure New Zealand Cricket didn't pick him for the term of his contract. As it happened, the league folded and Bond got a proper farewell, playing one more test, which was a thriller, 15 ODIs and 11 T20Is before he hung them up for good.

Bond sacrificed two years of his international career to the ICL because he had signed a deal and his word, or his signature, was his, um, bond.

That's the other thing you have to know about the Cantabrian: he is one of the straightest shooters you will meet. A former policeman, some can find his honesty blunt and even confronting, but Bond never expects anything from others that he doesn't demand of himself.

'Bondy's a guy who tells it as it is,' Nathan Astle once wrote. 'You know where you stand with him, which I think is a very good thing. If there's something on his mind, he'll tell it to your face and then move on, which is something I applaud.'

His international career might have been too fleeting, but he has stayed in the game with various coaching roles with New Zealand Cricket and T20 franchises, and the odd commentary gig.

No matter the job, he has stayed true to his principles.

* * * * * * * *

If you want to pinpoint the exact moment Bond announced his talent to the world, it would be 26 January, Australia Day, 2002. As was tradition, the all-conquering Australian team was playing a one-day international at Adelaide Oval, a beautiful swatch of green grass just north of the Torrens River, its historic stands, gate, scoreboard and embankment overlooked by the impressive Anglican cathedral St Peter's.

Watching cricket at the Adelaide Oval could be likened to a religious experience, although the Father, Son and Holy Ghost would do well to block their ears and avert their eyes from some of the carry-on from the bank in front of the scoreboard. Only the thirstiest of souls tend to congregate there and, on 26 January at least, only the most parochial.

Stephen Fleming won the toss and batted first. Brendon McCullum, in his first and ill-fated series, was quickly removed by Glenn McGrath, but Nathan Astle (95) and Lou Vincent (55) laid the foundation for a big score that never quite happened, despite a six-hitting cameo from Chris Cairns. As the players traipsed from the oval for the dinner break on that sweltering day, it was generally accepted that the run rate required of a tick under five per over was easily achieved and with a batting line-up that was uniformly world class, the hosts held all the aces.

All but one.

Like McCullum, the VB Series was Bond's first one-day international assignment. Unlike McCullum, it was going well. Probably a bit better than well. He'd taken three wickets on debut against Australia at the Melbourne Cricket Ground, and while the South Africans had given him some tap in Hobart, he'd rebounded well to take 2 for 28 in an upset win against Australia at the Sydney Cricket Ground and 4 for 37 against the Proteas at the Gabba, a game defined by Chris Cairns' match-winning century.

So when Australia Day dawned, it really needed to be Australia's day, or else their destiny in their own tournament would be in the hands of others. The bowlers had done half the job, now it was time for their Ricky Ponting-led batting line-up to complete it.

Dion Nash, a man who like Bond would have played a lot more for New Zealand were it not for back injuries, claimed Mark Waugh caught and bowled off a leading edge for a duck in the opening over, then Bond went to work. He tempted Ponting into nicking behind to Adam Parore for no score. Damien Martyn, tormented by Fleming's Great-Wall-of-China off-side field setting all summer, was dropped and then caught in the point cordon for 2.

'The way Bondy had the Aussies on the back foot was sensational and Flem suddenly had a weapon he could navigate,' McMillan would write in his biography, *Out of the Park*. 'The rest of our attack became better bowlers overnight as batters took more risks against them rather than Shane.'

It was the start New Zealand needed, but Adam Gilchrist was looking ominous. He was a remarkable player. He wasn't muscular like a typical power hitter but tall and lean. He gripped the bat high on the handle and hit through the line with astonishing effect. Even his thick edges seemed to race away for fours. With the total on 26 in the eighth over, and with 21 of them to Gilchrist's name, Bond decided to go length. Instead, the ball came out hot, turned into an unplayable yorker and ripped through his defence. Wow. It was one of those moments where every cricket fan in New Zealand was watching their screens and thought, 'We've got a proper bowler here.'

That single ball, regardless of whether he was trying to bowl back of a length or not, made a profound impression on Gilchrist and had a transformative effect on Bond's career.

'It was simply too good for me,' Gilchrist would say. 'During my career two balls stood out for me that I felt I could do nothing about. One was a beauty I got from Shoaib Akhtar on my test debut and the other was that one from Shane. It was quick, it was full and it swung late. There aren't many days when you walk off the field and you're not feeling disappointed but that was one of them. You just accept the fact that it was too good and there was nothing you could do about it.'

Bond would take 5 for 25 that day and New Zealand would win comfortably and, with a few shenanigans in between, Australia would eventually be locked out of the finals of their own tournament. In his autobiography, *Looking Back*, Bond explained how that Gilchrist delivery and dismissal altered his mindset.

'All of a sudden I was 10-foot tall. I was walking back to my mark thinking, "I can do this; I'm going to run in and bowl this now." Just like that, everything about the way I approached my cricket was changed. Rather than hoping I could hang in there and compete with these guys, I was planning how to get them out.'

The astonishing thing about the pace of change was that earlier in that same summer, Bond was a uniformed police officer, working out of a kiosk on Cathedral Square, keeping an eye out for trouble of a different kind than that posed by Gilchrist and Ponting et al.

* * * * * * *

Bond's rise from policeman to the New Zealand squad wasn't without controversy, but before we get to his selection in the New Zealand A team to tour India, a decision that sent a well-meaning Central Districts administrator into a paroxysm of anger, we need to understand how, in this era of full professionalism, one of the country's greatest bowlers became part of the thin blue line in the first place.

Despite going to an unfashionable cricket school, Papanui High, Bond's talent had been such that he was part of Canterbury age-group squads that were always dominated by the larger-than-life personality and talent of Craig McMillan. Bond was not a standout.

'There were no real signs at an early age that Bondy would end up being one of New Zealand's greatest-ever fast bowlers,' McMillan would later say.

Upon leaving school, Bond would join the High School Old Boys club and form a four-pronged pace attack with Stu Roberts, Chris Flanagan and Geoff Allott. Of that quartet, only Flanagan would not play for New Zealand, though he did play more than 20 first-class games for Canterbury. Bond never took a lot of wickets for Old Boys, but he showed enough promise to be drafted into the Canterbury senior squad. As an indication of some of the barriers he was breaking, on one of the first sponsors' evenings he attended, a tweed-coated man approached him to ask whether he had attended Christchurch Boys' High or Christ's College. When he mentioned where he in fact received his secondary education, the gentleman eyed him up and down and simply said, 'Haven't you done well, then?'

Bond's first over in first-class cricket was flayed for 16 runs by former Cantab Llorne Howell, who was now playing for Central Districts, but he soon had Mathew Sinclair out nicking behind and finished his first season with the Plunket Shield (known as the Shell Trophy) and 21 wickets at a decent average of 25.

Bond was also attending teachers' college, but discovered quickly that teaching wasn't in his future, so when he was offered a place in the New Zealand Cricket Academy, just down the road in Lincoln, for the 1997 year, he jumped at the chance. It was at the academy that Bond realised for the first time in his life that despite modelling himself on his hero, Sir Richard Hadlee, he was actually an in-swing bowler, not an out-swinger.

His reintroduction to the vagaries of vertebrae occurred during the 1997–98 season, when he broke his back during a club game. It was during this period of inactivity that he made some tough decisions about his life. Although he was just 22, he was frustrated by his progress as a cricketer; frustrated not just by his propensity for picking up injuries but also by the fact that one day he would seem to bowl quick, the next he would barely be above medium pace. At that point in his life, he didn't see cricket as a financially viable career decision so while recuperating from his stress fracture, made the call to go to university in 1998 and to kickstart an application to join the police. Bond did a year of property valuation at Lincoln University and received news in 1999 that he had been accepted to police college. There was a cricket itch that he needed to scratch first, so having recovered from his broken back, he and partner Tracey went north for a season of league cricket in Barrow-in-Furness, a town on the windswept Morecambe Bay, not far from the romance of the Lake District and the less romantic Sellafield nuclear power station.

'Along came Bond, like a storm blown in from the Irish Sea. Within weeks, his name would be on everyone's lips, while severely testing the punning capabilities of the headline writers at the *Barrow Evening Mail*,' wrote Crizzbuzz of Bond's impact in the North Lancashire and District League.

Bond was a sensation for Furness CC. With future Black Caps teammate Daryl Tuffey just across the estuary at Millom, the two New Zealanders went hammer and tongs all season to try to earn their respective clubs a championship. Furness won on the last day of the season, Bond's 130 wickets being the difference maker, smashing past South African Andre Nel's record of 102 for Millom in 1998. Bond also batted No. 4 and scored a few runs, too, so after a Kon-Tiki tour, he returned home and at least entered policing feeling better about cricket than when he applied.

'Being in the police taught me a lot of things about life and a lot of things about myself,' Bond recalled in *Looking Back*. 'What it didn't do was end my career. In fact, I came out a better player and, I would like to think, a more rounded individual. I learned that there was a world outside of cricket but the flipside of that was that I knew the utter dedication I would need to succeed once I started playing seriously again.'

Within months he would be playing and starring for New Zealand on their tour to Australia, but as a precursor, he was called into the New Zealand A squad — despite the name it is essentially a 2nd XI — to replace the injured Scott Styris for a month-long tour to India on the recommendation of Dayle Hadlee. This outraged Central Districts convenor of selectors Basil Netten, who intimated the decision had nothing to do with talent and everything to do with location.

To be fair to Netten, a CD stalwart, his accusations of a Canterbury bias in national selection issues wasn't totally unwarranted then (and haven't been for much of New Zealand's cricket history), but on this occasion he was dead wrong. Bond was exactly the sort of bowler New Zealand had been crying out for and his performances in India helped NZ A win the tournament — no mean feat in alien conditions.

It was the last time Bond's selection was ever called into question — well, not due to his playing ability, at least.

* * * * * * * *

Bond's start for New Zealand was hugely promising, but it was also fitful. On the strength of his exploits with the 'A' side, he was called in as a replacement for the test series against Australia in 2001–02 and in his first three innings at the bowling crease took the wickets of Steve Waugh in Hobart, Matthew Hayden in the first innings at Perth, and Justin Langer in the second. He had turned heads without necessarily getting the rewards, but that changed in the VB tri-series to follow, where he would walk away with the player of the series award.

He missed the following series against England at home due to a foot injury but was fit again by the time Bangladesh arrived. Bond went with the Black Caps to the West Indies in early winter, where he took five-wicket bags in back-to-back tests during the team's first successful series in the Caribbean. That was followed by a short stint at Warwickshire before heading to Sri Lanka for the Champions Trophy and a successful home test and ODI series against India on extremely juicy wickets.

That provided the lead-in for New Zealand's tilt at the World Cup in South Africa, a campaign made more difficult by their decision not to go to Kenya for security reasons, costing the side what would have been considered two easy points. It was a mixed tournament for Bond, with the highest of highs sitting right next to unfathomable lows. He bowled pretty well against Sri Lanka in the opener, a match New Zealand lost after getting their tactics wrong. He went wicketless in a critical win over the West Indies and got pumped around the field against South Africa in Johannesburg to the tune of 1 for 73. His mood was lightened by Stephen Fleming's incredible match-winning century.

After a break of more than a week due to not travelling to Nairobi, Bond came back with 3 for 33 and 3 for 29 against overmatched Bangladesh and Canada line-ups, before going wicketless in a six-wicket win against Zimbabwe.

The next match against Australia was pivotal. In a complicated system, the top three teams from each of the two pools qualified for the Super Sixes, where you carried your points scored against other qualifiers through to that phase, and a quarter of the points you scored against non-qualifiers. Because they had forfeited their match against Kenya and lost to Sri Lanka, the other qualifiers from their pool, it meant they only carried four points into that stage compared to Sri Lanka's 7.5 and Kenya's 10. In the Super Sixes you only played the teams that had qualified from the other pool, so they effectively had to beat Zimbabwe, which they did comfortably, and at least one and possibly both of Australia and India. On a strange-looking St George's Park wicket in Port Elizabeth, Fleming won the toss and inserted Australia, resulting in one very grumpy fast bowler who had been led to believe his team would bat first.

'I remember thinking, "My key bowler thinks I'm an idiot",' Fleming recalled for *Looking Back*. 'I was under no illusion as to what he thought of my decision.'

Probably still sulking, Bond bowled poorly in his first over, but by the time he had uprooted Ian Harvey's middle stump Australia were 84 for 7. Bond finished with 6 for 23 but Australia somehow scraped together 208 for 9 thanks to Michael Bevan and Andy Bichel.

New Zealand replied with a pitiful 112, despite having a batting line-up that featured all-rounders all the way to No. 10.

'I walked out to bat at No. 11 when the match was as good as lost,' Bond would write. 'I was dark. I couldn't hide what a foul mood I was in. On a personal level it was a landmark game for me. . . but at the time it was about the most hollow, gut-wrenching feeling I could imagine.'

There would be another gut-wrenching feeling to come when the team went to Sri Lanka for a one-day series. Dambulla is a town about 150 km from Colombo, but Bond would feel each and every one of the ruts and potholes as he was ferried by car from the interior town to the capital to fly back to New Zealand after aggravating his back in the nets, and then putting paid to it properly in the tri-series ODI against Pakistan. Bond left that field having taken 2 for 7 off five overs and wouldn't bowl for New Zealand in an international again for more than two years.

Bond took four months off after the Sri Lanka tour, built his strength up at training and decided to try to play in a club match.

'One ball was all it took. Bang, the back went again,' Bond would write.

One of the ironies of Bond's injury history is that nobody worked harder and nobody was more conscious of eliminating the sort of behaviours that contribute to injuries, but that didn't stop his supposed frailty being a constant source of derision on sports radio.

'It amazes me the criticism he has endured about the injuries. Just how many of those voicing their opinions have had their spine fused back together? Not many I'm guessing,' McMillan would say. 'Shane was probably the most professional guy in our team in terms of the amount of fitness work he did. Despite his run of injuries, he worked so hard. It must have been demoralising, dealing with setback after setback, having to start from scratch again.'

It was, but all Bond could do was get back to work, to look after his body. He did a lot of work with renowned boxing trainer Kevin Barry Sr. Bond didn't just love the training and the strengthening of his core. He loved the life lessons and Barry Sr's rough-hewn philosophies based around loyalty, honesty and, in particular, being true to yourself.

Working with Barry Sr helped clarify what he wanted out of life and that was to use his skills, and therefore his body, to maximise his potential and help set up his family. He took pride in his blue-collar upbringing and loved his mother, Jude, for all the sacrifices she made for him and his sister Tracey, but he wanted his wife, also a Tracey, and their three kids to have some of the creature comforts he never had.

One of the things he could do was eliminate risk, so his partying days stopped, just like that.

'When I first came into the side there were times, particularly during one-day series, where I felt we should have been drinking less than we did. If we got on a roll we tended to celebrate each win as if it were a final and I fell into that culture a bit at the start. As I got older and decided what I wanted to do with my life — which was basically to be the best fast bowler I could — I just learned to say no. Because my body wasn't the most reliable, I couldn't take the risk of getting injured because I was tired or had been out drinking, so I just completely shut down that side of touring. I was non-existent socially. Even if we won a test, I'd only have a couple,' he wrote.

'Did I ever miss it, knowing that the guys were out having a good time, relaxing and enjoying themselves? One word — no. I wanted to finish my career knowing that I did everything I could to give myself the best chance of being the best. I'm proud that I achieved that. I'm not the sort who goes stir crazy in my room. [Having young kids at the time] it gave me the chance to catch up on sleep, do a bit of gym work, some video analysis and just watch telly. Not the most exciting lifestyle in the world, but there you have it.'

With what now seems to be a staggering lack of foresight, Bond regained his strength and was selected for the test and ODI tour to England in 2004. He never made it past the warm-up game against Kent before he was on a plane back home again. The recriminations were more testing this time. Bond had lost faith in the NZC-prescribed rehabilitation process and sought more radical intervention, consulting with Dr Grahame Inglis.

The renowned orthopaedic surgeon gave Bond no guarantees, saying he had only performed the procedure he was about to recommend on two athletes, neither of them cricketers. He warned that Bond was unlikely to be able to bowl as quickly post-surgery as he had done in the past. Still, it was a simple choice. The other option was to keep doing what had not worked for the past year.

The surgery, which essentially fused some troublesome vertebrae together with a titanium rod and some pins, was a success. After many anxious days and nights wondering if he'd be able to pick up his kids let alone bowl again, Bond came back brilliantly on a tour to Zimbabwe, taking 10 wickets in the second test and six wickets against India in a tri-series ODI in Bulawayo, his victims including Sourav Ganguly, Rahul Dravid and Virender Sehwag, who would describe him at one point as the hardest bowler he had faced.

Playing at home for the first time in a long time, Bond was dynamite against the West Indies in the first test of their 2006 series at Eden Park, taking another five-wicket bag, but he injured himself in the process, missed the second test with a swollen knee and needed a cortisone shot to get him through the third. He made the plane to South Africa for a subsequent series but returned home without playing to get minor surgery on his knee. Bond returned by the end of 2006, bowling well in the Champions Trophy hosted in India — New Zealand lost the semi-final to Australia — before returning home to play a test and ODI series against Sri Lanka.

Everything was pointing towards the World Cup in the West Indies and Bond was in good form, enjoying a good run in the tri-series in Australia, also featuring England. Back home, he took another five-wicket bag against Australia, this time at the Cake Tin in a Chappell–Hadlee match, the highlight being a stupendous caught-and-bowled to dismiss Cam White, the quality of which was matched only by the Photosport photographer who captured him taking the ball millimetres off the turf.

Bond was feeling confident about the World Cup. Under John Bracewell, he felt the side had been primed nicely for a strong result. The team was experienced and expected to do well in the Caribbean conditions. In some respects, the World Cup was a disappointment, with poor organisation and underprepared grounds failing to ignite locals and television audiences alike.

Bond might not have taken big clumps of wickets as he had in South Africa four years and a few stress fractures ago, but he was close to unplayable at times. New Zealand went through pool play unbeaten, with Bond's 2 for 19 off 10 overs and 1 for 19 off eight overs important contributions to wins against England and Kenya, before he was rested for the final pool match against Canada.

In the Super Eight stage, another ICC tinkering with the tournament, he dominated the West Indies with 3 for 31, while

Bangladesh (2 for 15) and Ireland (2 for 18) found him difficult to score off. He was economical but went wicketless in a loss to Sri Lanka, while he took 2 for 26 off 10 when New Zealand beat South Africa at Grenada to book their spot in the semi-finals against Sri Lanka in Kingston, Jamaica. Bond was confident and, because it's how he's conditioned, he said so, stating that Sri Lanka was the team they wanted and that Sabina Park was where they wanted them.

A bout of diarrhoea before the game left him down on energy, and although he didn't bowl terribly, he was missing a spark, and under beautiful blue skies the Asian side piled on 289 for 5. During the lunch break, the clouds rolled in, and facing gloomy conditions and a suddenly swinging ball, New Zealand barely made it to 200. It was a lame end to a tournament that promised much but fell short in key areas.

'It was dreadful,' Bond would write of the tournament, 'there's no other word for it. It was without doubt the most boring tournament I had ever been to. There was so much down-time it was not funny. . .

'There was no feeling that we were at a big tournament. There were no crowds and no vibe and playing cricket in the West Indies was meant to be all about crowd noise and vibe. We could have been playing on the moon for all the atmosphere there was. It was weird.'

* * * * * * * *

Weird would be an apt way to describe how the final two years of Bond's career played out.

He would attend the World T20 in South Africa under Dan Vettori, when New Zealand were beaten in the semi-finals by Pakistan, but then came the bombshell: Bond had signed to play in a Twenty20 franchise tournament in India funded by a broadcaster, Zee Entertainment Enterprises, trying to get a toehold in that vast and lucrative market.

At the same time, India's governing body, the BCCI, was making plans for its own tournament that would become the global behemoth Indian Premier League, but at the time, the Indian Cricket League negotiations and contracting with Bond were far more advanced and, frankly, more lucrative. After some toing and froing with New Zealand Cricket, Bond was given a clearance to play in the ICL on the proviso he would be available for all international commitments.

Not long after he signed, he took another call from Justin Vaughan, NZC chief executive, though this one was far from welcome. Vaughan told Bond that under the little-known ICC Operating Manual paragraph 31.1, NZC would have to terminate Bond's contract and he wouldn't be able to play for New Zealand. Vaughan was not Bond's favourite person, but with hindsight it is clear how little sway in the matter he had. The BCCI was in the early stages of flexing its considerable muscle on the cricket world and having high-profile players in their country playing in a 'rebel' tournament was not going to wash.

Bond had signed on the dotted line, however, and was not going to renege on the deal he had agreed with the ICL's Australasian envoy, the late Tony Greig. Bond played a couple of tournaments for Delhi Giants, quite enjoyed the cricket and was paid very well, but once the BCCI decided it was the enemy, it never really stood a chance. The ICL matches were played at backwater venues without crowds and became a hotbed of corruption. In 2009 it folded, offering Bond a lifeline back to the Black Caps.

In terms of tests, that lifeline lasted five thrilling days against Pakistan at the University Oval, with Bond taking his fifth and final five-wicket bag in the first innings and, as Pakistan chased 251 on the final day, took his 85th, 86th and 87th test wickets to lead New Zealand to victory and secure him a man of the match award. He also tore a stomach muscle and, with his ability to stay on the park increasingly compromised, chose to promptly retire from red-ball cricket.

The hope was that Bond would be able to play through to the

2011 Cricket World Cup in India, and he looked on track when taking four wickets in the final Chappell–Hadlee ODI at the Cake Tin. What Bond knew but few others did was that that would be his last match for New Zealand in New Zealand. He was tired, he was constantly sore, and although the games were fine, he had lost his appetite to do the work to prepare for them. He had a nice IPL contract in front of him. It was time to walk away.

A month later New Zealand was in the West Indies for the World T20. Various people had been trying to talk Bond into staying a bit longer, getting through to the World Cup just over a year away, but Bond realised going to a tournament wasn't a worthwhile goal in itself, especially if his mind and body weren't going to allow him to give the best account of himself. In test cricket he had the tangible goal of 100 test wickets and although he didn't get there, it gave him focus. In T20 cricket he couldn't get himself fired up by stats because they were largely meaningless in those early, less analytical days. In ODI cricket he needed to be a wicket-taker, but he didn't feel he had it in him to be that guy any more.

In the West Indies, New Zealand needed to beat England to progress out of the Super 8s into the semi-finals. By the time he got to the final ball of his fourth over, it was clear England were going to win.

In *Looking Back*, he recalled the scene.

'"This is my last ball," I said to Dan on the way back to my mark.

'"Is it?"

'"Yeah, definitely, this is it."

'"Sweet," he said.

'So I ran in, full noise, delivered it and . . . got carved over midwicket for four by Bresnan.'

Not everyone gets to write the perfect postscript. With all the trials and tribulations Bond went through just to get onto the park, he knows that better than anyone.

CHAPTER 7
BRENDON MCCULLUM
(ONZM)

Debit: 2002							Last match: 2016
	Matches	Runs	Ave	S/R	100s	50s	Dismissals*
Test:	101	6453	38.64	64.6	12	31	209
ODI:	260	6083	30.41	96.37	5	32	277
T20I:	71	2140	35.66	136.21	2	13	44

Wins as captain: Tests 11 (win % 36), ODIs 36 (win % 58), T20Is 12 (win % 46)

*Includes catches as a keeper and a fielder

The morning of 18 February 2014 witnessed one of the more remarkable sights in New Zealand sporting history. It was a grey old Tuesday morning in the nation's capital, but there were queues of people lined up where Cambridge Terrace on one side and Adelaide Road at the other met the big green roundabout that is the Basin Reserve.

It was the last day of what was essentially a dead test. New Zealand had batted themselves to safety on the fourth day and the now-lifeless wicket was offering nothing to give New Zealand any realistic hope of running through a powerful Indian batting line-up on the final afternoon.

There were just 19 good reasons to gather. Brendon McCullum,

New Zealand's captain and No. 5, would start the morning on 281 not out, on the precipice of becoming the first New Zealander to 300, a figure made more mythical by Martin Crowe being dismissed on this same ground for 299 some 23 years earlier.

'It's a bit like climbing Everest and pulling a hamstring before the last stride,' Crowe would say more than once to describe the pain felt at falling short of the exclusive club.

McCullum's hamstrings were tight. So was the rest of his body. His mind was fraying slightly, too. On the fourth evening he had reacted scratchily when the 12th man had offered him encouragement to see it through to stumps. 'Listen, I'm on 200 and whatever, surely I'm kind of done here, eh?' The unwavering water carrier insists that it would be a tremendous achievement to bat the whole day on top of his work on day three so McCullum negotiated a deal and sure enough, when he saw out the day, the first thing he saw on his seat in the changing rooms were two cans of beer in an ice bucket and a packet of cigarettes. As an advertisement for the benefits of healthy living, it fell short; as a salve for an aching body and unfocused mind, it was just the ticket.

'I put my bat down, take my gloves off, open a can and just hammer it,' McCullum would write.

To that point it had not been a typical McCullum innings, though even that reads a little lazily because the diminutive right-hander had shown there was far more to his game than the swashbuckling middle-order cavalier he had become known as. Two of his more complete test innings had come under the cosh — 96 made at No. 3 against England at Lord's in just his fourth test (he'd batted No. 9 in the first innings so it was a sudden and dizzying promotion), and 225 opening against India at Hyderabad in 2010, his first tour since giving away the gloves and taking his selection chances as a batter alone.

Still, when he reached his first milestone at the Basin — somewhat fortuitously as he'd been dropped by Virat Kohli in front of the wicket early — he'd shown the sort of restraint not normally associated with his game. 'Fifty-one off 146 balls,' intoned Scott Styris from the tenuous safety of the broadcasting booths atop the creaking RA Vance stand, 'a very unusual McCullum innings.' When he baseball-batted Ishant Sharma over long-on for six to move from 94 to 100, it felt like his way of showing the 'usual' McCullum was still lurking in there; he just knew when to hide and when to show himself.

McCullum batted all through day four, first in partnership with BJ Watling, a man he had smoked many 'durries' with behind various grandstands and changing sheds around the world as they sought to calm frazzled nerves, and then James Neesham, a debutant with enough outward confidence to carry himself like a veteran.

At stumps, McCullum skolled his can of lager with the quiet satisfaction of knowing that he had done what he had set out to do: bat his side to safety and a series win. Still, when he went to bed that night after a pint with his dad Stu and New Zealand Cricket president Stephen Boock at the Cambridge Hotel, he did so knowing that the next 19 runs were the most important. Even if sleep came easily, it did not take long the following morning to understand the magnitude of the interest. Day four might have been one for the cricket purists, but the prospects for history on day five had captured the attention of the entire country, it seemed. When he flicked on the telly, front and centre was Crowe, a man McCullum had a complicated relationship with after he was elevated to the captaincy to replace Ross Taylor, Crowe's protégé. But here was Crowe, talking effusively about the significance of reaching the elusive triple century, what it would mean to all the players that had come before McCullum and all of those who had followed the team through thick and thin.

In his autobiography, *Declared*, McCullum wrote:

'I didn't really know it was that big a deal, probably because milestones have never really been my gig . . . I like to think that what's more important is the fact that we've batted for two-and-a-half days to save a test match against the number-one team in the world, which means that, with a day to play, we've as good as won the series. That's what I've been thinking is significant.

'Then we get to the ground and everybody is asking "How are you feeling?"

'"Yeah, not too bad. A bit stiff."

'Yeah, but how does it feel turning up to the ground on two hundred and eighty? How does that feel?'

'To be honest, I was feeling a lot better before you asked.

'Then we're out doing our warm-ups, our stretches, in our little circle, having a laugh and a chat, and I turn around and just for a second clock the stands and the grassy banks of the Basin. Man, there are a lot of people here! An hour before kick-off on the last day of the test match! Then I start hearing people yelling out to me. And I see the signs they're carrying and the numbers still pouring through the gate.

'Back in the changing room, I have one last durry and walk out there with Jimmy. All the guys are clapping us out. As I step towards the boundary rope, I take a moment, look at the crowd, and I get it that they've come to see a bit of history . . . I don't normally get nervous, but now I am. Mainly because I just don't want to let people down . . . If I get out for anything less [than 300], this innings will be a disappointment not just for me, but for the nation.'

The next 10 overs would be a seminal moment in McCullum's career and, indeed, New Zealand cricket. After a nervy start in overcast conditions — McCullum edges his score up by just three singles in the first five overs — he starts to find his groove with a flicked four through midwicket off Sharma and an imperious pull off Zaheer Khan. The following over from Sharma sees near-calamity. On 293, McCullum gets an edge to a leg-cutter and his head is on a swivel as he turns to see it drop inches short of MS Dhoni's gloves.

The Basin collectively exhales, while the camera pans to show his father sitting alone, chewing his nails. He didn't get time to bite them to the quick. After a brief diversion where Jimmy Neesham became the third New Zealander behind Bruce Taylor and Scott Styris to score a debut century at No. 8, McCullum pounced on a ball from Khan that was neither very short nor very wide and slid it powerfully behind point to the boundary.

'The next five minutes I'll never forget. The crowd won't stop cheering, won't sit down,' McCullum would write.

As a headline in the global behemoth that is ESPNcricinfo would say, 'the sprinter had just run a marathon'. In doing so he had found something that had been elusive throughout his career: near-universal adoration.

Crowe, who late in his life had become an insightful and reflective columnist, wrote the following about McCullum's innings and his metamorphosis as a cricketer.

'McCullum is the true leader, marching his men forward with exemplary and extraordinary example.

'With New Zealand 30 for 3 in Auckland, he strode in and dismantled the Indian attack for 224, setting up a stunning, close-fought victory. To then contemplate a dire situation with a stirring rearguard action only days later, in the second test, and occupy the crease longer than any Kiwi has ever done, speaks volumes of his character and his stamina. For a man with career-threatening back and knee injuries screaming at him, it simply defies all odds.

'From the little I know of Brendon, he is a sensitive, intensely proud, even emotionally driven, human. By removing the emotion from his game he allowed the right energy to flow through his game, settling him into a zone of fierce focus and determination, where he was always aware the job was never done. He showed that with responsibility he could seek a new wisdom, a better way, and that a large picture can only be created one fluent stroke at a time. His defence was immaculate, his footwork aligned and flowing, to making the bowler bend down to field, his concentration built one over at a time.'

The triple century was, to a degree, indicative of where McCullum was as a player in the autumn of his career. If he had spent his spring and summer as a freakishly athletic wicketkeeper, seemingly more capable of frustrating the watching public as he was of entertaining them with dashing cameos, 2014 was a revelation. He would become the first New Zealander to score 1000 test runs in a calendar year — a feat you would have got long odds on McCullum achieving ahead of more studious run-gatherers like Glenn Turner, Crowe, Ross Taylor and Kane Williamson.

It had been presaged in December 2013 with his first test century in three years, and his first as captain, against the West Indies at Dunedin, but that gave little clue as to the sheer volume of runs that were about to ping from the middle of his Puma-branded bat. Against India, his match-saving 302 was preceded by a double century at Auckland that set up victory. A poor personal tour of the West Indies was followed by a tour to the UAE to face Pakistan where he got better every innings, scoring 18, 39, 43, 45 and, finally, a 279-ball 202 to lead New Zealand to one of its most improbable comeback victories — a test overshadowed by the death of Phillip Hughes.

His final act of the year told you everything you needed to know about how McCullum viewed the game. Test cricket was returning to Christchurch for the first time since the devastating 2011 earthquake that had killed 185 people and left many buildings, including the old home of cricket at Lancaster Park, uninhabitable and unusable. It was the first test at Hagley Oval, against Sri Lanka. The evening before the test, Canterbury Cricket CEO and former New Zealand captain Lee Germon cried when he handed the players their test caps, thankful that his kids would get a chance to enjoy what he did as a child and watch test cricket in their home city.

New Zealand lost the toss on a misty Christchurch morning and were in a measure of trouble at 88 for 3 when the skipper strode to the middle in the first over after lunch, with Kane Williamson on 34 not out. The next wicket fell 126 runs later at 214, with Williamson dismissed for 54. In between times McCullum has smashed a 74-ball century, surpassing the fastest test century by a New Zealander, a record he had set one innings earlier in Sharjah.

McCullum was seeing it like a beach ball and another double century was at his mercy, but on 195 and facing just his 134th ball, he was caught on the long-off boundary attempting his 12th six. He would have smashed Astle's 153-ball record for the double-ton. To the roundheads among us, it made no sense. The game was so far advanced and McCullum was in such good form against an attack that was on its knees, why wouldn't he have just milked the remaining five runs to bring up his fifth 200-plus score? It's a question McCullum would have no truck with. To see the world through his eyes, he was on a roll, hitting with the wind against a spinner, Tharindu Kaushal, on debut. He'd been out pfaffing around as milestones approached in the past, so why wouldn't he try to reach this in one hit in those circumstances?

It was the inveterate gambler in McCullum coming out, but it was also the start of something else — a patchy and overly frenetic end to his international career.

But we'll get to that soon.

*   *   *   *   *   *   *   *

McCullum is not the best player to ever take guard for New Zealand, but he might well be the most influential.

As a player he rode the first wave of Twenty20 and gave instant legitimacy to the Indian Premier League, which has quickly grown to be one of the richest sporting leagues in the world.

As a captain he changed not only New Zealand's fortunes, but the way they played and approached the game.

The South Dunedin scrapper is still leaving an indelible mark on the game as coach, instantly transforming the fortunes of the England test team. So thoroughly revolutionised has been the style of cricket played under his mentorship and New Zealand-born captain Ben Stokes that there is a term for it — Bazball.

The title, which McCullum is known to hate, comes from his nickname Baz, a shortening of his middle name Barrie.

McCullum was born into cricket. As soon as he was able to walk, and possibly even before that, McCullum and his older brother, former international off-spinner Nathan, would call Culling Park, the domain of Albion Cricket Club, the oldest continuous cricket club in New Zealand, their second home.

Dad Stu McCullum blazed a trail as an attacking opening batter in the strong Otago teams of the early 80s. Those teams had hard heads like Warren Lees, Boock, John Bracewell and the Blair brothers, Bruce and Wayne. They were noted for playing an uncompromising brand of cricket on the field and for enjoying themselves off it.

Ahead of McCullum's last test in 2016, his brother Nathan was interviewed about what life was like in the McCullum household.

'We'd follow Dad down to Albion on a Tuesday and Thursday night, hanging out the back waiting for someone to hit us catches. We'd join in the fielding with the older guys.'

The McCullum sibling relationship was competitive, but Nathan is fiercely protective of his younger brother's legacy, believing he has been unfairly typecast.

'People drop that word "talent" like it was something that was dealt to you, but for Brendon it was hours and hours of playing with mates at the school, at home, at the park. Cricket, golf, basketball, soccer, you name it. We'd play for hours on end.

'It was practice without us realising it.'

Brendon once described himself as the ultimate optimist, because that's what cricket-obsessed kids in Dunedin, a city not noted for the length and consistency of its summers, had to be.

'I was the kid in South Dunedin who lived for Saturday mornings, when I'd pull back the curtains and hope it wasn't raining. The bedroom I shared with [Nathan] faced southeast, so once I'd drawn back the curtains, I could see over the top of the fence, the curving pylons at Forbury Park Raceway that held the lights for the night trots, and above them the sky over St Kilda beach. I was often disappointed. "Scottish mist", the locals call it. I grew up not taking summer for granted. A day of sunshine was precious, because a day of sunshine was a day of cricket.'

His precocity was recognised early, and it was his father's former Otago teammate, John Cushen, who was credited with being the first coach to push Brendon out of his comfort zone. After clearing it with Stu, Cushen went against his better instincts and selected the knee-high-to-a-grasshopper kid to the 1st XI when still in his first year at King's High, a blue-collar boys school in South Dunedin. Almost immediately, McCullum demonstrated a fearlessness and *joie de vivre* that was infectious. In one college match against Southland Boys' High, McCullum was at the crease with one wicket left and needing 16 to win off the last over. Cushen decided that caution was the better part of valour and sent out instructions to block out the final over to ensure a creditable draw. McCullum tried to convince Cushen that he could get the runs but eventually relented and followed orders. Cushen remembered being blown away that this tiny kid, who had yet to develop the Popeye forearms that would bludgeon the best attacks in the world, believed in himself enough to suggest to a crusty old coach that he was good enough to risk a loss in order to chase a win.

It was an ethos McCullum would never lose, even when the losses started to mean a little more and that cavalier style would start to attract the sort of negative reaction reserved for those who it appears are not utilising their talents to the fullest.

McCullum's schoolboy sporting feats were not restricted to cricket. He was also famously picked to start at first five-eighth in the South Island schoolboy rugby side ahead of Dan Carter, a feat he insists says more about the shortcomings of the selectors than any playing primacy he might have enjoyed over the man who would become a three-time World Rugby Player of the Year and who is widely considered the finest No. 10 New Zealand has ever produced. McCullum was also a fine goalkeeper and while at King's played for the 1st XI football side for midweek games and for the 1st XV at weekends.

There was talk about him going into the Highlanders rugby system, but he'd also played two years for the New Zealand Under-19 cricket side, the last one as captain where he went on a run-scoring spree against a visiting South African U19 side that included the likes of Hashim Amla and Johan Botha. He scored three centuries in the 'test' series and, after a schoolboy career lacking in three-figure scores, he had come to the realisation that he could actually bat for long periods when he applied himself.

He made his first-class debut for Otago in the 1999–2000 season, catching eyes more for his agility behind the stumps than for his ability with the bat in front of them. In limited outings in his first two seasons he failed to pass 50 with the bat. There was a significant uptick at the crease in the 2001–02 season and while that form had not transferred itself to the white ball game, he was, on promise rather than productivity, picked as an opener for the New Zealand one-day side playing in a tri-series alongside South Africa in Australia. Not surprisingly, it did not go well. In his debut he was sold down the river by his opening partner Mark Richardson, who was making a rare and misguided attempt at making an impact in limited-overs cricket, run out for 5. It didn't get a whole lot better from there.

By the time he had returned from his first World Cup, in Africa, in 2003, McCullum had played 21 ODIs for his country, and had scored a paltry 193 runs at an average of 13.8. To make matters worse, with New Zealand needing a win to stay in that World Cup, a fired-up Shane Bond induced a nick from Rahul Dravid with India already reeling at 22 for 3 chasing 147 on a tricky wicket. McCullum grassed the simple catch and, with it, effectively the match. Earlier in the tournament he had been front and centre in a nightclub incident that had left star all-rounder Chris Cairns bloodied after being punched by a local following a claim that a shirtless and over-the-top drunk New Zealand contingent had been behaving boorishly.

Recalled McCullum in *Declared*:

'Rampant egos plus testosterone plus booze plus bulletproof attitudes are a volatile mixture when you're a long way from home. There was a lot of clubbing and all the stupidity that went with it — the worst of it an incident outside the Tiger Tiger nightclub in Durban at the World Cup in 2023, where Cairnsy got king hit by this big bugger. Cairnsy went down, blood coming out of his mouth, and was obviously in trouble. When the guy turned on me, I tackled him into a shopfront, tried to pin him with my shoulder as he beat the shit out of me. Luckily, security arrived, but it was pretty hairy there for a while.'

McCullum was making an impact on the cricket world, but not the sort that the New Zealand selectors, who continued to pick him on raw talent rather than results, were hoping for.

Fortunately for McCullum, his initial exposure to test cricket was far smoother. Picked to face a powerful South African side in 2004, McCullum started with a useful double of 57 and 19 not out, opening the second innings after a large hole appeared in the pitch that was potentially dangerous for New Zealand's left-handers Mark Richardson, Stephen Fleming, Jacob Oram and Daniel Vettori. In his third test he scored another half-century, this time in a losing effort.

Later that year he was elevated up the order, this time at Lord's where he struck a wonderful 96 at No. 3, putting on 173 for the second wicket with Richardson. He followed that innings with a half-century at Leeds and finally cracked three figures in Dhaka, when he scored 143 against Bangladesh.

He looked set for a long, hyper-successful test career and although the first part was true — he would become the first player to play 100 consecutive tests from debut, finishing with 101 — success was sometimes elusive and often relative. By the end of 2009 his average was still hovering around the 30 mark, a figure that was decent for a wicketkeeper, but one that most agreed was not representative of his batting talent.

In 2010, with his back ailing and fears of a shortened career, McCullum took the bold step of giving up the gloves, which after a few short detours would end up on the end of BJ Watling's arms, to fight for his place as a batter only. The move would pay immediate dividends on the 2010 tour of India, with scores of 65, 11 not out, 4, 225, 40 and 25, but it was something of a false dawn. In more trying new-ball conditions, McCullum's hard-handed defensive technique was often found out and this phase of his test career is only ever looked upon as a qualified success. Yet looks can be deceiving: though never as consistent one would like a top-of-the-order batter to be, McCullum's average of 39.9 as an opener was superior to his overall average and higher than some greats of the New Zealand game.

It was into the middle order, however, that McCullum eventually slotted and where he would enjoy his most significant successes as a test player.

In the newest, most dynamic format of the game, it would be a different story.

* * * * * * * *

Twenty20 cricket hit New Zealand in a whirlwind of beige, facial hair and bad hairstyles.

On a balmy, midweek Eden Park night, New Zealand took a

Getty Images

Stephen Fleming's class was never in question, although he struggled to turn 50s into centuries. Here, at his adopted home ground of Trent Bridge in 2004, he scored a sparkling 117.

Getty Images

Nathan Astle brought his one-day sensibilities to test cricket on his way to a thrilling double century — the fastest in history — against England at Christchurch.

Getty Images

New Zealand had rarely seen a talent like spin wizard Daniel Vettori, bespectacled and with flowing locks, bowling here on test debut against England in 1997.

Getty Images

Not just a brilliant fast bowler, Shane Bond was also a great 'what-if'
story. It's foot to floor at Gqeberha (Port Elizabeth) on his way to 6 for
23 against Australia at the '03 World Cup.

Getty Images

Adoration was a long time coming for Brendon McCullum, but here he acknowledges an ecstatic Basin Reserve crowd after in 2014 becoming the only New Zealander to score a test triple century.

Getty Images

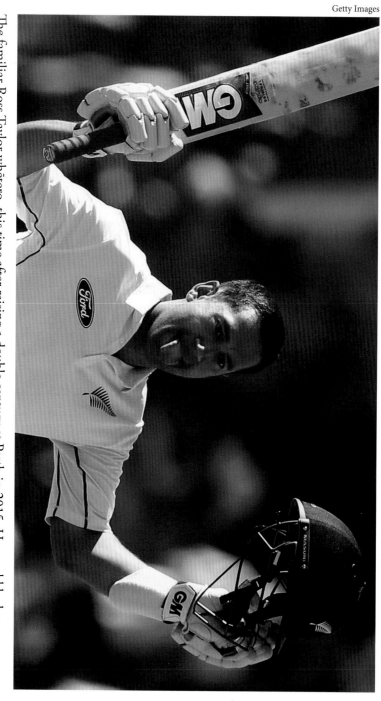

The familiar Ross Taylor whētero, this time after raising a double century at Perth in 2015. He would be last man out for a brilliant 290.

Getty Images

Rhythm and swing: Tim Southee's enduring excellence has played an underrated role in New Zealand's rise to a global force.

Getty Images

Martin Guptill struggled to do his talent justice in tests, but he was a match-winner in white-ball formats, like when he blitzed 237 against the West Indies in the 2015 World Cup.

Getty Images

Whether standing behind the stumps as keeper or in front of them as a batter, BJ Watling only ever had one thought on his mind — how can I help my team win?

Getty Images

Head still, eyes on the ball — Kane Williamson, on the way to 251 against the West Indies in 2020, has broken most New Zealand batting records there are to break.

Getty Images

He might not possess the typical fast-bowler's visage, but don't be fooled, whether bowling with red ball or white, Trent Boult has a killer instinct for wickets.

Getty Images

Neither particularly big nor fast, Pretoria-born Neil Wagner has combined relentless hostility and 100 per cent effort to become one of New Zealand's greatest test bowlers.

Getty Images

The unassuming Tom Latham has proven to be one of New Zealand's most reliable and prolific test openers, and an adaptable ODI wicketkeeper-batsman.

Getty Images

The Black Caps galvanised the country during their 2015 World Cup campaign, highlighted by the Grant Elliott-inspired penultimate-ball victory over South Africa in the semi-final at Eden Park, playing an ultra-aggressive brand of cricket, while at all times remaining humble.

Getty Images

The victory over India in the inaugural World Test Championship final was the culmination of the greatest era in New Zealand cricket history. The team is in celebration mode in the changing sheds at Southampton.

Getty Images

As if to reject the idea that their best days were behind them, the Tim Southee-led Black Caps pulled off their most improbable test victory, defeating Brendon McCullum-coached England in 2023 by one run after following on at the Basin Reserve.

festival approach to its first T20I. It was against the old foe, Australia, and it had all the fun of the fair, with New Zealand opting to don retro beige strips in honour of those first New Zealand sides to compete in the Australian-hosted one-day tri-series of the early 80s. They took the field in head bands, terry-towelling hats, aviator-style sunglasses and Hamish Marshall had teased his curls into an Afro that would not have looked out of place at Studio 54 in the heyday of disco.

Australia, on the other hand, while up for a laugh — Glenn McGrath pretended to reprise the underarm delivery, for example — took the cricket side of the game much more seriously, with captain Ricky Ponting giving a glimpse as to the possibilities of the format as he played genuine cricket shots on his way to 98 not out off 55 balls, setting his side up for a 214 for 5 total that was never seriously challenged, despite a quickfire 36 (24 balls) from McCullum at the top of the order.

At that point in its evolution, a T20I was seen as a nice pipe-opener to a series before the 'real' cricket could begin, but at least two of the New Zealanders on the field that night — Stephen Fleming and McCullum — took the time to look around the stadium and drink in the future.

There were 30,000 people in Eden Park, a crowd so large and unanticipated that the park operators and New Zealand Cricket found themselves hopelessly under-resourced and unable to get the bulk of them to their seats in time for the start.

'Obviously none of us predicted just how much and how quickly it would change the face of the sport, but we had gone into the match thinking it was all a bit of a laugh and we came away thinking very differently,' McCullum would write in his book *Inside Twenty20*.

'The things we kept coming back to were the size of the crowd and the noise they generated. Most of us had never played in front of that sort of a crowd in New Zealand. All the pre-match banter about how ridiculous we could make ourselves look changed pretty quickly to, "Wow, we may have something here that we can really build upon".'

Fast-forward three years and McCullum is taking strike in front of another packed crowd, this time at M. Chinnaswamy Stadium, Bangalore, where the Royal Challengers of that city were about to take on McCullum's Kolkata Knight Riders in the first match of the Indian Premier League.

McCullum had been in lousy form in the lead-up to what, in hindsight, could be accurately described as one of the biggest cricket matches in history. He had barely middled a ball in the nets and at one point batting coach Matthew Mott, the likeable Australian now in charge of England's white-ball problem, refused to let McCullum hit any more balls, believing he was tying himself in knots by trying too hard.

In truth, McCullum was feeling the weight not just of expectation but of the massive US$700,000 price tag he came with. At the inaugural IPL auction, he had declined the opportunity to be picked up for a guaranteed $200,000, opting instead to take his chances on the market. With a reserve price of $175,000 that meant he was risking throwing away $25,000 — or the whole lot in the unlikely scenario that he was passed over — but after a good international season, he justifiably felt his stock was on the rise, and so it proved with Kolkata owner and Bollywood legend Shah Rukh Khan taking a huge punt on his talent.

In the lead-up to the game, while an extravagant opening ceremony took place, McCullum ran into Bangalore adviser Crowe behind the stands. He left quite an impression, with Crowe telling Ross Taylor, who was in the Royal Challengers squad but not the playing XI, that 'Brendon was fizzing'. Taylor would later recall Crowe as continuing: 'He's on the Red Bull. He'll either get a duck or 80.'

In a supercharged atmosphere, McCullum's poor form in the nets transferred to the middle where after seven balls, a lifetime in a T20 powerplay, his score stood at 0.

'Seven dot balls in Twenty20 is almost unforgivable unless you can quickly make up lost ground,' McCullum wrote in *Inside Twenty20*. 'The nerves compounded with every dot ball. I just didn't know where I was going to get a run from. The wicket felt fast, it felt bouncy . . . it was disastrous. I didn't know what was going on.'

Having played out a clumsy maiden to Praveen Kumar, McCullum walked down the wicket to Zaheer Khan in desperation and clubbed him over the infield for an unconvincing four.

That was not all she wrote.

When McCullum left the ground at the end of the 20 overs, he had 158 not out from just 73 balls.

As Royal Challengers Bangalore captain Rahul Dravid would later joke: 'The only good thing about it was that it finished in an hour and a half.'

Ten years later, ESPNcricinfo would rate the innings as one of the 25 most significant moments in the website's history, but for McCullum the innings was a double-edged sword.

'Among all the hubbub in the dressing rooms after the match it was something [long-time India captain Sourav] Ganguly said to me that has stuck with me,' McCullum wrote. 'He sat down next to me, smiled and said: "You know things are never going to be the same for you again." I probably only half acknowledged it. It wasn't that I didn't believe him necessarily, but more that I had no appreciation of the adulation or expectation that comes with cricketing success in that part of the world . . . I didn't realise that playing an innings of that magnitude on that stage would affect how I would be viewed in India from then on.'

He was an instant hero, but Indian cricket fans prefer their heroes to be infallible. McCullum would confess that he spent too much of the next couple of years trying to replicate or surpass his opening-night feat, rather than trying to play the right innings for the time.

He would finish his career with close to 10,000 T20 runs and seven hundreds. Of the T20 pioneers, perhaps only Jamaican Chris Gayle had a greater impact with the bat. It made him a wealthy man. T20 was a big part of McCullum's life and career, but unlike Gayle, it never came to define him.

* * * * * * * *

McCullum's playing career and his cricketing legacy might come to be recognised as two entirely separate entities.

His career was very good. Twelve test centuries — enough to be tied for fifth on New Zealand's all-time list — and 6453 runs (third), along with a bunch of catches and dismissals, give him some better-than-decent numbers.

He played some of the most memorable innings New Zealanders have ever witnessed. Along with those already highlighted, there was a stupendous 116 in a T20I against Australia at Lancaster Park, an innings that saw him scooping balls from the lightning-quick Shaun Tait over his own head for six. It's a shot that is more commonplace now, but in 2010 it was inconceivable to all but a few.

At the 2015 World Cup, he carved brutal half-centuries against Australia and England in pool play, and against South Africa in that stunning semi-final.

In his final test, against Australia at Hagley Oval, he broke the record held by Sir Viv Richards, the Master Blaster, and Misbah-ul-Haq for the fastest century. His 54-ball assault was two better than their 56-ball efforts.

Yet for all the great memories, there were periods, sometimes extended, where he seemed intent on destroying his average as much as he was destroying bowlers. At that 2015 World Cup, for example, when people recall McCullum's input, they tend to gloss over the fact he played a pivotal, perhaps *the* pivotal, role in getting New Zealand there and instead remember his contribution to the showpiece game, a three-ball duck.

'I forgot to watch the ball,' McCullum would later lament.

'He's complex. He's got contradictory skills. He's mercurial and you'll see both sides of that package in the same innings,' said Richard Boock upon McCullum's retirement. Boock, the brother of former international left-arm spinner Stephen, was a long-time cricket writer for his native *Otago Daily Times* and the *New Zealand Herald*, before he became a public relations manager at New Zealand Cricket. 'He's a fantastic player who everyone wonders if he could have been even better if he'd just done things more their way.

'If you were lucky enough to see him in full cry, it was more memorable than many of the so-called greats. His approach has touched a lot of people.'

Indeed, his approach still reverberates through the New Zealand game, and now with England where, at the time of writing, he had started his tenure as coach of the test side in spectacularly successful fashion, taking a moribund side and winning nine of their first 11 matches (in the previous 11 tests they had won two and lost six).

When he captained New Zealand, after a shaky start he convinced his team to play in a way that was authentic to them. For most of the six decades of New Zealand's international cricket existence they had tried to emulate England, the country where the best players — Martin Donnelly, Tom Pritchard, Glenn Turner, Sir Richard Hadlee, Geoff Howarth, John Wright, Martin Crowe and Stephen Fleming to name some — went to play on the county scene.

When the county doors closed as the international calendar became too packed, New Zealand hired Australians to key positions in the high-performance set-up and the players, whether consciously or not, tried to emulate a more hard-bitten, combative approach to their cricket.

This had limited success for a while but was not particularly appealing to a public that preferred the stoic humility (and success) of the All Blacks to the suddenly brash cricketers.

After the Cape Town humbling, McCullum, along with the rest of the management team, made a concerted effort to instil the best national characteristics into their cricket: innovative, occasionally daring, never submissive.

That, more than any numbers, is what McCullum should be most fondly remembered for.

In 2014, McCullum was recognised by the country's largest newspaper, the *Herald*, as its New Zealander of the Year. He had this to say:

'I'm never going to go down as a great player or have great stats. I spent too much time worrying about numbers when I was younger, but then I realised stats can tell you what you want to hear . . . What I'm most proud of is that I've learnt from my mistakes. I've changed from a keeper-batsman to a batsman and I've got better.

'I know I'm never going to go down as a great player but when I do decide to leave the game, at least I'll know I've made a contribution to it.'

A hell of a contribution, as it turned out.

CHAPTER 8
ROSS TAYLOR
(CNZM)

Debit: 2006   Last match: 2022

	Matches	Runs	Ave	S/R	100s	50s	Catches
Test:	112	7683	44.66	59.29	19	35	163
ODI:	236	8607	47.55	83.32	21	51	142
T20I:	102	1909	26.15	122.37	-	7	46

Captaincy: Tests 4 (win % 28.6), ODIs 6 (win % 30), T20Is 6 (win % 46.2)

There's an anecdote from Ross Taylor's schoolboy cricket days that paints a vivid picture of the player he would become.

As Paul Gibbs, a former first-class cricketer and Taylor's coach at Palmerston North Boys' High School, tells it, Taylor was batting for his 1st XI against Marist, one of the stronger clubs in the Manawatū premier competition, when he clearly edged one down the leg side and was caught behind.

(Taylor would later say, unconvincingly, that he 'wasn't sure' that he hit it.)

'It was one of those games when we were using player-umpires,' Gibbs said. 'Tradition dictates that when you're playing with team-mates as umpires, you walk when you nick one. I was standing at square leg and there was a huge appeal, but Rossco didn't walk, and from where I was standing it looked very out. Well, these men just unleashed everything they had at him, and from my point of view he got everything he deserved.

'It just transformed Ross. From there he was a different player. He took them apart [scoring a first-innings century]. Before the second innings I told him why I thought he should have walked and told him that I wanted him to use the second innings as a chance to bat time. Well, he smashed 116 in less than a session and went out. It was pretty hard to criticise him after that.'

That was the young Taylor and the Taylor he would become wrapped into one package: wide-eyed but not naive, outwardly cocky and inwardly sensitive, outrageously talented and a prolific scorer of centuries.

There is a danger that Taylor, who retired from international cricket in 2022, has not had the recognition he has perhaps deserved. Sure, it was a fine farewell — the player tunnel, the big-screen mementoes, the gathered family and friends — but did we actually realise the magnitude of the player that was leaving?

Possibly not.

Partly that's because his career ran concurrently with Brendon McCullum, a massive personality and arguably the most influential cricket figure in modern New Zealand cricket history, and Kane Williamson, the country's greatest batter. Partly it might be because his career ended in low-key circumstances, tests against Bangladesh and ODIs against the Netherlands, and partly because a lot of the valedictory focus went on his role as a groundbreaker, with Taylor just the second Samoan to play test cricket and the first to captain New Zealand.

It might have been partly, also, because his book *Black & White* landed on shelves shortly after he left the international game and restirred a lot of angst surrounding the end of his captaincy tenure, his treatment at the hands of New Zealand Cricket and the casual and sometimes overt racism he experienced in the sport. That was mostly a good thing. For Taylor it was no doubt long overdue redress, but it contributed to the fact we were talking about things to do with Taylor, rather than Taylor himself.

The simple, irreducible fact was this: Luteru Ross Poutoa Lote Taylor was a *great* player.

Test cricket has been played for close to 150 years and just 46 batters have more than his 19 test centuries, and only one New Zealander, Williamson, has more.

Only 44 players have accumulated more than his 112 test caps. One of those is Daniel Vettori, whose 113 caps includes one for an ICC World XI, so they share the New Zealand record.

Only 10 players have taken more than his 163 catches in the field, including Stephen Fleming (171).

In one-day international cricket he has been, if anything, better.

Only 11 players worldwide have scored more than his 21 ODI centuries and he is three clear of Martin Guptill, the nearest New Zealander. No New Zealander has as many as his 8607 runs and only four — Fleming, McCullum, Vettori and Chris Harris — played more than his 236 games.

If there was a format in which he never reached the heights expected of him, it was Twenty20, but he was still capped 102 times by his country — third at the time of writing behind Guptill and Tim Southee — and scored 1909 runs, bettered only by Guptill, Williamson and McCullum.

His longevity is beyond impressive, becoming the first player from any country to be capped 100 times in all three formats.

They're an amazing collection of numbers, but when he retired he was interviewed by Spark Sport and what he regarded as the key moment in his career was disarmingly simple.

'It was turning myself into a test cricketer because I didn't think I could get there,' he said.

* * * * * * *

Taylor's starting point on that journey was Masterton, the farming service centre that is the largest town in the Wairarapa. It is not a town or region known for producing cricketers — Sir Brian Lochore and Sir Bob Charles are the province's greatest sporting icons — but five months apart Taylor and Jesse Ryder, another child of the Wairarapa, were born.

Much has been made of the sliding-doors nature of Taylor and Ryder's careers, but although there were some uncanny similarities, it was the differences that enabled Taylor to forge a brilliant future and for Ryder to write one of New Zealand's most poignant 'I-could-have-been-a-contender' stories. Like Ryder, Taylor grew up in working-class surroundings, but unlike Ryder he had a loving, nurturing family unit.

Taylor was born Luteru Taylor and at home he was just as regularly called Kelu. He was only called the name for which he is now famous when the principal of his primary school kept mangling his Christian name. Its anglicised version would be Luther, and his grandmother, who was enrolling Luteru at school, just told him to forget it and call him Ross.

Taylor's mother Naoupu, or Ann, is Samoan and his father, Neil, is a Pākehā. Taylor and his sisters Rebecca, Elianna and Maria all grew up comfortable with both Pasifika and European cultures. The family regularly spoke Samoan in the house at the behest of Ann and great pride was taken in the achievements of those with Samoan heritage who made the All Blacks, particularly the former centre Eroni Clarke — whose son Caleb now plays on the wing — who was a cousin.

It feels important to mention this background for this one reason: unlike rugby, Samoans have not traditionally taken to cricket, despite playing a version of it themselves, kilikiti, in the islands. Unlike rugby, league and netball, cricket has not had a lot of Pasifika role models for young kids to look up to, with Murphy Su'a the only Samoan to have played for the Black Caps before Taylor started smashing all records. There are myriad reasons for this, but one that stands out is socio-economics. Cricket is not cheap, and Taylor has often referred to how his paternal grandparents played a huge role in allowing him to follow his sporting dreams.

'Dad was a factory worker while Mum worked at the New Zealand Housing Corporation. When she was made redundant things started to change. Money had always been an issue, but after that it got really tight. Mum's second job was cleaning the Work and Income premises. I'd go there after school to help her by cleaning toilets and sinks and getting rid of rubbish. I used to clean 10 or 15 toilets a day. As I got older, I came to understand what Mum and Dad had to do to make ends meet and the sacrifices they were making for their children. Later, whenever cricket wasn't much fun, I always tried to put things in perspective by thinking back to those days,' he wrote in *Black & White*.

'I had three hugely influential relatives on Dad's side: his mum, Grandma Sylvia, her husband, Grandad Jack, and our great-aunty who we called Aunty Mary. They were our babysitters when Mum and Dad were at work — there was always shortbread in their cupboards — and they funded a lot of trips to hockey and cricket tournaments that my parents couldn't afford.'

Cricket is expensive. Gear is expensive. Summer tournaments tend to take weeks, not days, so there are the accommodation costs associated with that. It has been an overwhelmingly white, middle-class sport in New Zealand for those reasons — although that is rapidly changing with the influence of South Asian immigration — with many kids dropping out of the game early not because they stop enjoying it but because it becomes unaffordable.

Taylor's financial situation might not have been rich, but his talent was. From a young age, he had an extraordinary capacity for self-improvement. His favourite tool was that most basic of practice equipment, the ball in a sock. In Taylor's case it was a hockey ball — another sport in which he excelled through the age-group levels — into a sock tied to a tree on his lawn. Taylor would spend hour after hour hitting the ball, getting used to the way it reacted off the bat depending on whether he was honing his front- or back-foot play. With a dad who worked long hours and sisters who didn't share his passion for the game, this was Taylor's cricket world, where he could imagine playing the best teams and players in the world. Sometimes his practice was so incessant it drove the neighbours to distraction, especially on those summer nights where the 'thwock, thwock' of bat on ball extended past 9 pm.

At both school and the Lansdowne club, Taylor scored his runs quickly and in bulk, and soon found his way onto the radar of local cricket luminaries, including Dermot Payton, a long-time opening batter for Central Districts and a renowned shaper of talent as a coach. Payton would run sessions at an indoor centre and would later recall that Taylor never missed one.

'I didn't have to instruct him. His shot selection was impeccable,' Payton would tell *Cricket Monthly*. 'Full and wide, cover drive. Full and on middle and leg, on-drive. Short and wide, cut. You could tell he was a talent. He was just so natural. It wasn't a case of rebuilding him or pulling apart his technique. It was near perfect.'

Another Central Districts legend who Taylor impressed at a young age was Mark Greatbatch. CD had a first-class game at Masterton's Queen Elizabeth Park and Taylor got to hang out with the team as a type of dressing-room dogsbody. The pay-off, if you can call it that, was he got a few throwdowns, but he did enough in one short session with Greatbatch for the burly left-hander to ring CD chief executive Blair Furlong, a man who knew a bit about talent having raised two first-class cricketing sons in John and Campbell, and told him bluntly to get this kid involved with the rep programme somehow, anyhow.

'There was definitely something about him,' Greatbatch said in *Black & White*. 'He was well ahead of his age in terms of skill and quality. He had a bit of rawness, but he had some power and was passionate about the game — loved it, lived for it.'

Greatbatch's other major contribution to Taylor's future came when he helped facilitate a move from Wairarapa College to Palmerston North Boys' High School for his final two years of schooling. The whole 'which-school-did-you-go-to?' discussion can be an extremely tedious and counterproductive part of New Zealand's cricket ecosystem, especially in the bigger cities where old school ties can grease the wheels of selection in some cases and stymie it in others, but there is no doubt that PNBHS had developed a reputation for hothousing cricket talent in a way that Wairarapa College could not match. In the years preceding Taylor's arrival, Black Caps Mathew Sinclair, Jacob Oram and Jamie How had cut their teeth in senior cricket while playing for the school, and fellow internationals George Worker and Adam Milne would follow.

Taylor didn't just learn cricket and, if you go back to the start of this chapter, the subtleties of cricket etiquette here, but as a boarder he gained an independent streak and an ability to fend for himself that he would never lose.

He was on a fast-track to the dream he'd formulated at 15 when, as someone who knew that academics wasn't for him, he decided there and then he was going to be a professional cricketer.

* * * * * * * *

There is some irony given what would happen in the years ahead, that Taylor's first national recognition saw him play for the New Zealand Under-19s against a South African team that included Johan Botha and Hashim Amla. Taylor was vice-captain. His

125

skipper? Brendon McCullum.

Taylor would play two years for the U19s and, after a trip to Lord's on the young players' scheme that has also seen players like Mark Waugh and Martin Crowe on the staff, Taylor returned to the NZC Academy based in Lincoln and started his first-class career. It was at the academy where he met fellow cricketer Victoria Brown and it was in his early days of first-class cricket he would meet Crowe: both were to have a huge impact on his life and career.

Brown and Taylor would marry, have three kids — Mackenzie, Jonty and Adelaide — and live a low-key life, just as it suits them, out of the spotlight in Hamilton. With a background in high-performance cricket herself, Victoria has been able to comfort and cajole in equal measure. One occasion the latter was used was when Taylor was wracked with doubt ahead of the second test against England at Birmingham in 2021, the final match before the World Test Championship final. Taylor had batted skittishly, something he has been prone to do when not in peak form, in the previous test at Lord's and had only scored in fits and starts since his last test century against England at Hamilton in 2019.

Taylor had started to think his place in the final might be in doubt, that coach Gary Stead had signalled his desire to move on when dropping him from the T20 side and that batting coach Luke Ronchi had lost faith in his ability to deliver on the big stage. According to Taylor, Victoria could see he was talking himself out of the team and, bluntly, told him to man up and score some runs. He responded with an 80 at Edgbaston and, for the record, his place was never in doubt for the final, even if he hadn't scored any, but the kick up the butt was well timed and necessary.

Theirs is an enduring love story, but so is Taylor and Crowe's, though it's fair to say that on first sight it was unrequited.

The famous and now widely accepted version is that Crowe was encouraged by Taylor's manager, Leanne McGoldrick, and

Greatbatch to check out Taylor with a view to mentoring him and taking his game to the next level. Taylor had made a bit of an impact since his arrival on the first-class scene in the 2002–03 season with his bravado and obvious eye–hand coordination, with his CD coach Graham Barlow saying, 'I don't want to say he's brilliant because he ain't yet, but he's giving us all a good thrill.' His raw talent was obvious, but so was the fact he didn't yet know how to construct an innings to suit what might have been needed on any given day.

'I remember playing against Ross in a domestic game and this young kid was just flaying at everything,' recalled Stephen Fleming as he spoke during the coverage of Taylor's last test.

Fleming, no doubt trying to get into the young batter's head, asked him if he actually wanted to play for New Zealand.

'There was a real talent there, but it was a matter of how it was going to be shaped and moulded. Fortunately he fell under the wing of one of our greatest who not only taught him about the game and set some goals that helped shape him, but his [influence] went outside of cricket and that's the greatest role a mentor can have.'

It very nearly didn't happen. Crowe attended a Plunket Shield (then known as the State Championship) game between Auckland and CD at Eden Park Outer Oval in the days between Christmas 2003 and New Year's. Plenty of CD players were in the runs — Peter Ingram, Sinclair and Craig Spearman all scored centuries — but Taylor's contribution to the match was a frenetic 10 off 14 balls in the first innings and 14 off nine in the second.

'The ball was going all over the place at Eden Park Outer Oval,' Taylor would later recall. 'I saw him walking into the ground and around the boundary as I was batting and I thought, "Geez, there's Martin Crowe." Tama Canning and Kyle Mills were making me look silly. At that stage I didn't really trust my defence. My best form of defence was attack . . . probably not what was required on the first morning of a first-class game.'

Crowe would famously tell McGoldrick that her client was 'nothing but a dirty slogger'. He was, however, convinced to reconsider when Taylor rang him in 2006, then paid his own flights to Auckland to speak with him in person and tell him, emphatically, that he intended on breaking the then-New Zealand record of 17 test centuries and would like the holder of that record to be on his side when he did so.

That year he had made his one-day international debut for his country and by year's end, after just three ODIs, would have his first century, an unbeaten 128 against Sri Lanka that would be immediately followed by a night in hospital as he, caught up in the excitement, forgot to hydrate during his explosive innings. The ODI runs were nice, and Taylor would remain a brilliant 50-over cricketer throughout his career, but he wanted more: he wanted to be New Zealand's best test player, too. Only then would he feel like he'd made it.

Explicit goal setting is not for everyone. It wouldn't work as well for, say, Williamson, who for his own peace of mind needed to be process driven, not outcome focused. Taylor was cut from a different cloth — he, like Crowe before him, paid careful attention to the process but also needed the extrinsic motivation that statistical goals provided.

From New Zealand Cricket's perspective, the melding of minds between Taylor and Crowe would end up being immensely productive.

Taylor made his test debut in 2007 on a tour to South Africa that ended up like most tours to that country — in sound defeat, with the debutant not getting to 20 in all four bats in the two tests he played. Taylor was dropped on his return home, missing the two tests against a feeble Bangladesh line-up, but re-called for the marquee three-test series against England. It was in this series that New Zealanders cottoned on to the idea that, in Taylor, they might have a middle-order fixture for years to come. In the first test in Hamilton, he scored a lovely 120, an innings noted for a series of delicious straight drives, and followed up with a double of 53 and 55 in the second test, before the series was rounded off with 74 at Napier. Barring injury or unavailability, Taylor's place in the side was rarely, if ever, discussed again (though, for reasons that will become obvious, his career does have a pre- and post-captaincy division to it).

It is interesting watching highlights of those early days. The 23-year-old Taylor was upright and although his lightning-fast hands were a feature of his game, there was an elegance and a looseness that was not so apparent in the years to come.

New Zealand would travel to England for a reciprocal series in 2008 and Taylor batted poorly in the first test at Lord's, a numbing experience after Crowe, whose name is twice on the famous honours board there, had filled his head with dreams.

'Whether that rubbed off on me and I put extra pressure on myself, I'm not sure, but I was all over the place and in a really bad headspace. To turn that around, to score 150, will go down as one of my best knocks.'

That 154 not out to be precise came at a gloomy, pre-refurb Old Trafford. He scratched out his guard in a pool of Daniel Flynn's blood after the left-hander had his cage rattled and his teeth extracted by a nippy James Anderson bouncer. In difficult conditions, Taylor was unstoppable and set New Zealand up for what should have been a convincing victory until an inexplicable second-innings collapse followed by the pitch suddenly losing all life on the fifth day gifted a win to the hosts.

It wasn't until India arrived in 2009 that Taylor embarked on the first consistently prolific period of his test career. Between the first innings of the second test at Napier — where he and his old mate Ryder (201) enjoyed a 271-run fifth-wicket partnership — Taylor went a staggering 20 test innings without a single-figure score, compiling three centuries, including a then-New Zealand record for the fastest test century when he smashed 138 against Australia, and six half-centuries. In that run he boosted his batting average from an acceptable 32.74 to 43 and took complete command of the No. 4 position he would keep for the rest of his career.

If the universe was trying to warn him that life and sport were not meant to be as easy as he was perhaps demonstrating them to be, it did so in the ODI game, where Taylor endured a miserable 2007 World Cup, his only notable score (85) and in fact his only score above 10, coming in an early match against Kenya. It was a rare prolonged slump in a format that suited Taylor's strengths — his hockey career had helped him slap the ball powerfully over midwicket and behind point.

* * * * * * * *

In 2011, seemingly headed towards the peak years of his batting career, Taylor was appointed captain following Daniel Vettori's well-signposted intention to step down from his leadership roles.

He had been playing great cricket, including banishing the memories of the Caribbean World Cup by scoring consistently at the 2011 version, held on the subcontinent, the highlight being a match-winning unbeaten 131 against Pakistan — always a nettlesome opponent for New Zealand at World Cups.

Taylor's elevation was not a controversial decision — most in the media and on public talk forums warmly welcomed the appointment — as much as it was a contentious and ultimately damaging process.

Taylor was pitched into a highly public run-off for the role against the guy he had replaced as vice-captain in slightly mysterious circumstances. In 2010, the *New Zealand Herald* ran a story on the front page headlined: 'Taylor is vice-captain of New Zealand, but don't tell a soul.'

The story continued:

'Ross Taylor has been made vice-captain of the national cricket team . . . but keep it to yourself, because New Zealand Cricket does not want anyone to know.

'Key players were told of the 25-year-old's appointment when the Twenty20 and one-day squads for Bangladesh were announced this week. But the public were going to be kept in the dark [due to] an ongoing sensitivity around the demotion of wicketkeeper-batsman Brendon McCullum. McCullum, 28, was relieved of his deputy duties in October, shortly after Andy Moles resigned as national coach.

'McCullum said at the time that he was disappointed but still had "some fairly big goals I want to achieve for New Zealand, including the captaincy".'

At the time, some of the decisions taken by NZC looked misguided, and in hindsight they're even worse, essentially pitting two of their best players against each other. When Taylor 'won' the role of captain under the coaching of traditionalist John Wright, a damaging and unfair narrative had taken root: Taylor was the establishment guy who had been pushed ahead of the players' champion.

It would end up damaging both men, but more so Taylor. As McCullum would write in *Declared*, 'It wasn't good for cricket, it wasn't good for Ross, it wasn't good for me, it wasn't good for our relationship or any team with the two of us in it . . . the public selection process put a lot of pressure on our relationship that didn't need to be there.' There's a telling line in Taylor's book where he recalled thinking at the time that other people wanted him to get the job more than he actually did, which might have been reflected in his occasionally diffident captaincy.

What wasn't in doubt was that Taylor played very well as captain. He scored 56 in treacherous conditions in Hobart to lead New Zealand to that rarest and most beautiful of things — a test win in Australia. He scored an unbeaten century against Zimbabwe, a century in Bengaluru and, most stunningly, a double of 142 and 74 as his team beat Sri Lanka on the Teardrop Island. The performance was notable because coach Mike Hesson, who had taken over following Wright's resignation, had informed him earlier on the tour that he would be recommending a change of captaincy when they returned home.

The fallout in the public domain and at a personal level was enormous. Taylor was badly bruised. He didn't travel with the team to South Africa and even those who didn't believe he was a particularly strong captain were horrified by the way it had transpired. He returned to the team for a home series against England with a groundswell of public support behind him, even if he admits his 'reintegration' — a term Taylor hated because it implied that him missing the South African tour was a transgression — into the team that had effectively rejected his leadership took some time. From this point on, Taylor became even more overtly goal-oriented and statistically focused. The results were incredible and, to some, ironic in that they gave the Hesson-McCullum reign real impetus.

In the 2013 home series against the faltering Windies, Taylor rattled off 217 not out, 16 not out, 129, 131 and 2 not out. The 131 at Hamilton was a particular gem as Sunil Narine (6 for 91) was getting it to turn square with both his conventional ball and the carom. It took all of Taylor's considerable wits to combat him.

Taylor was a different batter by now. His backlift was shorter; he stood lower. He wasn't as pretty, perhaps, as his early days, but he was highly functional. He needed only the merest hint of width, and sometimes no width at all, to slide the ball either side of point.

Crowe, by now stricken with the blood cancer that would eventually take his life, wrote movingly about this period in his popular ESPNcricinfo column.

'The moral of the story so far is of a man, humble and gentle in nature, being stung by a painful experience and taking his time to heal and learn from the experience. Many would have succumbed to such an ordeal. Instead, Ross chose to focus on his true essence for living: to love and be loved. His family has been extraordinary. His wife, Victoria, a cricketer herself, has been unbelievable in support. Becoming a father has given Ross the real focus of his life.

'He will fulfil his dream and achieve whatever goal he sets himself, for he sees life clearly and succinctly. There will be other obstacles, mostly top-level bowlers gunning for his scalp, yet he will find a positive way to express his love for cricket and the privilege he feels representing his country and family . . .

'This flurry of expertly crafted hundreds in the last three weeks has been a wonderfully courageous way to end a tough yet important year in his life. Ross Taylor is a good, honest story of pain and pleasure; and he is a greater man for coming through it.'

Taylor entered a curious period of his career, marked by the sort of inconsistencies that he'd largely eliminated from his game. Having scored three test centuries in three weeks to end 2013, he scored just one in 2014, against Pakistan in the United Arab Emirates, and one in 2015, the small matter of 290 at the WACA, the highest score by a visiting batter in Australia. Taylor had started to look especially fidgety early in his innings.

In a piece with *Cricket Monthly*, Taylor had explained his methodology when it came to getting under way in tests.

'To be consistent, the first thing you need to do is to survive your first 20 to 30 balls,' he said.

'To do that you need to trust your defence. More often than not, if you get through those first 30 balls, batting becomes easier regardless of whether it's a flat wicket, spinning wicket or if it is seaming around. Some days that might happen earlier, other days it stretches out to 40 balls. The more you play the more accustomed you get to different conditions and environments [but] no day is the same. You can be in good nick and have a bad night's sleep and suddenly you're struggling. You can be in good form and wait six hours to bat and by the time you get to bat, you're spent. You can be out of nick, squirt a couple through the gully for four, and all of a sudden something clicks.'

Too often in this period it wasn't clicking for Taylor, and the reason wasn't that he had lost the desire. He just wasn't seeing the ball as well. Literally. He was suffering from an ailment known as pterygium, or surfer's eye, and needed an operation.

With his eye back in full working order, Taylor started ticking off more milestones including, while on tour to Zimbabwe, passing his mentor Crowe's record for runs in tests.

While Taylor remained a highly effective test batter through to the end of his career, scoring five unbeaten tons, two against Zimbabwe and one each against the West Indies, Pakistan and England, plus a double hundred against Bangladesh at the Basin Reserve, it was his ODI batting that turned heads in his later years.

The brilliant World Cup hundred at Pallekele in Sri Lanka against Pakistan was the start of a prolific period for Taylor. He scored a century against Zimbabwe in Bulawayo, against the West Indies in Basseterre, against England in Napier and Bangladesh in Fatullah. In a five-match series against India at home, he went 55, 57, 17, 112 not out and 102, before kick-starting his next series, against Pakistan, with 105 not out in Dubai.

Given his lead-in to the 2015 World Cup saw him score 59 not out and 102 not out against Pakistan back to back, he would end up having a mediocre tournament, nicking behind in the final for 40 being an appropriate way to end the month. He quickly put that disappointment behind him on New Zealand's tour to England, scoring back-to-back centuries in a series victory.

He scored centuries against Australia and South Africa in the home summer of 2016–17 but was even more spectacular a year later. He opened a home series against England with a century, and after missing out with the bat in the second match and sitting out the third, found himself at the crease at Dunedin's University Oval in the fourth chasing a massive 336 to win. He was also nursing a torn hamstring which he popped running between the wickets shortly after bringing up his 19th ODI century.

What followed was perhaps Taylor's signature innings. Knowing that running twos was out of the question, Taylor swung for the fences and did so with incredible success. His 181 not out saw New Zealand home with three balls to spare and became an instant classic. He was likened to West Indian legend Gordon Greenidge, who was noted for playing better when he was limping.

'[The] physio came out and asked if I wanted to stay in or come out. I'm glad I stayed in. I couldn't run any twos, so I didn't want to put any pressure on the other guy. So I had a go, and hit a couple out of the screws,' was Taylor's understated way of describing his knock.

He was understatedly good at the 2019 World Cup, too, his final major tournament for New Zealand, scoring important runs against Bangladesh and the West Indies. Then a heady 74, when he showed an innate appreciation of the conditions, in the semi-final at Old Trafford against India proved the difference between the teams. His World Cup batting odyssey ended unluckily at Lord's when he was on the end of a shocking decision but which couldn't be overturned due to New Zealand having exhausted its one review.

In 2020, Taylor would have one more big series, scoring 109 not out, his 21st ODI century and his 40th and final international ton, against India, following up with an unbeaten 73 in the next match.

* * * * * * * *

That series might have been a nice sign-off for his ODI career, which did rather peter out with an anaemic home series against the Dutch, but Taylor had one more big occasion for New Zealand.

Despite his anxiety and lack of form, Taylor played the World

Test Championship finale at Southampton and he did find himself at the crease at a pivotal point, with New Zealand 44 for 2 in a nervy chase for 139 and immortality. Wickets had fallen in clumps in this match, and Taylor and Williamson knew theirs was the pivotal partnership.

They faced 31 dot balls in a row as India built pressure, and it took Taylor 19 balls to get off the mark.

Two long and magnificent hours later, he shuffled a half step down the wicket and flicked Mohammed Shami imperiously over square leg for four to win the match.

His 47 not out might not be prominent on any spreadsheet of his career, but it might just be the perfect way to remember a guy who'd grown up wanting to be a professional cricketer and who ended up not just doing that but being one of the best this country has ever produced.

CHAPTER 9
GLORY AT THE ROSE BOWL

NEW ZEALAND V INDIA – WORLD TEST CHAMPIONSHIP FINAL

At The Rose Bowl, Southampton, 18–23 June 2021

INDIA		FIRST INNINGS					SECOND INNINGS					
		Runs	Mins	Balls	6s	4s		Runs	Mins	Balls	6s	4s
R.G. Sharma	c Southee b Jamieson	34	88	68	–	6	lbw b Southee	30	121	81	–	2
S. Gill	c Watling b Wagner	28	108	64	–	3	lbw b Southee	8	48	33	–	–
C.A. Pujara	lbw b Boult	8	85	54	–	2	c Taylor b Jamieson	15	129	80	–	2
V. Kohli*	lbw b Jamieson	44	196	132	–	1	c Watling b Jamieson	13	43	29	–	–
A.M. Rahane	c Latham b Wagner	49	190	117	–	5	c Watling b Boult	15	69	40	–	1
R.R. Pant†	c Latham b Jamieson	4	31	22	–	1	c Nicholls b Boult	41	149	88	–	4
R.A. Jadeja	c Watling b Boult	15	102	53	–	2	c Watling b Wagner	16	60	49	–	2
R. Ashwin	c Latham b Southee	22	36	27	–	3	c Taylor b Boult	7	38	19	–	–
I. Sharma	c Taylor b Jamieson	4	28	16	–	–	(10) not out	1	17	6	–	–
J.J. Bumrah	lbw b Jamieson	0	3	1	–	–	(11) c Latham b Southee	0	6	4	–	–
Mohammad Shami	not out	4	9	1	–	1	(9) c Latham b Southee	13	20	10	–	3
Extras	(lb 3, nb 2)	5					(b 1, lb 8, w 1, nb 1)	5				
TOTAL (92.1 overs)		217	447				(73 overs)	170	359			

BOWLING	O	M	R	W	O	M	R	W
Sharma I.	25	9	48	3	6.2	2	21	0
Bumrah	26	9	57	0	10.4	2	35	0
Shami	26	8	76	4	10.5	3	31	0
Ashwin	15	5	28	2	10	5	17	2
Jadeja	7.2	2	20	1	8	1	25	0

NEW ZEALAND		FIRST INNINGS						SECOND INNINGS				
		Runs	Mins	Balls	6s	4s		Runs	Mins	Balls	6s	4s
T.W.M. Latham	c Kohli b Ashwin	30	158	104	-	3	st Pant b Ashwin	9	59	41	-	-
D.P. Conway	c Shami b Sharma I.	54	222	153	-	6	lbw b Ashwin	19	80	47	-	4
K.S. Williamson*	c Kohli b Sharma I.	49	294	177	-	7	not out	52	147	89	-	8
L.R.P.L. Taylor	c Gill b Shami	11	81	37	-	2	not out	47	127	100	-	6
H.M. Nicholls	c Sharma R.G. b Sharma I.	7	35	24	-	1						
B-J. Watling†	b Shami	1	6	3	-	-						
C. de Grandhomme	lbw b Shami	13	48	30	-	1						
K.A. Jamieson	c Bumrah b Shami	21	30	16	1	-						
T.G. Southee	b Jadeja	30	60	46	2	1						
N. Wagner	c Rahane b Ashwin	0	12	5	-	-						
T.A. Boult	not out	7	15	8	-	1						
Extras	(b 4, lb 16, nb 6)	26					(lb 11, nb 2)	13				
TOTAL (99.2 overs)		249	489				(73 overs)	140	207			

BOWLING	O	M	R	W		O	M	R	W
Southee	22	6	64	1		19	4	48	4
Boult	21.1	4	47	2		15	2	39	3
Jamieson	22	12	31	5		24	10	30	2
de Grandhomme	12	6	32	0					
Wagner	15	5	40	2		15	2	44	1

New Zealand's 21st-century cricketing success can be neatly, if not totally accurately, divided into two sections. The first successful period ran until Stephen Fleming's retirement in the summer of 2007–08. During that time they had turned themselves into a consistent force at home and a one-day team to be feared, even if they tended to underachieve at World Cups.

Then followed the years of instability as coaches came and went as regularly as high-performance strategies were adopted and ditched at headquarters in Christchurch.

Things reached their nadir in 2013 when the Black Caps were dismissed for 45 after winning the toss and batting first in South Africa, but it has been a long, sustained period of joy since.

Well mostly, as with any generalisation there are notable exceptions. The years 2008–13 were not all nettles and gorse bushes, and

2013 onwards hasn't been all fields of clover. There has been, even in the best of times, no sustained period of success against our closest and fiercest rivals to the west and the last World Test Championship cycle, the defence of the title no less, which ended in March 2023, was at best underwhelming and at worst insipid.

Two years previously, however . . .

The World Test Championship win was not only the culmination of the golden years, the golden generation, but it was also cleansing. Writing in the *New Zealand Herald*, I described the victory as an anaesthetic for the pain that still lingered after the tied drama of the World Cup final — a tie that saw England lift the trophy on boundary countback.

'There was an element of surrealism in watching the Black Caps achieve this feat while sitting in the cold and dark of a midwinter's morning. The colour of the clothes and the ball might have been different, but two years ago a lot of these same blokes were poised to do something similar at a famous ground 130 km north of Southampton, only for their hearts to be torn from their chests.'

It was a minor miracle the championship happened at all, following years of procrastination at ICC level followed by a global pandemic that did a good job of shutting down sport, from professional to community level, around the world.

The championship was first seriously proposed in 2009, with Martin Crowe a firm proponent of the concept. As well as being a brilliant player, Crowe must rank as one of the sport's most important innovators. His brainchild Cricket Max was the obvious precursor to T20, and he saw value in giving context to test cricket. Although the first final might not have got maximum cut-through with the global media or British public, that was largely through circumstance. When Australia and India meet in 2023's final, the concept will likely have been elevated to another level. Regardless of who wins that test, neither cricketing giant will be the first name on the mace.

Originally proposed to replace the little-loved Champions Trophy in 2013, the WTC was originally proposed as a tournament to be run as a league across a four-year cycle, before the top four teams would meet in a semi-final and final in England.

In 2011, however, faced with a raft of financial problems and the demands of sponsors for content, the ICC reneged on the proposal and pushed back the start date to 2017. It reinstated the Champions Trophy for 2013 in England, much to the chagrin of test-cricket luminaries. Again in 2017, the proposed tournament was cancelled and replaced with the eighth edition of the Champions Trophy, but in 2019, after much debate about the format, which was now reduced to a two-year league cycle and a one-off final, the WTC was officially kicked off by the 2019 Ashes.

Then, Covid.

Despite a few series being wiped out, India and New Zealand advanced to the final — the latter getting a big boost by Australia being docked points for a slow over rate. It also helped that they carved through their final home summer by winning four out of four tests against the West Indies, three emphatically and one in the nick of time when Mitchell Santner thrust his left hand high into the Mount Maunganui sky to pull down a catch and dismiss the final Pakistan batter Naseem Shah with just 4.3 overs remaining in the test.

The tournament nearly didn't happen at all, but New Zealand became inaugural WTC winners. There'll only ever be one first winner. This is how they did it.

* * * * * * * *

The choice of venue, Southampton's Rose Bowl, might seem curious given it carries neither the gravitas nor nearby population of London's two test grounds Lord's and The Oval. Nor does it have the long-standing history of Headingley, Trent Bridge, Edgbaston or Old Trafford.

One thing it does have that all the previously mentioned, apart from Old Trafford, don't, is an on-site hotel, which was the determining factor in taking the match there in the midst of the coronavirus pandemic.

That enabled the ICC to create a 'bubble' environment without too much difficulty and apply social-distancing rules. What was less simple to organise was the weather, which started dismally: 18 June, a Friday, was completely washed out. This in itself wasn't too big an issue because the match was scheduled over six days to mitigate against weather interruptions and the inevitable slow over rates in such a high-pressure game.

Day two dawned only slightly brighter, but it was fine enough for a toss and a little more than two sessions of cricket before bad light interrupted, then ended, play. Crucially, Kane Williamson won the toss and gave his beautifully balanced five-pronged pace attack — Tim Southee, Trent Boult, Kyle Jamieson, Neil Wagner and Colin de Grandhomme — first use of a wicket that had a green tinge.

Southee and Boult are masterful operators with a new Kookaburra, but they seemed less comfortable with the darker Dukes ball used in England. Searching too hard for swing and too desperately for wickets, they were guilty of overpitching and Rohit Sharma (34) and the gifted but inexperienced Shubman Gill (28) cashed in. The 2.03-metre Kyle Jamieson made the initial breakthrough, having Sharma caught in the slips, and Wagner quickly followed with the wicket of Gill. Boult returned to have Cheteshwar Pujara trapped in front, but when captain Virat Kohli and Ajinkya Rahane saw India through to 146 for 3 at stumps, it felt like New Zealand had ceded the advantage of the toss.

In just the third over of day three, the test turned on its heel as Jamieson got the ball to nip back and pin Kohli in front for 44. It was a telling moment. During the recently completed Indian Premier League, Kohli had tried to convince his Bangalore teammate to bowl to him in the nets with a red Dukes ball to help him prepare for this match. Despite the discrepancy in experience and influence, Jamieson held firm and refused. This moment alone justified the awkward situation. Aside from the experienced Rahane (49) and a cameo of 22 off 27 balls by Ravichandran Ashwin, the rest of the Indian line-up succumbed meekly, with 217 the total. Jamieson starred with five wickets, while Boult and Wagner picked up two apiece.

When day three ended with New Zealand 102 for 2, they looked to be in the box seat thanks to solid starts from Latham (30) and Conway (54). Day four, however, never started and the test had become not only a race between two good teams but a race against time.

It might not have seemed like it at the time, but New Zealand's spluttering innings probably saved the test. After a delayed start to day five, New Zealand struggled against India's pacemen, with Williamson (eighth man out for 49) the only one to show genuine resistance, though there were handy contributions from Jamieson (21) and Southee (30). A meagre lead of 32 meant a second-innings shootout was in prospect, though when India got to 64 for 2 at stumps, a draw was heavy favourite.

Jamieson again provided the test with a perfect jolt, nicking out both Kohli and Pujara early on the sixth and final day. Unlike the first innings, New Zealand's seam attack was in perfect sync, with Southee's 4 for 48 and Boult's 3 for 39 complementing Jamieson's breakthroughs. Arguably the most decisive single moment of the test came when Henry Nicholls, fielding at gully, turned and chased a Rishabh Pant (41) skyer, eventually taking an outstanding catch at what amounted to a deep backward point.

New Zealand was left chasing a modest 139 to win the WTC mace, one of sport's most exquisitely crafted trophies. There were early jitters when Latham (9) used his feet to run past the ball and Conway (19) got his front pad in front of a straight one. Ashwin had both wickets and can be a devastating operator when he gets his tail up, though normally in drier, more spin-friendly environs.

There was a sense of unease, especially when Williamson overturned a poor leg-before decision against him on review, which I tried to capture in my report for the *Herald*.

'Taylor can be a skittish starter. The Indians knew that. Another wicket right then and they would have been just a couple more good pieces of cricket away from exposing New Zealand's collection of cultivated boofers and unconventional bashers that starts at No. 7 and continues through to No. 11 . . .

'They got lucky, the pair of them. Beaten outside the off stump more times than they could count, they rode their luck and their reservoir of skill and experience.

'Williamson reached 50, dropped on the way by the luckless Jasprit Bumrah, and the partnership reached 96 when Taylor — it had to be Taylor — whipped Mohammed Shami over square leg for the win.'

When Taylor hit the winning runs, the eruption in the New Zealand viewing area and from the small but vocal contingent of Antipodeans in the bleachers could have been heard on the Isle of White.

That euphoria soon gave way to something else: a feeling of relief that Taylor talks about in *Black & White*.

'Despite being inundated with quality New Zealand [gin], it was a comparatively subdued celebration: I sat next to Kane drinking chardonnay, talking to home . . . and just letting it sink in. It was equal parts elation and relief: to have lost a third World Cup final would have been unbearable.'

Despite having some fortune in making the final and despite the WTC format still being a little rough around the edges, New Zealand's win was largely embraced by the wider cricket community. Writing in ESPNcricinfo, Andrew Fidel Fernando said: 'In the end, though, test cricket's biggest prize found its way to a team that truly adored it — New Zealand, who have invested heavily in red-ball cricket, frequently treated the format with the dignity it deserves, and never spoke ill about the league. After everything the World Test Championship has been through, the mace is currently where it deserves to be, cradled in the ultra-soft hands of BJ Watling, like Jenny at the end of *Forrest Gump*.'

Perhaps the most glowing testimony came from across the Tasman Sea, where New Zealand's efforts at the bat-and-ball game have usually, and often with justification, been treated with some derision. Fairfax columnist Greg Baum was having no truck with those compatriots who felt it was a hollow victory.

'It's not that New Zealand punches above their weight. It's that they punch above everyone's weight,' he wrote.

'How mighty is their feat? Let's go back to the weigh-in. This final was cricket's smallest country against its biggest. It was five million people and a few bandwagoners versus 1.4 billion. Cricket New Zealand's annual revenue of $55 million is barely more than Cricket Victoria's, and less than Surrey County Cricket Club's. India's is $700 million that we know of. In India, cricket is everything. In New Zealand, it sometimes gets to No. 2.'

Baum traversed New Zealand's reinvention as a cricketing power who did things without rancour and said it wasn't just the result that mattered but that the match was a slow-burn classic, saying that each team 'stared and stared and stared' before India blinked.

'And so it is that India rule and run world cricket, but New Zealand reign over it.'

New Zealand brought the trophy, the mace, back to New Zealand and toured it triumphantly around the country. It took pride of place at Mount Maunganui's Bay Oval when the Black Caps played their first test at home following the win, the first home test of the new cycle. With it sparkling and gleaming in front of the pavilion, kids and parents posed to have pictures taken with it. Meanwhile, out on the pitch, New Zealand, sans an injured Williamson, promptly lost to Bangladesh, something they'd never previously managed to do, home or away, in the 21 years of the Asian country's test-playing existence.

The mace started to represent something else: it had the unmistakable feel of an end of an era, although that may end up being a fatalistic way of looking at it.

It was, unquestionably, the culmination of an era — a hell of an era at that.

CHAPTER 10
TIM SOUTHEE

Debut: 2008   Last match: 2023

	Matches	Wickets	Ave	5w (10w)	Economy	S/R
Test:	94	370	28.98	15 (1)	2.97	58.4
ODI:	154	210	33.46	3	5.43	36.9
T20I:	107	134	23.72	1	8.16	17.4

Also: 1976 test runs, six 50s and 73 catches

Wins as captain: Tests 3 (win % 50), ODIs 0 (win % 0), T20Is 13 (won % 59)

You would have got long odds on Tim Southee emerging as one of the statesmen of New Zealand cricket in the years immediately following his debut as a callow yet free-swinging teenager, armed with a smile so innocent and toothy he looked like he'd walked through the gates of McLean Park in a singlet and pair of Red Band gumboots before changing into whites.

Yet here we are, with 15 years under his belt, not only watching him lead his country in the most cerebral format of the game but also still finding it hard to talk about him as one of the finest cricketers we've produced.

That's the thing with Timothy Grant Southee: it's unlikely this country has ever produced such a roundly underestimated cricketer

146

— one with an entirely appropriate middle name because, to excuse the dreadful pun, we've become so used to taking him for granted. Worse than that, despite cricket being a very segmented sport where players often specialise in one facet of the game, often to the detriment of others, as a nation of pundits we too often obsess over the things Southee is not very good at — defending spinners and DRS reviews, for example — rather than what he has proven quite brilliant at.

With that in mind, it is important to front-load this appreciation piece on Southee with facts, not feelings. This is done not solely with the intention of dazzling with numbers but to illustrate this obvious yet often overlooked point: you can count on one hand the number of New Zealand bowlers better than him and still have some digits left to spare.

You might want to whisper this next bit: in some metrics he compares quite favourably to the one and only Sir Richard Hadlee, the country's one and only cricketing knight. Yes, just mentioning him alongside the Great Man can lead to scorn and derision, but if you ignore the noise and look at the numbers, he matches up well in not all but some.

Southee, born in Whangārei in December 1988, had at the time of writing 714 international wickets, the most by any New Zealander and enough to stand at 13th on the all-time list. While this is a modern statistic in that it heavily favours those like Southee who have played the entirety of their careers in the Twenty20 era, it will soon become mainstream, and with Trent Boult limiting his appearances, Southee will not be overtaken by any current bowlers. His national record should be safe for at least 15 years and probably longer.

Southee's 370 test wickets puts him behind only Hadlee's 431, while his 15 five-wicket bags — perhaps the closest comparison a bowler has to a batter's century — is third behind Hadlee, who compiled a scarcely believable 36 (third all-time), and Vettori's 20.

As an aside, it was interesting when compiling this to note

that while Southee had played 94 tests to Hadlee's 86, the Great Man had bowled more deliveries (21,918 to 21,608), which clearly demonstrates how Hadlee wasn't just the focal point of the bowling attack, he often was the bowling attack, which is one reason why he has so many bags of wickets.

Southee is one of just five New Zealanders to take 200 one-day international wickets, his 210 placing him third behind Vettori (297) and Kyle Mills (240) and ahead of the Chrises, Harris (203) and Cairns (200). With just 154 appearances, Southee, who hasn't always been a frontline choice in ODIs, has played significantly fewer ODIs than the other four.

Only two New Zealanders have taken 100 T20I wickets, Southee's 134 leading Ish Sodhi's 115, though they are likely to soon be joined by Mitchell Santner (91). He has the best figures by a New Zealander in T20Is, 5 for 18 versus Pakistan at Eden Park on Boxing Day 2010.

He has the fifth-most catches of any New Zealander in test cricket (73) and the second-most in T20Is (53).

In almost no respects can Southee the batter ever be compared to Sir Vivian Richards, or even Andrew Flintoff, but at the moment his 83 test sixes sits one above the red-headed English all-rounder and one behind the West Indian legend.

Southee is also on the brink, along with Australia's Mitchell Starc, of joining an exclusive 21-strong club of test cricketers who have 2000 runs and 200 wickets. It is a club well represented by New Zealanders, with Vettori (4531 and 362), Chris Cairns (3320 and 218) and Hadlee (3124 and 431) already ensconced. Given the way Southee's batting has been lampooned over the years, he will be perhaps the least likely of the inductees into this august yet imaginary club.

Yet while all these numbers bolster the argument that Southee is a modern great, if there was any debate, they still can't get to the essence of what makes him the cricketer he is and why he is regarded by one and all as one of cricket's great 'team men'.

On that score, there are two aspects of Southee's career that stand out. One can be accurately tracked by data, the other more immeasurable. First, Southee keeps getting better as he gets older. Second, there is nobody who loves playing for his country more.

He might be at the forefront of the modern Black Caps evolution and be a big-stage player in cricket's splashiest age, but Southee is in most respects an old-fashioned cricketer with old-fashioned values.

* * * * * * * *

Southee's career has been one long outswinger with the odd period of scrambled seam, and that journey started on the fields of Maungakaramea and has taken him around the world and back.

He is the third and youngest child of Murray and Joanne, brought up on a sheep and beef farm in Waiōtira, in rural Northland. It's not an easy place to pinpoint on a map, but if you drew a line between Waipū and Dargaville and dropped a pin about halfway along that line, you'd be near enough.

Just a few kilometres up the road was Mid Western Rugby Club and Maungakaramea Cricket Club, the latter being the focal point of the community in summer and a club that has produced a disproportionate amount of first-class cricketers, given the small and widely dispersed population that it serves.

With a father who played rugby for North Auckland and an older brother, Mark, who was mad about the game, rugby played a huge part in Southee's childhood. When recalling his footy career for *Rugby World*, Southee recalled how he and his brother made their own Ranfurly Shield out of a log and some tin foil, then filled Murray's discarded empties with water to pretend they were having a beer after the game. Being the youngest, Southee didn't win many 'challenges', but he got used to winning a bit more when he made the trip south to board at King's College.

Southee attended Whangārei Boys' High in Year 9 and 10, making the 1st XI in his first year, but accepted a cricket scholarship to King's for his senior years. He got the surprise of his life when he was selected for the 1st XV as a reserve lock in his first year at King's. In his second they won the prestigious Auckland secondary schools competition and in his final year, having carved out a position for himself at blindside flanker, he made the Auckland secondary schools and Northern Region A team.

It wasn't a career of bloodied noses, cracked ribs and soft-tissue injuries that awaited, however.

'I finished school that year and got a cricket contract with Northern Districts — the rest as they say is history,' he told *Rugby World*.

As good as Southee was as a schoolboy rugby player, he was better at cricket. He was playing alongside men for Northland aged just 15, playing against internationals in Hawke Cup qualifiers.

At the World Under-19 championships in Malaysia in 2008 he was named player of the tournament when he took 17 wickets at an average of 6.64.

(Trent Boult took 11 wickets at 10.9; Kane Williamson's top score was 37, Australian Steve Smith's was 39 — it was a bowlers' tournament!)

At national age-group tournaments, Southee had often dominated and not just with the ball — his long, clean hitting was also a feature and there were genuine hopes he might turn into an all-rounder.

Which brings us to his test debut.

Southee had played just 11 first-class matches for ND when he was selected to play the touring English, first in a T20I — back when the format was still, at international level at least, considered a light and frothy way to kick off a tour — and then in the third test of the series.

Southee ripped through Michael Vaughan (2) and Andrew Strauss early, before coming back with the second new ball to account for century-maker Kevin Pietersen. Early on day two Southee forced Stuart Broad and Ryan Sidebottom into mistakes to claim 5 for 55 on debut. Not a bad start. It was Stephen Fleming's final test and while he signed off with a typical half-century, Southee ensured that the future would be looked forward to as much as the past would be lamented.

Southee didn't stop with just taking wickets. Amid the dying embers of the test, the No. 10 ensured it sparked to life again briefly with a 40-ball unbeaten 77, combining with the rabbit's rabbit Chris Martin (5) to add 84 for the final wicket in a heavy loss. It was an innings that included nine sixes, many of them huge, as exclamation points. As a spectacle, it was an absolute hoot, but it was also, in retrospect, a bit of a millstone around Southee's neck. Many punters correlated runs with technique and assumed the selectors had unearthed a genuine all-rounder from the wilderness of rural Northland. Even a cursory examination of the footage from that innings reveals a slogger — a decent slogger, but a slogger nonetheless — but the idea persists that Southee has sold his batting talent short.

There was another interesting side note from that test, and that was the press calls after the first day's play. Pietersen, KP, was wheeled in first and spoke at length about what a good century he had just scored. Once his oratorical tap had been turned on there were real fears it might never cease, but that was nicely balanced out by Southee's slightly dumbstruck appearance minutes later, when a broad smile and an 'aw shucks' was about as deep as it got. There was no mistaking the hardened professional from the teenager that day.

It was emblematic of the first few years of Southee's career. The talent was obvious, but oftentimes he just looked happy to be there. He went to England, played at Lord's, went wicketless and didn't feature again in the series. He toured Australia and took five wickets for the match in Brisbane, but none in Adelaide, where he also conceded his first 'century'.

Back home, he didn't feature in the first two tests of a series against India or the first two tests of the home series against Pakistan next summer. His career was more stop than start.

'I remember the first time I was dropped,' Southee said in an interview after he reached 300 wickets. 'I was pretty upset as a 19 or 20-year-old. The first thing my old man said to me was, "You're obviously not working hard enough." That was a bit of a reality check and something that stuck with me as well. You can never work too hard at what you're doing.'

Southee had also earned a reputation as being a bit too fond of the social side of touring, but his teammates always maintained that he was never a big drinker and always kept himself in great shape. Perception can sometimes equal reality in the eyes of the public and that baggage was not helped when Southee was identified as the player involved in a mid-air clinch with an inebriated young woman en route to the 2011 World Cup in India. A fellow passenger towards the expensive end of the plane had been troubled enough by what she saw to call into a talkback radio station during a stopover to report the incident and pretty soon the story mushroomed to include the front page of the *New Zealand Herald*.

'After a difficult summer on the pitch, rumours were rife yesterday that one of New Zealand's rep cricketers had found a different kind of form in the airspace over the Indian Ocean,' the *Herald* reported.

'Medium pacer Tim Southee was accused of getting a little too close and personal with a female passenger from first-class on board an Emirates flight . . . A passenger on the flight from Sydney to Dubai told a radio station the incident was the worst possible sort of lewd behaviour, a claim hotly denied by Southee and his employer.'

An internal NZC 'investigation' found the incident to be blown out of all proportion and barely even worthy of mention, but the context around it would have proved educational for Southee. It had been an unsettled time, with Andy Moles removed as coach amid rumours of player power out of control. Any sign of misbehaviour, no matter how trivial, was latched on to by the public because it played into the narrative that the Black Caps were, as Brendon McCullum would later describe it, overpaid and underachieving prima donnas.

Southee was, for a couple of awkward days, the central figure in this bubbling cauldron of public dissatisfaction because, although he might not have been a prima donna and at that point in his career he was very unlikely to be overpaid, he was underachieving.

By midway through 2012, four years after his explosive debut, Southee was kicking around test cricket with a bowling average in the mid-40s, and while his ODI numbers were better, largely due to a five-wicket haul against Pakistan in Wellington in 2011, they were not outstanding enough for him to be considered an automatic selection.

So disillusioned were some becoming with Southee's apparent lack of development that he was cited as a reason McCullum missed out on the captaincy in 2011 because he had the temerity to include Southee on his leadership ticket as a potential vice-captain. Leaks from the appointment process at the time suggested this was, in the eyes of the panel, a deal breaker.

Little did they know. To be fair, outside of McCullum, little did anybody know.

* * * * * * * *

Southee's test career was revived in the unlikeliest of venues.

On a tour to India in 2012, Southee had missed the first test, a chastening innings defeat in Hyderabad, where Ravichandran Ashwin took six wickets in each innings and New Zealand's preferred seam attack of veteran Martin, Trent Boult, Doug Bracewell and James Franklin struggled to make a dent in India's batting armour.

In the second test, Martin's in-swing was out and Southee's out-swing was in.

Sharing the new ball in a test for the first time with his ND teammate Boult, Southee bowled Gautam Gambhir, had Cheteshwar Pujara out hooking, strangled Suresh Raina down leg side, had centurion Virat Kohli trapped leg before not playing a shot and, for his 50th test wicket, dismissed MS Dhoni. For dessert, he dismissed two tailenders caught behind to end with 7 for 64, and although New Zealand lost by five wickets, he had the pleasure of disturbing the great Sachin Tendulkar's stumps in the second innings.

Southee was back; the firm of Boult & Southee was just getting started.

The latter was important because at this point in their history, with Mike Hesson having just taken the coaching helm from John Wright and Ross Taylor still captaining, the team was ranked eighth in the world.

Southee stayed hot in the subcontinent, taking another five-wicket bag and eight for the match in an upset win over Sri Lanka at Colombo, but missed the tour to South Africa that followed, McCullum's first as skipper, after rupturing the ligaments in his thumb while fielding. It was one of the rare times Southee has been unavailable for his country and it was a good one to miss.

He returned for the home-and-away series against England. After a rust-filled return in the home series, he was back to his brilliant best at Lord's, taking 4 for 58 and 6 for 50, to get hold of what remains his only 10-wicket haul in tests.

It had taken a while, but the seamer had found his groove. He swung the new ball early at a decent but hardly life-threatening pace range of 130 to 135 kph. Being supremely fit and a rhythm rather than a shoulder bowler also allowed him to bowl long spells.

In home series wins against the West Indies and India in the 2013–14 summer, his wicket hauls per innings were 4, 2, 2, 3, 4, 3, 3, 3, 3, 2. On the 2014 autumn tour to the Caribbean he took 10 wickets across the two tests they won in Kingston and Bridgetown but struggled in the loss at Port of Spain.

It would be wrong to say wickets slowed to a trickle, but a four-wicket haul against Sri Lanka was his best return between then and the home World Cup in 2015.

Southee did not actually have a great World Cup, yet ask any New Zealand cricket fan about the spell they'll remember most from the tournament and invariably they will point to his one-man demolition of England at Wellington Regional Stadium. Southee took 7 for 33 and then New Zealand blitzed the chase for 124 in just 12.2 overs. It was a phenomenal display of swing bowling, with the crowd rising as one when Southee took his seventh wicket bowling to a field that had four slips.

Southee took just four more wickets for the entire tournament, going wicketless in the semi-final and final and his one-day fortunes seemed to be the inverse of his test status. The more and more indispensable he became as part of New Zealand's test line-up, the more tenuous his place became in the ODI team.

* * * * * * * *

Something curious happened between late 2016 and 2018. Imperceptibly, by stealth almost, Southee, approaching 30, went from a very good test bowler to great. His bowling average in 2017 was around 32. There is nothing wrong with that at all in the modern era when batters have far less fear about attacking the quicks, but it is out of world-class range. Having played as many tests as he had by then, that average becomes increasingly difficult to shift.

The spur for his rise from good to great might have been a truly remarkable win against Pakistan at Seddon Park in November 2016. Southee took 6 for 80 in the first innings, but with weather having a big say, the tourists took tea on the final day at 158 for 1, the draw a formality. New Zealand's attack, however, went ballistic, taking the final nine wickets in 25 overs, Southee contributing two to take man of the match honours.

Williamson was skipper by now and it was around this time that the fulfilment of the leadership promise was taking shape. Southee had for some time occupied the alpha corner of the dressing room and often used humour to cut pretenders down to size, but observers say it was around this period that, with his sense of playfulness still intact, he saw the benefit of building up those around him.

One of those who particularly benefited was Neil Wagner, the South African immigrant whose wholehearted approach to cricket was viewed with some curiosity by New Zealanders used to a slightly more sedate mentality. It took a while for Wagner to gain acceptance in Southee and Boult's corner of the room, something the former admitted to the *Herald* that he regrets. 'I'd imagine it was difficult for him — it was a bold thing to do at the age of 23, moving to another country. Looking back, we made it harder for him [to fit in] than we needed to.'

Wagner, who takes his own place in this book, is now recognised as part of the most prolific pace triumvirate in New Zealand test history.

If 2017 laid the platform, everything from 2018 on has been a spectacular adornment to his career.

What is not acknowledged enough is the role Southee played in guiding New Zealand through to the World Test Championship final. While Williamson's mountains of runs created headlines, as did Wagner's broken-toes heroics and even Mitchell Santner's stunning caught-and-bowled intervention against Pakistan at Mount Maunganui, Southee's often understated brilliance too often went unnoticed or ignored. Often it was more convenient to mock his batting, which, admittedly, was often preposterous.

Jarrod Kimber, a global cricket writer who uses statistics to take subterranean-deep dives into players, once wrote that Southee's achievements get overlooked because 'there always seems to be a bigger story' floating around.

'Not to mention that he's also old news,' Kimber continued. 'Like he's not actually that old. But he's been around since he was a teenager. And since he came on the scene, New Zealand seemed to find a new seamer every couple of years. First Boult, then Wagner and now Jamieson — but it's Southee who is third all-time to Vettori and Hadlee.

'He's done all this being a relatively old-fashioned cricketer. Along with [James] Anderson, he's probably one of the few true outswing bowlers left in cricket. He's evolved beyond our traditional notion of an outswing bowler. But that's still what he is, someone who bowls many abnormally swinging balls at and around off stump . . .

'[Southee] has been incredible for a while, we just haven't noticed. There have been bigger teams, other wickets and his own teammates stealing the show.'

He *has* been 'incredible' for a while now.

Since the start of 2018, Southee has played 36 tests and taken 162 wickets at an average of 25.8. He has taken six-wicket bags against England at Hagley Oval and at Lord's, again, and one against Sri Lanka at the Basin Reserve. He has taken five-fors against Australia in Perth, India home and away and against the West Indies, Sri Lanka and South Africa.

He took his 300th test wicket, just the third New Zealander to do so, against Pakistan at Mount Maunganui. Southee's response at the close of play was typically understated, though he did confess to having confused his mate Wagner in the process.

'It's special, and obviously not many people have been able to do it and the two that have [Hadlee and Vettori], they are two of our greatest-ever cricketers — so it's nice to be in that bracket,' he said. 'When I was a kid, all I wanted to do was play cricket for New Zealand, and I guess to sit here after a reasonable time of doing that and achieving a couple of things along the way . . . it's a pretty cool feeling.

'You obviously know you're reasonably close. So, yeah, the guys kept reminding me. Wags [Neil Wagner] was actually one ahead of everyone else; he thought it was the first one and came in and gave me a big hug, and I was thinking, "What's going on here mate?"'

In this rich period, Southee even found time, very curiously, to be dropped by coach Gary Stead for the final test of the disastrous 2019–20 three-test tour to Australia, despite taking 12 wickets across the previous two and despite fellow senior pro and captain Williamson being absent through illness. Southee, the presumptive skipper for the SCG test, was instead running water while the Tom Latham-led side crashed to a 0–3 whitewash.

The decision caused a stir and would be one of the last mistakes New Zealand made before lifting the WTC mace 18 months later. Southee would get credit for not dropping his lip, although he did tell the *Herald* that it stung.

'Any time you are left out, it bloody hurts,' he said, perhaps referencing a test in Dunedin against South Africa where he also missed the playing XI. 'It was about not showing my disappointment to the group. The last thing they needed was a senior guy kicking cans. We had a number of discussions about it, and you've got to respect the coach's decision. I had to stomach it and move on.

'But it hit especially hard because I felt I was taking a few wickets leading into that game. I didn't see it coming.'

Southee doesn't get dropped much now, certainly not in tests when he was somewhat surprisingly elevated to captaincy in 2022 as Williamson relinquished the leadership in one of the formats in a bid to tax his mind less and extend his career.

Southee took the team to Pakistan, where they were unlucky not to win one or both of the tests that ended in draws, the final one a thriller that had New Zealand needing one wicket and the hosts 15 runs before bad light ended play three overs early (if ever there was an official's ruling that proved that cricket as a sport could still get in the way of itself, that was it).

Returning home, Southee saw his side spanked by an England team energised under the coaching of former New Zealand captain McCullum at Mount Maunganui and, despite some hearty hitting that led to his second-highest score in tests, was instructed to follow on at the Basin in the following match.

They were desperate times. It felt like the confirmation of the end of an era. While writing in my cricket-heavy newsletter *The Bounce*, this author stated:

'New Zealand have been outclassed at the Basin Reserve, just as they were in the somewhat confected pink-ball test at Mount Maunganui. Being outclassed is one thing, being out-everythinged another. Out-bowled and out-batted, that's a no contest, but more worryingly, out-fielded, out-thought and out-bodylanguaged.

'They're just not in the game; passive onlookers at their own party as England commandeer both the keg and the Spotify playlist.'

Yes, it's embarrassing to read that back now, but there was a truth to it. New Zealand were dying and half-buried, but Southee instead helped engineer one of the greatest test wins of any nation, any time. They beat England by one run to become just the fourth team to win following on. If that wasn't a sign that this team under Southee still had some intestinal fortitude, it was confirmed one test later when they defied the rain and Sri Lanka's best efforts to win a test off the final ball at Hagley Oval, and they required no such drama to complete a 2–0 series win in Wellington.

The Southee captaincy reign, if nothing else, has got off to a start that has been wildly entertaining, almost impossibly so.

Those two words, wildly entertaining, could also be used to describe his batting, although other, more traditionally inclined, followers of the sport might choose less generous terms.

The slogger that cleared his front hip and pasted England all around McLean Park in 2008 is still the slogger who cleared his hip and pasted England all over the Basin Reserve in 2023.

In between there hasn't been a lot to get excited about. Five half-centuries and just 24 scores of 25 or more in 94 tests, and one 50 in ODIs, does neither his eye nor his batting position justice. Southee often found himself coming in at No. 8, a position Vettori worked diligently to add to the all-rounder class. Diligent is not a word that sits easily alongside Southee's batting.

Fielding, however, is a different matter entirely.

Although there are no metrics that can definitively answer the proposition, you could make a strong case that Southee is the greatest fielding fast bowler in New Zealand history. It's difficult to think of anybody globally, excluding all-rounders like Ben Stokes, who are obviously superior.

Southee is a good mover in the outfield, but what separates him from most quicks is his bucket hands in the slips, which became his preferred position to 'rest' as opposed to the normal habitat of fine leg or third man.

* * * * * * *

Southee's white-ball career is not as neat and tidy to assess. On the surface, his economy rate, particularly in 50-over cricket, looks a little bloated for a bowler of his class, but then you consider the big-bat, small-boundary era he has played in and it starts to look a little better. Throw into the mix the fact that he invariably bowls in the powerplay and at the death, and the body of his work starts to look a lot healthier.

Southee had played 107 of the 175 T20Is New Zealand has played since his debut, 154 of the 258 ODIs and 94 of the 126 tests. He has played 355 of the 559 international cricket matches New Zealand has played in each format since he made his debut.

He has been around so long he feels like part of the furniture, yet there is no indication that Southee, whose economical action does not lend itself to the usual injury problems associated with pace bowlers, is nearing the end.

He is 34 years old and cites James Anderson, who is still playing test cricket at 40, as his inspiration.

'I'd love to play for as long as I possibly can,' he has said. 'I love doing what I've done and have been fortunate enough to do it for a period of time now. Obviously there's high standards that come with representing New Zealand. And as long as you can [live up to] those standards, then age is a number.'

Southee has given a lot to the Black Caps — there could still be a lot more to come.

CHAPTER 11
MARTIN GUPTILL

	Matches	Runs	Ave	S/R	100s	50s	Catches
Test:	47	2586	29.38	46.6	3	17	50
ODI:	198	7346	41.73	87.3	18	39	104
T20I:	122	3531	31.81	135.7	2	20	68

Debut: 2009   Last match: 2022

There's a conversation I can remember as clearly today as I could back in 2007 when it took place. I was sitting in Shane Bond's lounge and we were going over some things for what would eventually become his book, *Shane Bond: Looking Back*.

He was lamenting some of the structures in the New Zealand game that he felt were an impediment to producing good players, particularly around the preponderance of two-day, two-innings club and school cricket. He felt the onus should have been on first-innings points, not outright wins, because all the system did was promote 'rubbish cricket' where spinners were just used to encourage the slog and batters did not learn to bat time any more effectively than they would in a limited-overs match.

At that point Bond was prevented from playing international cricket due to signing with the 'rebel' Indian Cricket League, but he had been turning out for Canterbury. Like many times in New

Zealand cricket's history, there seemed to be any number of effective medium-pacers doing the rounds, but that had never been an issue, so I asked Shane: 'Have you seen any batters that have impressed you on the domestic circuit?' With only a moment's hesitation, he replied: 'Not many, but there's a kid in Auckland, a redhead called Martin Guptill, who hits a cleaner ball than Nath [Astle]. He could be special.'

I remembered that conversation less than two years later when I sat in a makeshift press box at an Eden Park being rebuilt for the 2011 Rugby World Cup and watched Guptill shuffle down the wicket, realise he hadn't got the pitch of the ball but still deposited Chris Gayle into the upper tier of the West Stand to bring up a one-day international century on debut.

I remember that conversation now as the country contemplates a 2023 World Cup tilt without its best player, the injured Kane Williamson, while a contract-less (his choice) Guptill contemplates his future.

I remember that conversation now, also, as I contemplate this conundrum: Martin Guptill, New Zealand's most prolific white-ball run-scorer, might be remembered as much for what he didn't do brilliantly as for what he did.

* * * * * * * *

Let's get it out there before we get to the good stuff.

Guptill's test career was not a success. It wasn't an abject failure either, but the numbers do not correlate with the prodigious talent.

'I don't think he was an opener in test cricket,' Ross Taylor, his best friend in cricket, wrote in *Black & White*. 'Had Gup, with all his natural talent, been given an extended opportunity, he would have been a fantastic five or six for New Zealand for many years.'

It is moot, of course. Guptill's sample size for opening in test cricket is large, 75 innings at 27.5, but his outings at Nos 5 and 6 are few (eight innings at 49.6). To make a conclusive judgement based on four tests in the middle order would be foolish, but we can say with some authority that Taylor was right in that Guptill was not a reliable test opener. 'You've got to be a bit different to be an opening batter in test cricket — that's why Wrighty was so good,' Taylor continued, somewhat esoterically. 'I think Guppy's too normal to be a test opener.'

Guptill himself seems pragmatic about the situation and puts his lack of productivity at the top of the order against the red ball down to a failure to play to a tempo he was comfortable with. While the art of opening the batting is as much about denial of your instincts as it is about talent, when you're as good at hitting a moving object as Guptill is, sometimes you've got to be more committed to doing that. Instead, he thinks, he might have been too wrapped up in trying to be a 'traditional test opener'.

'Even in my early days of first-class cricket there was quite a big disparity in my strike rates. It would have been up at 80 to 90 in one-day cricket and then it would have dropped back to 30 to 40 in first-class cricket,' he said. 'Having a survival instinct rather than still trying to score runs probably hindered me a bit.

'I'd go to drive one and in one-day cricket I'd probably smash it because I had the intent to score runs, whereas in first-class cricket I'm a little bit more reserved and I go tentatively at one, nick off and I'm out. Now I'm getting a bit older and having played a lot more cricket I'm probably more confident with how I wanna play first-class cricket. I sort of showed that when I came back into the team in 2015. I had a year to 18 months back in the team before I got dropped again and I showed a little more intent — I was probably scoring around that 50 to 60 strike rate for the most part, which is a much better tempo for me.'

It is fascinating to hear Guptill talk about regrets. Because cricket, and particularly the batting side of cricket's equation, is a sport built upon managing failure, you will often hear batters use phrases like, 'It's just the way I play', to mask deficiencies. Guptill has almost turned that on its head, admitting that his test career never lived up to its potential because he didn't play the way he played. He looks at his excellent record for Auckland in the Plunket Shield — if you take the test numbers out of his first-class equation, he averages more than 45 — and realises he left a lot of runs on the table in five-day cricket.

He also rues not taking up the opportunity, like his mate Taylor did, to work with Martin Crowe on a more formalised basis earlier in his career. 'I started working with Hogan 2014, but I actually had the opportunity in 2010,' he said, 'but I was young and stubborn, not wanting to change things — it was really stupid on my part. I thought I was better than I was. Things could have been much different if I started with him earlier, but by the time I did I only had two years with him before he passed away. I could have been a massively different player; the consistency [in test cricket] could have been there, but you never know. The time I did have with him was invaluable — we did a huge amount of work in the Eden Park indoor nets in the winter of 2014 and that was the start of my golden patch.'

It is worth noting, for posterity if nothing else, that Guptill scored three test centuries and 17 50s in his career, with numbers that are comparable, and in some cases superior, to players who are remembered with some fondness from previous generations, like Ken Rutherford, Jeremy Coney, Jeff Crowe, Mark Greatbatch and Bruce Edgar.

Ask the 36-year-old Guptill sitting in front of you now what he'd tell the 19-year-old Guptill who was about to make his first-class debut and he doesn't hesitate.

'I'd tell him what I tell the young Auckland guys I play with now. I'd say, "Look, batting is about scoring runs. You're not just there to soak up dot balls and be there all day; you still have to score runs. Base your game around scoring runs and where you want to score."

I would definitely tell myself that coming into first-class cricket back at 19 years old.'

Perhaps the hardest player in the book to assess, Martin Guptill's frustrations at test level only rarely spilled into his white-ball cricket where he was an explosive force at the top of the order and a proven match-winner.

'Gup is one of the best ball strikers and the best ODI opener I played with,' Taylor wrote. 'His innings of 189 not out against England in Southampton in 2013 and 237 not out against the West Indies in Wellington in 2015 — the highest individual score in a World Cup game — are the best ODI innings by a Black Cap that I've seen.'

It is there we need to dwell, but not before we learned how he got there.

* * * * * * * *

Whether by chance or outrageous fortune, Guptill is a Westie, which is either used as a term of endearment or for gentle ribbing, for all those who grew up or live west of Auckland's Blockhouse Bay Road.

He went to Kelston Primary and Avondale College, but his cricket education came somewhere in between, at Ken Maunder Park, where his dad was a stalwart of the Suburbs New Lynn club, a team renowned for playing a hard-nosed brand of cricket befitting the community it served.

The term 'stalwart' does not do Peter Guptill, who died in 2017, justice. He played for SNLCC for 35 years, 21 of them in premier grade, where he scored a tick under 12,000 career runs, getting close but never quite cracking his way into the Auckland side. A true clubman, he then went on to serve on committees, chaired the club and served as president from 2012 to 2015.

'Dad played cricket right up until his mid- to late forties. He was still in love with the game and being the youngest one in the family,

I just wanted to keep up and play cricket really. My older brother Ben and I basically grew up at the club on weekends, watching Dad play and hanging around Ken Maunder Park.

'The club is still important to me. I grew up playing there, it's been a big part of my development. My uncle played there as well, so it's a real "family ties" sort of thing.'

As a 'tiny' 12-year-old, Guptill was playing with 15-year-olds Ben and Michael Bates, the latter a left-arm paceman who played two ODIs for New Zealand in 2012. Playing ahead of his age group helped his development, but it nearly all came crashing down when Ben ran over his left foot in a forklift while they were at the family haulage business.

'It was a fairly traumatic time for everyone,' Peter would tell the *Herald* in 2009. 'The doctors originally set the crushed toes [the outside three] and gave them a couple of weeks to heal. When they hadn't shown any signs of healing they made the decision to amputate. We had no choice. It was difficult for Martin.'

Guptill said the naivete of youth got him through what was a time of uncertainty. The toes were starting to go gangrenous, so having them removed was far preferable to waiting for a miracle that in all likelihood would never arrive and having to have his foot removed at the ankle. That grim prospect that would have put paid to any hopes of a professional cricket career, however fanciful that might have seemed to a 14-year-old who already had designs of following his father and brother into the family trucking business (Guptill earned his heavy vehicle licence in 2009).

'It was December 2000, so I couldn't play cricket for a bit. Those summer holidays were a bit stuffed after that. The good thing about being that young is that natural resilience; you bounce back pretty quickly. I mean, I played the last game of the season, in the first term of 2001, so it didn't knock me down for too long.'

While lying in Middlemore Hospital feeling sorry for himself, he got the sort of visit most kids only dream of, when Jeff Crowe, the Black Caps manager who had played cricket against Peter, arranged for Stephen Fleming, Jacob Oram and James Franklin, with an average height of 1.94 metres between them, to come for a visit before a one-dayer against Zimbabwe at Eden Park.

'It's pretty daunting seeing these guys you watch on TV walk through your door taking up the whole doorway so I was like, "Wow!"'

Guptill does not believe the injury has affected him apart from cosmetically — wearing jandals can cause sideways glances from kids, for example — though he does note that most of his soft-tissue injuries have occurred in his left leg, so there might have been some compensatory overuse of muscles, but 'that's probably clutching at straws, really'.

'My balance has always been pretty good. It hasn't really held me back running or anything like that. It's just one of those things that happened, and you move on quickly. It's just part of me and you wouldn't know unless I was in bare feet.'

Guptill played his first senior club game for SNLCC shortly after his 16th birthday. He can remember exactly how he went out. If there's one thing you'll learn when you talk cricket with Guptill, it's his incredible recall. 'It was against Eden Roskill. I got caught down the leg side in my first innings. Less than ideal, but that's just the way it goes. Yeah, it definitely hit my gloves.'

He said he never stood out as a young player. He made age-group rep teams, but he was physically small and nothing more than a steady player. He cited Marc Ellison — a 'manchild' — as the Auckland kid everybody assumed would make it, while he was little more than an afterthought. Ellison has gone on to live a peripatetic cricket life that included stints at club level in Australia and England, before settling in Belfast where he has played first-class cricket for the local Northern Knights franchise.

Guptill had enjoyed a winter at the Academy, so cricket was

starting to loom larger when Dipak Patel pulled him aside at his third national under-19 tournament, this one at Lincoln, and told him he was leaving to get on a plane to make his Auckland debut in a one-day match against Canterbury at Eden Park Outer Oval.

Guptill was so green he didn't know the code to the gate to get into Eden Park, so was standing forlornly outside with his gear, desperately trying to reach coach Mark O'Donnell to let him know he wasn't late. It was just as well he got in on time because although he was batting No. 3, he was facing the second ball of the match after Tim McIntosh fell to the first. His first two scoring shots were pulled sixes off Chris Harris and Stephen Cunis, but it obviously didn't impress one Black Cap much because Guptill's other vivid memory of that debut was being roundly abused by Craig McMillan on his way to 28, second top score in Auckland's sickly 100 all out.

'Ross [Taylor] wouldn't have taken it. He would have bitten back, but I was so young I didn't know what was going on. I just wanted to play,' he said of his introduction to the more verbose side of adult cricket.

His nascent senior career was interrupted by the Under-19 World Cup in Sri Lanka, in a team captained by Ellison and also including future Black Caps Tim Southee, Colin Munro, Hamish Bennett, Todd Astle and Roneel Hira. It was not a successful tournament, with the team never coming to terms with the conditions and losing the plate final to Nepal (Munro was batting No. 10!), with Guptill's most significant contribution coming with 42 against the United States.

Back in friendlier climes, Guptill made his first-class debut for Auckland at the end of the 2005–06 season, falling to Wellington's Mark Gillespie for a duck in his first bat and responding with 99 in the second, one of the more curious combinations of scores on first-class debut.

'I can remember my thought process pretty vividly,' Guptill says, of his 99. 'Jesse Ryder was bowling. We were 200 and something for 1, so we were ahead of the game, and I remember thinking, "Oh, third man's back so I'll run it down there." Then I was like, "Nah, just wait for the ball and play it on merit." I overthought it, got one outside off stump and ended up nicking it behind. I was kicking myself a wee bit there, but you get offered 99 on debut and you'd take that any day of the week — better than getting two ducks. Touch wood, to this day I haven't got a pair in first-class cricket.'

Guptill's elevation to the national side seemed a matter of time after his 596 runs were a whopping 126 more than next-best James Marshall in the 2007–08 one-day State Shield charts (now the Ford Trophy). He was selected for New Zealand A tours to Australia and India, so was firmly on the radar by the time the 2008–09 season rolled around with the West Indies in town. He was in good form, having got that maiden first-class hundred he'd missed by a run on debut and following it with another century in a one-dayer against Northern Districts. He was getting ready to catch a plane to Christchurch with the Auckland team when selector Glenn Turner called to tell him to unpack and that he was instead going to be playing a one-dayer at Eden Park in place of the struggling Jamie How. The plan was to bat Guptill at No. 3, but he was whisked straight in as an opener after Jesse Ryder was dropped after a late night out saw him miss a team meeting.

Guptill looked born for the big stage on the way to an unbeaten 122 from 135 balls and showed he had a flair for the dramatic by hitting an enormous six to raise three figures. 'I hit it on top of the West Stand,' he recalled. 'I ran down and it wasn't there, so I had to keep going through with it.'

By the end of the summer, he had made his international bow in T20Is and tests as well, and although the rise had been rapid, he was the opposite of young and brash. Guptill admits he was a relatively timid presence in the Dan Vettori-led Black Caps, preferring the don't-speak-unless-spoken-to approach to fitting in.

'As a young guy, I didn't want to put a foot wrong.'

He preferred to do his talking in the middle, but despite a regular output, it wasn't until his 54th ODI that he added his second ODI century, 105 against Zimbabwe in Harare. On the same tour he would add his second test century after a maiden 189, batting at No. 5, against Bangladesh in Hamilton — a test where he put on 339 with Brendon McCullum for the sixth wicket.

Following the Zimbabwe tour, the centuries would come thick and fast in the ODI game. On a tour to England, he scored back-to-back unbeaten centuries with 103 not out at Lord's and 189 not out at the Rose Bowl, an innings Taylor rates as one of the best he's seen, but not one that makes Guptill's top three.

Those are, in chronological order . . .

237 NOT OUT VS WEST INDIES, WORLD CUP QUARTER-FINAL, WELLINGTON, 2015

'I remember the first ball so clearly. Jerome Taylor came running in, it was pitched up and swinging away and I just punched it between mid-on and the stumps for four and thought, "Oh yeah, I'm on; I saw that one pretty well." I'd come off a hundred against Bangladesh in the previous game, but I'd sort of stuffed it up in the end. I got a cramp on 98 or 99 — I tucked it off my hip and my calf just cramped up — and then I got to my hundred the next ball before slogging out. I should've kept going because we lost a couple of quick wickets and Dan Vettori ended up hitting one over cover for six to bring us close and Southee might have popped one on the bank to win it. It got a lot closer than it should have — a bit touch and go [New Zealand won by three wickets with seven balls to spare], so there was no real feeling of celebration for me.

'At the Cake Tin I wanted to do well, and it wasn't a particularly fast hundred — I think I got it off 111 balls or something like that [well, exactly like that]. We took the batting powerplay and three balls later I just remember sticking my front foot down the middle of the wicket to Darren Sammy and just basically slogging him over, I want to say forward square leg rather than cow corner, and I've got a good piece of that and it went up on the roof. Everything is a blur from there. I think the next 52 balls I scored 137 runs, so everything just started hitting the middle. The runs just kept adding up and we got about 390 [393].'

Guptill's memory might be close to photographic, but his capacity for understatement is getting in the way here. This was, it has to be noted, a World Cup knockout match in front of an expectant and slightly nervous crowd, not a meaningless bilateral match to provide the necessary content for a broadcasting deal.

In an article for *The Nightwatchman*, I wrote: 'It was the innings of his life — it is difficult to conceive he will ever be able to bat better — but for us New Zealanders who over the previous few weeks had learned how to love the game again, it felt like the innings of all our lives.'

What he also failed to mention was that there were genuine questions over his place in the side on the eve of the tournament. In the lead-up, New Zealand played a seven-game series against Sri Lanka, and Guptill was conspicuous for his lack of results.

'In the nets I was hitting it as well, but it wasn't translating onto the field. I scored one 50 against Sri Lanka in seven innings, finished the series with a duck [his third of the series] and didn't know what the hell was going on. We then played Pakistan in two ODIs and I got 30-odd in Wellington [39] and 80-odd in Napier [76] so I was like, "Okay, this could be the start of something here".' It was. Guptill scored 547 runs in the tournament — more than anybody else.

180 NOT OUT VS SOUTH AFRICA, HAMILTON, 2017

'My number one. Definitely my best ODI innings in New Zealand. It was such a difficult wicket. It was slow and it turned, not a typical Hamilton wicket. We bowled first and opened with two spinners.

We've never done that before, not even in India or elsewhere on the subcontinent. We opened up with Jeetan Patel and Mitchell Santner, and Southee ended up bowling 10 overs of off-cutters [even Kane Williamson bowled a few overs]. South Africa got to 279 thanks to AB de Villiers [72 not out off 59 balls] who made it look pretty easy, but he makes any wicket look easy, doesn't he?

'I was coming back from a hamstring injury and actually retore it on the field, so I was batting pretty much on one leg and everything clicked from ball one. Everything hit the middle of the bat and I was finding gaps left, right and centre. The other guys couldn't really get it away, yet I was popping it over cover, pulling fours and nudging ones at will. They had a pretty decent attack — Kagiso Rabada, Wayne Parnell, Chris Morris, Dwaine Pretorius, Imran Tahir and JP Duminy — so it wasn't an easy attack to score against. Rossco [Taylor] and I put on 180. He had scored about 40 off 80 balls at one stage and people were thinking he was scoring too slowly, but the way I look at one-day cricket is big partnerships like that, it doesn't matter how they're formed, they set big totals and chase down big totals. That's the foundation. Ross got out [for 66 off 97] and [Luke] Ronchi has come out to bat at No. 5 and we won in a couple of overs.'

Again, probably not the whole story. When Ronchi came in, New Zealand still needed 23 to win. He scored 1 not out off one ball as Guptill went ballistic. His innings contained 15 fours and 11 sixes, and he scored close to 65 per cent of New Zealand's total. New Zealand won by seven wickets with five whole overs to spare.

114 VS AUSTRALIA, SYDNEY, 2016

This Chappell–Hadlee knock is something of a forgotten gem, coming as it did in a heavy loss, but Guptill's innings contained some truly magical shots, including bopping Mitchell Marsh over long-on for a 100-metre six to move from 98 to 104.

'I only got half the job done that game. I was pretty pissed off not to take us deeper and give ourselves the chance of winning the game, but, again, it was just one of those innings where you feel like you're in a zone and it doesn't matter what they bowl to you, you're going to hit it in a gap.

'I was actually none off 10 balls, then hit [Mitchell Starc over the mid-on for four. The next over I walked at [Josh] Hazlewood and hit him back over his head for six, and then I don't know what happened, but everything seemed in slow motion. Starc was bowling pretty quick, but I remember flicking him off my toes for six and it felt effortless. It was the first time I had faced Pat Cummins as he was coming back from his back injury. I got a bit of width from him and could put it in front of point or behind point at will. It was one of those days where you got the same ball but could choose to put it in a couple of different areas.

'Jimmy Neesham and I had a run-a-ball 92-run partnership and then he decided he wanted to take on Starc and came off second best, which pissed me off a wee bit cause we were making it look pretty easy. We lost another wicket and were really on the back foot. Anyway, I brought my hundred up and then Adam Zampa dropped it short. [Twelfth man] Glenn Maxwell's on the field for some reason and I slapped it above his head, but he caught it on the second go.'

* * * * * * * *

If it were those innings alone, he'd hold a special place in our cricketing history, particularly the World Cup fireworks, but Guptill has done much more than that.

At 18 ODI hundreds, he trails only Taylor's 21, and his 7346 ODI runs trails only Taylor (8607) and Stephen Fleming (8007). Only one player has scored at least 2000 runs for New Zealand in ODIs at a higher strike rate than Guptill's 87.29, and that's his opening partner for many of his explosive knocks, Brendon McCullum (96.37).

With 23 all-format international centuries, only Williamson (41), Taylor (40) and Nathan Astle (27) have more.

He scored two T20I centuries, one against South Africa in East London and the other against Australia at Eden Park. Only Colin Munro (3) has more, though nobody comes close to his 3531 runs, with Williamson the next highest with 2464. At the time of writing, he is one of just three New Zealanders to have played 100 T20Is along with Taylor and Southee.

But the numbers can't tell you the sound the ball makes off the middle of Guptill's bat. The sound is deeper and resonates longer than most. As soon as you hear that sound you know the ball is travelling a long way and it is getting there in a hurry. It's not just aural pleasure, either. The sight of a Guptill lofted straight drive is one of the sport's great visual treats, particularly when he keeps his head down in an almost exaggerated fashion, holding the pose like a golfer trying to drive the green on the 18th at the Old Course, St Andrews. The full swing, the long levers, there might not be a single shot in New Zealand white-ball cricket that is so instantly identifiable with one player.

Yet for all his white-ball brilliance, he'd never be described as the luckiest cricketer to walk the flat green fields.

In a star-crossed 2019 World Cup final, Guptill found himself the central character in three of the most dramatic moments in cricket history — moments that happened just minutes apart.

On 220 for 7 chasing 242 to win, Ben Stokes skyed James Neesham to long-on, where Trent Boult waited. He caught the ball just inside the rope and with Guptill nearby calling for him to throw it in the air, Boult held on for a split second too long, standing on the rope as Guptill signalled six. Worse was to follow. With nine needed from three balls, Stokes scuffed a full toss to Guptill at deep midwicket. Coming back for two, Guptill's throw looked to be zeroing in on the stumps when a diving Stokes inadvertently diverted it to the boundary instead. Conceding five runs instead of two was rotten luck; having it erroneously ruled as six runs was rotten officiating.

Finally, and most desperately, Guptill was on strike for the final ball of the Super Over, with one needed to tie and two to win. He flicked Jofra Archer's well-directed yorker neatly into the outfield but slipped ever so slightly while taking off. Jason Roy's throw beat him back and England had, famously, gut-wrenchingly, 'won by the barest of margins'.

You have to be a fairly phlegmatic sort of bloke to bounce back from that sort of pain, but that's what Guptill had done until the start of the 2022–23 season, when he was hit by another sort of blow, being informed by the New Zealand selectors that while he would still be a squad player, he wasn't a first choice for the white-ball playing XIs. It seemed premature, but he's been around long enough to know that coaches and selectors have their own needs and wants, and there has been a sense that New Zealand needed to reinvigorate its programmes with talent. With the sand starting to slip more freely through the hourglass of his playing career, he made the call to hand back his New Zealand contract to become available for franchise tournaments such as Australia's Big Bash and the Pakistan and Caribbean super leagues.

'At my age I don't want to be playing as much and it just felt like the right time. I have two kids [a daughter Harley and son Teddy] and I still feel like I have a lot to offer, but how things have unfolded, I'll go out and find cricket where I can.'

It feels a little strange to contemplate a white-ball era without the tall, red headed right-hander at the top, but if he never plays for his country again, he can retire in the knowledge few have come close to doing what he's done.

CHAPTER 12
BJ WATLING

Debut: 2009   Last match: 2021

	Matches	Runs	Ave	S/R	100s	50s	Dismissals*
Test:	75	3790	37.52	42.61	8	19	275
ODI:	28	573	24.91	68.37	-	5	20
T20I:	5	38	9.5	65.51	-	-	3

*Includes catches as a keeper and a fielder

Unflashy and uncomplicated, the cliché you fall back on when talking about players in the mould of Bradley-John Watling is that they made the most of limited talents. Like many clichés it has an element of truth, but it also conceals the true story: Watling was a remarkable talent, his abilities were just of the less-expressive kind.

Ian Smith, one of New Zealand's greatest at the position, called wicketkeepers the drummers in the band. It was the title of his biography, in fact. The batters and bowlers are the lead guitarists and singers, the stars of the show, but the keepers are the steadying presence that keeps the team in rhythm. A sloppy drummer can condemn a rock band to mediocrity, no matter how technically proficient those around them might be; likewise, a sloppy keeper can fail to bring out the best in his bandmates on the field.

Watling would have been the type of keeper Smith had in mind with his analogy. The nuggety right-hander only ever approached his cricket with two questions in mind: What does my team need now? How do I go about providing it?

Because of his unobtrusiveness, Watling's excellence can often be overlooked. The feeling is exacerbated, too, because he has been replaced so seamlessly in the side. Wellingtonian Tom Blundell is in many ways a BJ Watling facsimile. He is quietly efficient and mostly mistake-free behind the stumps, and he already has four test centuries and a couple of back-to-the-wall classic innings to his name. He has taken the Watling template and added his own flourishes to it.

'I'm just so stoked for him,' Watling said of Blundell. 'I was lucky enough to work with him [as a coach] at Wellington and he's impressive. He's made every post a winner whether it's with the bat — I mean, he scored a hundred on debut — or as a keeper. I just enjoy watching New Zealanders do well.' It's a typically magnanimous response and while it might even be possible that Blundell will end up being remembered as a better keeper-batter than his predecessor (statistically he is tracking that way), it would in no way diminish Watling's legacy.

Brendon McCullum, who knows plenty about the demands of being the team's keeper, mentioned once that Watling had come into the team when it was on Struggle Street, he had been part of the team during their rise from the basement towards respect, and was a part of the team that achieved something close to dominance.

'That's not a coincidence,' he said.

In a podcast with former Chiefs rugby star Dwayne Sweeney, McCullum explained that Watling's contribution could never be calculated just by runs and catches.

'BJ is such an integral part of the Black Caps, not just performance wise, but culturally.'

Watling, never at his most comfortable when being showered with praise, deflected.

'You can feel the culture change and shift through better performances and more confidence, but I was lucky to be part of a New Zealand era that saw some of our best-ever play at the same time. We had Kane Williamson, Baz [McCullum], Ross [Taylor], Trent Boult, Tim Southee and Neil Wagner all playing at the same time. Good things are going to happen when you have that much quality on the field.'

Kane Williamson, when asked about the qualities the team would miss on Watling's retirement, said: 'He's the guy who keeps the team honest.'

The word 'honest' is critical in the BJ Watling story. When he was a teenager, Watling got a tattoo. Stories that start with young men getting inked are often cautionary tales. They often end in laser removal of ex-girlfriends' names, of rock bands that are no longer cool, of imagery that loses meaning and looks silly on ageing bodies. They're stories of regret.

Watling didn't just get a tattoo, however. He got a credo, an instruction manual for his life.

'LOYALTY. HONESTY. SELFLESSNESS.'

That's what it says on the box and that's exactly what his teammates always got from him.

He is the guy who gets the toughest questions from the guy staring back at him in the glass. Nobody you talk to, not in cricket circles at least, can remember him ever letting himself down.

* * * * * * * *

It took a while for the keeper in Watling to come out at the highest level.

Of his first 40 first-class games, just five were spent behind the sticks. It wasn't until his ninth test that he earned the big gloves. Even then, there were doubts.

If you were to judge his wicketkeeping solely by the eye test, he was not a natural. He didn't appear to possess the soft-handed glovework of Ian Smith, the overt confidence of Adam Parore or the ground-covering athleticism of McCullum. There were times, especially early, when Watling looked like a stopper. Perhaps cruelly, there were the occasional murmurings from the safety of the press box that Watling the keeper looked like an accident waiting to happen. What he did possess, however, was something no critics could measure: a maniacal desire to improve.

By the end of his career, Watling looked like a keeper's keeper, which is about as high a praise as one gloveman will bestow upon another, but even in those early days, the ones when he looked at his most ruffled, he had the happy knack of catching the ones that were nicked, and that's not a bad base to work from.

There were plenty of nicks, too. Whether it was Tim Southee swinging it away from the right-hander or Trent Boult swinging it away from the left-hander, the outside edge was always in play. Then, of course, there was Neil Wagner pounding away, looking to brush gloves and coax inside edges.

Not surprisingly, these combinations feature highly in the list of New Zealand test bowler-fielder combinations.

Southee induced 73 nicks that Watling caught (he added two more as a fielder), which is the seventh-most prolific combination in the world (Dennis Lillee and Rod Marsh, who played 13 years together, lead the way on 95) and comfortably a New Zealand record. The next-best New Zealand combination is Boult and Watling, with 57, and third is Wagner and Watling with 54 (one more as a fielder). The famous Richard Hadlee and Smith duo has 43.

Some of those numbers are due to happy accidents in terms of where careers coincide with each other, but there was no accident behind Watling's continued selection or his continued ability to catch the deflections. His 265 dismissals place him ninth on the all-time wicketkeeping list and of those above him, only Brad Haddin

(270 in 66 tests) has played fewer than his 75 tests. Watling's number becomes even more impressive when you consider he played just 67 as a designated keeper. His dismissals per inning — 2.09 — ranks among the best to have ever played the game.

The art of wicketkeeping, however, is a difficult one to write about. Unless the keeper possesses a range of eccentricities, like long-time England keeper Jack Russell who had the same hat for the entirety of his career, ate Weet-Bix every lunch break and blindfolded builders and contractors before driving them to his house to do work, or his countryman Alan Knott, who used to bolster his chamois leather inners with strips of plasticine and dunk his hands in hot water before taking the field, there is a limited amount to say.

Their value is measured by their ability to go unnoticed — the drumming analogy is apt again — and by their ability to 'not'. If a keeper does 'not' drop catches, does 'not' let through byes and does 'not' shut up in the field, they have done a great job. It is not, there goes that word again, necessarily an arcane art, but neither is it fully understood. It's an incredibly important part of the bowling and fielding equation, but some of the calculus is hidden from view (though not always from the stump mics). Suresh Menon, the Indian television personality and comedian, once said that 'you don't have to be mad to be a wicketkeeper, but it helps'.

The keeper must cajole and encourage. When the days are long and the sun is hot, the keeper's job is to ensure the energy does not flag in the field.

As author William Fiennes wrote in *Wisden*, keepers must talk and talk and talk, 'and not just the relentless dreary chiselling at the batsman's sporting and sexual self-esteem — now the keeper had to be chief of geeing-up and morale-boosting too, as if he were the afternoon's host and compère, calling everyone "buddy" and filling the pauses — "Good areas, Frankie!" — like a radio DJ scared of dead air'.

They're also expected to have an analytical brain, relaying information to the bowler and captain about a batter's faults and tendencies. Like a good poker player, they will sometimes bluff, making the batter think they're doing something they're not.

The modern game has raised the bar for the keeper-analyst role. With the Decision Review System in place, the keeper plays a key role in deciding whether teams should review caught-behind and leg-before appeals that have been rejected. A good review is, by definition, as good as a wicket.

There is another thing about wicketkeeping that is not immediately obvious to the casual viewer. It hurts. If a keeper plays for any length of time, they will end up with callused hands, cracked knuckles and dislocated and, in many cases, permanently disfigured, fingers. The constant bending and squatting, often followed by explosive sprints to the stumps, wreak havoc on knees, hips and back in particular. One of the main reasons there was a place for Watling behind the stumps was because McCullum gave away the gloves due to his aching back making it difficult to get out of bed in the morning, let alone prepare for and play international cricket.

It is physically taxing, maybe not as much as fast bowling, but without the opportunity to rest at fine leg in between.

A keeper can never switch off in the field, which is perhaps why they tend to be punchy, here-for-a-good-time-not-a-long-time batters. If you were to describe a typical keeper-batter they would be aggressive, they'd score quickly and often extravagantly; they'd be the batter that provided the zest before the tail.

That's not who Watling was.

* * * * * * * *

From a very young age, Watling hated getting out.

It might have been the South African in him. Born in Durban in 1985, Watling immigrated with his mother Linda to New Zealand when he was nine and still at primary school. Throughout his career Watling has made a note of thanking his mother, a schoolteacher, for raising him alone and instilling into him the values he holds dear.

'I didn't get to know my father,' he said.

In South Africa, if you're old enough to walk you're old enough to play cricket with a hard ball on grass wickets, so Watling got a nasty culture shock when he arrived in a new country and found the game he loved being played with plastic bats and balls.

His mother once described how unimpressed her son was with her for 'ruining his life' by bringing him to this place that didn't play cricket properly.

The first place Linda found a job was Tokoroa, a South Waikato town of 15,000 people noted for its proximity to the Kinleith Mill and the forestry industry. It has a reputation for producing rugby internationals — Keven Mealamu, Richard Kahui, Isaac Boss, Sean Maitland and Quade Cooper to name just five — but test cricketers were thin on the ground.

Watling often played for teams that weren't very good. He got used to batting through innings. He liked the feeling of remaining undefeated, of showing resolve where others couldn't or wouldn't. If there were 50 overs to use, why not try to use them all? This attitude stayed with him upon arrival at Hamilton Boys' High School. He was a small kid from a small town living with his aunty. Early on, his game was not expansive, but he was always a tough out.

It was at HBHS where he came under the tutelage of Chris Kuggeleijn who'd had a brief international career. Kuggeleijn loved Watling's fight, his willingness to punch above his weight and his insatiable appetite for work; Watling loved Kuggeleijn's attitude to life, his homilies and his motivational toolbox, which included the Dale Wimbrow poem 'The Guy in the Glass'.

On the weekends the 1st XI played senior cricket in Hamilton, where they were frequently informed as to how 'shit' they were and how they were likely to soon wear a bouncer to the head. It was a bit basic, a bit silly, but it did make going back to play midweek inter-school fixtures feel like a bit of a doddle.

HBHS won back-to-back national secondary school titles, but not everything came to Watling as he felt it might have. One of his abiding memories of youth cricket was not getting picked for the Northern Districts Under-19 team in the first year he qualified. 'That was disappointing,' he said. 'I did not enjoy that at all, but Kuggs was the coach and kept me grounded.'

Watling quickly banished the negativity, making not just the ND U19s the following season, but also the New Zealand side as their keeper and opening batter. A year later, while still in his teens, he was making his senior ND debut, scoring a typically gritty 37 in the first innings at No. 8 — he was keeping in Pete McGlashan's absence — and a solitary run when promoted to open in the second. Shuttling up and down the order was to become a theme.

There was nothing in those early years of the Plunket Shield that marked him out as a future test star. He scored a couple of 50s in each of his first two seasons in first-class cricket, but his average was hovering around 20. In his third full season he had a breakthrough of sorts, scoring 90s against Canterbury and Central Districts and home-and-away centuries against Otago, his first a big one, 153 at University Oval.

It was, however, an incredible feat in club cricket in 2008 that first thrust Watling into the national spotlight. Playing for Old Boys in the three-day Hamilton club final against an Eastern Suburbs team that won the toss and chose to field, Watling compiled 378, the only serious threat to his innings coming when it seemed he might have to cut it short to attend the Northern Districts end-of-year photo and prize-giving. 'I had a quick shower, ironed a shirt and I wasn't too late, although I missed the team photo. I'll have to get inserted,' he said after the knock.

A year later, he was opening the batting for New Zealand.

* * * * * * * *

Watling would have been quite happy to make a career as a dogged opening bat. It suited his skills and his mindset.

In his first test against Pakistan at Napier he scored 18 in the first innings before falling to the canny Mohammad Asif, a seam bowler with a beautiful action whose career was dogged and eventually ended by a series of cheating scandals involving failed drugs tests and match-fixing claims. In the second, Watling was on 60 not out and was poised to lead the New Zealand charge for a last-session victory when the heavens opened.

Watling also scored a half-century on debut for New Zealand in one-day cricket, against Sri Lanka in Dambulla, but struggled in his limited opportunities, most played in Asia, and could not force his way into John Wright's 2011 World Cup squad.

(It should probably be noted here that Watling actually debuted for the Black Caps in a T20 series against Pakistan in the UAE in 2009. He would play one match in Sri Lanka in 2012 and two more against the West Indies on the island of Dominica in 2014, and that was the sum total of his T20I career.)

Watling played sporadically for New Zealand in tests and ODIs, trying to nail down a place in the top three, until 'the idea was thrown out there that Baz's bad back might mean he needed to give up the gloves'.

We tend now to look back on that period as a natural changeover from McCullum to Watling behind the stumps, but it didn't work like that. Watling played a test in Ahmedabad at No. 3 with Gareth Hopkins as wicketkeeper and McCullum opening, and another in Bulawayo at No. 5 with Reece Young the keeper. He kept and scored an unbeaten century, his first, against Zimbabwe in Napier in January 2012, but played his next test in Kingston, Jamaica, as an opener, with McCullum at No. 3 and Kruger van Wyk as the gloveman.

It was not until the miserable New Year's test of 2013 in Cape Town that you could say the Watling as wicketkeeper era started — and the team celebrated that momentous occasion by being rolled for 45, with his contribution a golden duck (he did redeem himself somewhat in a lost cause with a fighting 42 in the second innings). A pair of fighting 63s in the next test at Port Elizabeth, now known as Gqeberha, again in a heavy defeat, established Watling as the man to provide top-order-like sensibilities into the middle order.

Although he never cracked it in one-day cricket — 'I definitely would have liked to have played a lot more white-ball cricket and I honestly didn't stop trying until I was 32 or 33, but I just didn't take my opportunities' — that remained his role for New Zealand, with one notable exception, until the very end.

Like his keeping, his batting wasn't always silky smooth, but when New Zealand needed him most, it was damned effective. He would take strike knees bent, bat held up and at an angle like a tower guardsman preparing for rebels to storm the gates. From that solid base he would deflect and nudge until he felt secure enough to throw pressure back on the bowler.

His eight test centuries put him up there with New Zealand's best, as does his average of 38.11.

It is tempting to call Watling a throwback, but it would be more accurate to call him unique or template-busting. He batted the majority of his career at No. 7, but he was no dasher. Quite the opposite. His strike of 43.4 was what you expect from a top-three player, not fifth-drop. Adam Gilchrist, the freakishly good Australian keeper-batter, went at a strike rate high of close to 84 at No. 7; Quinton de Kock 74 in the same position; McCullum 64.

New Zealand didn't need Watling to be a dasher. They had around him, at various times, Colin de Grandhomme, McCullum,

Southee, James Neesham. They needed a solid role player, not another compiler of dashing cameos.

Watling soaked up a lot of balls at No. 7. It was enervating for the opposition bowlers. Once you have a team five down you have visions of making quick inroads. Often the second ball is in your hands or not far off. Tailenders don't much like a brand-new cherry, but Watling loved it. He was the reliable wing man to the established top-order player and the safety blanket for the tail.

He will be most remembered for the two rearguards he formed with McCullum and Williamson respectively, both at the Basin Reserve and both record partnerships.

In 2014, coming to the crease on a pair and having scored just 1 and 11 in the first test, he joined skipper McCullum with the total on 94 for 5, with New Zealand still 151 runs from making India bat again and still a long, long way from forcing a draw and a series victory. The skipper would go on to score 302, but he would not have got that far if it hadn't been for Watling providing not just run support but spiritual support also.

Watling scored 124 in a marathon 367-ball, eight-and-a-half-hour marathon, but also played a vital role in pulling McCullum back from the brink when the skipper, not noted as a compiler of epics, started to look like he wanted to ad lib rather than play to the script. Both now reformed nicotine addicts, they were back-of-the-changing-shed smokers back then and Watling would use the cigarette as a carrot. 'Come on Baz,' he would say, 'just 20 minutes more and we can have a pole [smoke], a coffee and a chat.'

It might not have been the sort of motivational advice the surgeon-general would recommend — interestingly, McCullum and Watling were both consistently in the top three for fitness in the team, in part, Watling would later say, to compensate for his 'terrible habit' — but it worked.

The other intriguing point about Watling's 124 is that if you challenged anybody to recall a shot he played, they might not remember a single one except maybe the flick off his pads for four from the bowling of Zaheer Khan to raise three figures. He wouldn't mind that at all, but Watling's innings was a study in mixing long periods of dogged defence against very tight bowling, with the occasional sparkling boundary. It was also the longest innings played by a New Zealand wicketkeeper, which counted for absolutely nothing in Watling's eyes — though the eventual draw and series win did.

When asked about his knock at the time, he didn't talk about it at all.

'We just really wanted to win that series,' he said. 'The motivation to [do] that was obviously apparent, cause Baz was in a mood to bat long periods of time, and I was lucky enough to be at the other end for a good part of that. Had the best seat in the house, really.'

The 352-run partnership was a New Zealand sixth-wicket record, but it didn't last long.

Back at the Basin a year later, a Kumar Sangakkara double-century had earned Sri Lanka a 125-run first-innings lead. New Zealand was again staring down the barrel when Watling joined Williamson at the crease at 159 for 5 with a lot of time left in the game. It would be the last wicket Sri Lanka took. Williamson would notch his first test double-ton, while Watling would again be forwarded for nomination for best supporting actor, scoring what was then his test-highest 142 not out. The 365-run stand eclipsed the sixth-wicket record and earned a plaque at the Basin to sit alongside the one that had been laid just a few days earlier to commemorate the 352-run record.

Ask Watling what his favourite innings are and you get a sanguine response.

'I tend not to look too deeply into each innings because sometimes a 50 or 60 can be just as important to the team's needs, but they never get the same attention as a century. One of my favourite moments, though, was when Trent Boult got his first test 50 in Bangladesh, and I think we put on a record partnership for the 10th wicket.'

Typically, he distracts from his own performance, which was a brilliant 103, his century brought up with a slog-sweep for six and a more exuberant expression of joy from Watling than is customary.

On a flat wicket in Chattogram, New Zealand was in danger of wasting a Williamson century when they were 282 for 7 with neither Watling nor Doug Bracewell off the mark. Bracewell scored 29 and Sodhi just 1 before Watling and Boult (52 not out) started their rearguard. They didn't surpass Brian Hastings and Richard Collinge's 151-run New Zealand 10th-wicket partnership record, but the 127 was a record overseas, passing the 124 set by John Bracewell and Stephen Boock in Sydney in 1985.

There are two other Watling specials that cannot go unmentioned, both playing huge roles in New Zealand victories against England. The first came at Headingley in 2015 and followed a silly loss at Lord's from a seemingly impregnable position, despite Watling's double of 61 not out and 59. At Leeds, New Zealand and England couldn't be split after posting 350 runs each in the first innings. The test was finely poised when New Zealand found themselves 141 for 4 when Watling, playing as a specialist batter because of a back injury (that led to Luke Ronchi's debut), scored a glittering 120 at a very un-Watling-like strike rate of 74. New Zealand would end up winning convincingly on the final day thanks to the spin twins of Mark Craig (3 for 73) and, wait for it, Williamson, who took 3 for 15.

The second was his first double-ton and his eighth and final three-figure score in tests. It came in November 2019, during the first test to be played at Mount Maunganui. For Watling, it was one innings after an unbeaten 105 in a crucial win in Colombo — the win that after a rocky beginning kick-started New Zealand's World Test Championship campaign. At Bay Oval, Watling ground out 205, sharing big partnerships with Colin de Grandhomme (65) and Mitchell Santner (126) as New

Zealand compiled a match-winning 615 for 9.

Watling followed up with 55 in the second test at Seddon Park to cap a prolific spell, but the harsh truth is the remainder of his career was a struggle. He, like most of his teammates, endured a poor tour to Australia and his struggles contrasted with that of Blundell who, brought in as an opener for the Boxing Day and New Year's tests, scored a century at the MCG. A lean home series against India followed, then a hamstring niggle restricted him to just one test against the West Indies. He did pass 50 for the final time in a two-test series against Pakistan, but on the eve of the tour to England that preceded the WTC final, he announced he would be stepping away from the game.

Watling had started to doubt whether he had the energy levels to work himself out of his batting rut and, with wife Jess having just given birth to a second child, felt that more of the 'selflessness' tattooed on his arm was required at home than in the changing sheds.

'My wife Jess has been a constant source of stability and support, and I'm certainly looking forward to being able to spend more time with her and the kids,' Watling said in the press release announcing his impending retirement. 'I also owe a big thanks to my mum for steering me in the right direction early on and always being there for me.'

Watling didn't score a lot with the bat in that 75th and glorious final test, but there was one more chance to show what he was all about. On the sixth and final day of the Rose Bowl match, Watling broke his finger fielding a poor throw from Williamson in the 53rd over, with India six down. Watling soldiered on, screaming in pain as he collected one delivery. He continued, even taking a catch to dismiss Ravi Jadeja, before giving the gloves away to Blundell only when the end of the innings was in sight. The finger would later require surgery.

His retirement would have never been articulated like this because it would not have been fair on either, but Watling would have known that there was a guy who had been waiting in the wings who had more to give the cause than he could muster. One of the principal tenets of selflessness is knowing when it's the right time to step away, yet few manage it because it is human nature to think you have one last big campaign or performance in you.

Watling, like most things in his career, got it right, diverting his energies now to coaching which, he says, feels more like an addendum to his playing career than the start of another one. 'Towards the end of my playing career I really enjoyed the leadership aspect, so this feels like an extension of that,' he said.

Watling knows what good coaching can do to impressionable minds. He was just a schoolkid when his coach Kuggeleijn read his favourite poem to the team.

For it isn't your father, or mother, or wife
Who judgement upon you must pass
The feller whose verdict counts most in your life
Is the one staring back from the glass.

CHAPTER 13
KANE WILLIAMSON

Debut: 2010   Last match: 2023

BATTING	Matches	Runs	Ave	S/R	100s	50s	Catches
Test:	94	8124	54.89	51.46	28	33	76
ODI:	161	6554	47.83	80.97	13	42	64
T20I:	87	2464	33.29	123.01	-	14	41

BOWLING	Matches	Wickets	Ave	5w
Test:	88	30	40.23	-
ODI:	155	37	35.4	-
T20I:	77	6	27.33	-

Wins as captain: Tests 22 (win % 55), ODIs 44 (win % 51), T20Is 35 (win % 51)

Towards the end of the 2022–23 summer, a season that meteorologically speaking never really arrived for much of the country as it wallowed in the after-effects of extreme weather events including Cyclone Gabrielle, the general consensus was that Kane Williamson was struggling.

The concept of a 'struggle' is both open to interpretation and relative. Williamson was not far removed from a test tour to Pakistan where he had scored 200 not out, 36 and 41, but after three successive failures against England, two at his hometown Bay Oval and in the first innings at the Basin Reserve, questions were being asked as to whether the tennis elbow that had plagued him for years and the constant grind of being a three-format cricketer was starting to erode his baseline skills.

What happened over the next month was a timely reminder of the breadth of Williamson's talent and his capacity to fight.

At the Basin Reserve, England's brilliant but occasionally maverick captain Ben Stokes enforced the follow-on when the home side's first innings ended 226 runs shy of England's 435 for 9 declared. The follow-on is a rarity in modern cricket, but Stokes did so safe in the knowledge that New Zealand, in his words, had to 'play the perfect game' from there to escape defeat. He did so also in the knowledge that Williamson, New Zealand's batting talisman, had compiled scores of 6, 0 and 4 in the series and had looked particularly vulnerable to James Anderson's outswing, nicking limply behind in the first innings.

This time, bolstered by a 149-run first-wicket partnership between Devon Conway and Tom Latham, Williamson sought redress. For the next 447 minutes and 282 balls Williamson played an innings that was marked not by his usual clipped finesse but by heart and character. When he was unluckily dismissed, strangled down leg side by a nondescript ball from the part-time medium pace of Harry Brook, he had 132, New Zealand had 455 and from there they would set themselves up for a remarkable one-run victory, becoming just the fourth team in test history to turn a follow-on into victory.

If his 26th test century was one for the ages, his 27th, just a fortnight later, might have been even better.

Chasing 285 to beat Sri Lanka, rain on the final day saw it turn into a limited-overs affair. When play finally started for one extended 53-over session, New Zealand needed 257 more runs off 53 overs with Williamson 7 not out after scratching and clawing his way through to stumps the previous day (in the first innings, against a sneakily excellent Sri Lankan pace attack, he'd posted 1, his fourth single-figure score in his past five innings).

With three balls in the day to go, he'd added 110 to his overnight score. Some of the class of previous campaigns had returned, but this was a dig high on grit as well. He was on strike while Neil Wagner — nursing a bulging disc in his back and a torn hamstring — paced edgily at the other. New Zealand needed five runs to win; Sri Lanka needed two wickets. Given how bleakly the day had started with torrential rain causing surface flooding throughout the Canterbury region, it was remarkable that all four results remained possible as the shadows lengthened across the park. To prevent boundaries and make running twos very difficult, Sri Lanka captain Dimuth Karunaratne had every fielder bar the wicketkeeper patrolling the Hagley Oval ropes.

Asitha Fernando, who had bowled superbly, went for the wide yorker but missed his length slightly. With that wide line, however, he knew he was protected by the two men patrolling the long, square boundary on the off side. Williamson had another idea. He essayed a hybrid cut-cum-drive and, like the sound of a starter's pistol, the ball cracked from the middle of his blade, splitting the boundary riders with a precision that was surgical.

'We saw his class,' captain Tim Southee, a man who has inherited an economy of emotion from his predecessor in the role, gushed. 'That last boundary was just an unbelievable shot. To beat two good fielders on the boundary to the big side [of the ground]. Just the calmness in which he did it is good for the group.'

Although the winning run from the final ball would come via a bye, it wasn't without skill either. Williamson swished and missed at a bouncer that was very high then turned and sprinted. Wagner reached the striker's end when keeper Niroshan Dickwella missed his shy at the stumps, but as Fernando gathered in his follow-through and turned to throw at the bowler's stumps, Williamson, who had started his sprint deep in his crease and on the back foot, was floundering a long way from safety. Fernando's throw broke the stumps and while Williamson will never be accused of wearing his heart on his sleeve, he looked anything but convinced he had made his ground. His pained expression as he asked the umpire why it wasn't called wide — he could be seen mouthing, 'Mate, it was so high' — is about as close as you will see Williamson get to dissent. Never before had the final scheduled ball of a test gone to the third umpire to determine whether it would be a win or a draw. In frame by agonising frame we saw Williamson sprint, lunge and . . . beat the throw by centimetres.

A split-second slower or a fraction later in the dive and we would have witnessed an epic draw, rather than a second consecutive thrilling win.

In a match report on ESPNcricinfo, Alagappan Muthu wrote: 'If ever there was a time to get carried away, it was this. And yet all he did was bow his head in sweet relief. Honestly, people open their mail with more excitement than Williamson winning a five-day match off its final ball.'

Williamson's poker-face demeanour shouldn't be mistaken for a lack of passion, however.

'He just loves it,' said his captain Tim Southee in the aftermath of the drama. 'He's a world-class player and world-class players are able to perform in different conditions and different situations and he's done that his whole career. Even when he was young, he was the guy we leaned on.'

A week later New Zealand travelled back to the Basin and Williamson took his form with him.

His 28th test century, which came in a crushing innings victory, was a delight. It was different from the previous two: silkier, a return, perhaps, to more carefree days. Commentator Mark Richardson, a famously stubborn opening batter who came awfully close to a chapter in this book himself, said something upon Williamson reaching three figures that was revealing.

'When [Williamson's] in touch and scoring runs, he's as close to batting perfection, I think, as you get — technically, tactically and mentally.'

The 215 runs that he would eventually score — his sixth test double century, putting him in rarefied air where only Sir Donald Bradman (12), Kumar Sangakkara (11), Brian Lara (9), Wally Hammond, Virat Kohli and Mahela Jayawardene (all 7) have taken breath before — did feel close to perfect, particularly the coaching-manual cover drives.

While the strokeplay during the Basin ton might have represented something of a turning back of the clock, this wasn't the Williamson of the mid- to late 2010s. It was something different. At 32, maybe there wasn't quite the sparkle of his pomp, but there was something else — something less spectacular but possibly even more admirable.

Williamson would never have articulated it in this way, he probably wouldn't even know how, but he had developed the ability to bend a game to his considerable will.

* * * * * * *

The Williamson success story is, in effect, an origin story.

If you were looking to artificially create the type of hothouse environment where genius flourishes, you could do worse than replicate Williamson's childhood.

The first truly remarkable event in Williamson's life occurred at birth when his parents, Brett and Sandra, discovered that when Kane emerged on 8 August 1990, he was just part one of a two-part package.

'There were complications with the pregnancy, and no one could work out why,' Brett outlined in an article in *Cricket Monthly*. 'Sandra spent three nights in hospital and the doctors still couldn't work out what was wrong. Kane popped out first, a few minutes later Logan's head appeared. There was pandemonium in the ward.'

The twin thing guaranteed Kane and Logan would each have a permanent childhood playmate, but they were just joining a crew — they have three older sisters, Anna, Sophie and Kylie — that placed a high importance on sport and being active.

Sandra was a basketball rep and Brett was well known on the club cricket circuit. The kids took their sporting passions, modified them to their own needs, and ran with them all over the playgrounds of Pillans Point primary and wherever else they had room for games.

From a very early age, Williamson's eye–hand coordination was raising eyebrows. Brett once recalled seeing Kane the toddler shooting a small ball into one of those mini basketball hoops you stick to the door of your bedroom — nothing remarkable in that, except he appeared to be shooting with proper basketball form.

While Williamson played everything he could when younger and was a fine rugby player and basketballer — another tick for the column of those who rail against early 'specialisation' — his overriding passion mirrored that of his father, cricket.

When you ask Williamson about his earliest memories of cricket it is of him commandeering Brett as soon as he got home from work, walking through a gate in the back fence — their Tauranga property backed onto the Pillans Point School fields — and having throwdown after throwdown. Without explicitly doing so, father was inculcating son with the traits that would become the hallmark of his batting from fields as modest as the Tauranga Domain to hifalutin Lord's: high elbow, play straight early, bat for a long time. Brett would encourage Kane to use his feet, to chip the ball back over his head; and when Dad read an article about the poor standard of pitches in New Zealand providing a roadblock to good back-foot play, he paid special attention to that part of practice. It is perhaps not surprising, then, that Williamson is the best back-foot puncher of the ball through the off side New Zealand has ever produced.

This culture of play as practice, or practice as play, that was instilled in Williamson from such a young age is why he chafes at descriptions like natural talent.

'It's hard to know what natural is,' he told *Cricket Monthly* in 2015. 'Talent or 10,000 hours [of practice], which one is it? Everyone is gifted, I guess, but you get some that seem exceptionally so. I'm not one of them. You get others that spend a bit more time practising; I was constantly playing and practising from a really young age. I didn't necessarily look at it as practice, I was just having fun.

'The ball in the sock, Dad giving throwdowns, anything I was doing then I was putting a lot of time into it — basketball, rugby, volleyball, soccer. It wasn't just cricket. I'd tried doing everything for as long as I could, but cricket started to take over.'

When it took over, it did so spectacularly.

Word started emerging early of a teenager in the Bay of Plenty who was starting to turn heads with his prodigious run-scoring.

Doug Bracewell, a Tauranga-raised contemporary of Williamson, remembered bowling to him in an inter-school game and thinking, 'Geez, how good is this kid?' He soon got to watch him first-hand as part of Bay of Plenty and Northern Districts age-group rep teams. 'We had an annual tournament that we went to every year. I reckon he went two or three years without being dismissed,' Bracewell recalled. 'The only time he wasn't batting was when they retired him.'

Often the bloke retiring him was his dad, who was also not averse to reversing the batting order if his son was dominating. Brett was more interested in making sure everybody had the opportunity to enjoy their cricket in the way his son was.

Even at such a nascent stage of his cricket journey, there was a serenity to Williamson that made him stand out. Even at the age when hormones started to race through a boy's body and emotional regulation and sound decision-making became more of a challenge, Williamson rarely beat himself up if he failed. To him it was an integral part of the process. He could never understand how anybody could have so much arrogance as to think that a bowler is not good enough to get them out. When this type of rationale is baked into your DNA, it enables you to remain even-keeled in times of success and also when the runs are not coming.

The choice of the term 'even-keeled' is deliberate, too. One of the most successful pieces of sporting merchandise in New Zealand history has been the sailor's hat, created by the Alternative Commentary Collective to be emblematic of Williamson's sea-captain status — 'the steadier of the HMS *Black Caps* ship'.

'There has been success and failure and there'll be plenty more of both,' he said in 2015. 'You can't hold on to success for too long or hold on to failure. You've got to let both go. It's easy to fall into the trap of getting a hundred and it feels good so you want and expect more, or you fail and you don't know why. You want success too badly. Sometimes you have to accept you're going to have both and neither will last forever. Let them come and go.

'That's the challenge. It's not something that is done easily by any means. It's a challenge for everyone. It's very easy to be found wanting and sometimes the wanting is the struggle. You try to stay calm and relaxed, but like I say, I can talk about it, but the challenge is to live it.'

Williamson's mastery at the crease, particularly in the longest format, has seen him mentioned as part of cricket's mythical batting Big Four alongside England maestro Joe Root, India's talisman Virat Kohli and Australia's idiosyncratic genius Steve Smith. All share a hunger for runs, but perhaps none see the runs as a by-product quite the way Williamson does. It's almost wrong to say Williamson has a hunger for runs, because his needs are more basic than that: he has a hunger for batting.

* * * * * * *

Trying to pick Williamson's career highlights is like trying to pick a few good paintings from the Uffizi or a couple of decent tunes from The Beatles' discography.

He scored a century on debut in India in 2010, a sign that he was a special talent, but it's almost jarring when you think back on the 194-run fifth-wicket partnership with the fabulously talented but wayward Jesse Ryder, the memory of him getting an awkward hug from Daniel Vettori and the likes of Andy McKay and Tim McIntosh clapping him from the players' area.

It was a New Zealand squad alright, but an easily forgotten one, and it was jarring for Williamson in another respect: that Indian team contained players like Sachin Tendulkar, Rahul Dravid, Virender Sehwag and VVS Laxman, players who had made up the bulk of Williamson's make-believe backyard cricket teams in battles with his brother and friends.

His immediate success was not altogether surprising given the hype — none of it generated by himself it must be noted — that surrounded his schoolboy run-scoring feats which had seen him score an estimated 40 centuries by the time he had left school, to his ascension to the Bay of Plenty senior reps by the age of 14, scoring 60 on debut against a Counties team that featured Daryl Tuffey, and first-class cricket for Northern Districts at 17.

Early in the 2011–12 season he scored 284 not out for his Northern Districts first-class side and showed his contempt for personal milestones when he happily obliged and backed captain Brad Wilson's declaration with a triple century fast approaching, even though ND would end up winning by an innings with more than a day to spare.

The runs weren't flowing quite as freely for New Zealand, however, and when he was dismissed for a duck in the first innings against South Africa at Seddon Park his test average sat in the mid-20s with the debut century still his only three-figure score. Although there were some doubts as to whether his skills would transfer easily to the white-ball game, at this point, March 2012, his record was significantly better in ODIs, with two centuries and an average in the mid-30s.

There was no question that his place in the side was secure, but there were the first whispers that perhaps his talent had been oversold to the public. His first century at home, against a wickedly strong South African pace attack that included the metronomically accurate Vernon Philander and the lightning-quick trio of Dale Steyn, Morné Morkel and Marchant de Lange, hushed the doubters.

Chasing a nominal target of 389, Williamson, promoted from No. 5 to 4 for the injured Ross Taylor, strode to the crease with the score 1 for 2 and played an innings of genuine character, defying everything South Africa threw at him on the final day. That included a bunch of strong words as Williamson on 7 correctly stood his ground as Alviro Petersen claimed a catch at backward point that replays suggested had brushed the turf. Two runs and plenty of balls later, there was a break in play as Williamson took time to catch his breath, having had his box split in two by a Steyn nip-backer. 'I'm not going to apologise,' Steyn muttered in the direction of the prone batter. Teammates who were coming and going speak in awe of that day, about how quickly and aggressively the South Africans were bowling and how much fun — yes, fun — Williamson was having.

When stumps were drawn, Williamson, in tandem with his age-group mate Bracewell, had earned his side an improbable draw and himself a second test century. Oh, and the cracked box was kept for a long time on the mantelpiece as a wince-inducing heirloom.

New Zealanders discovered they had a talented young player in their midst; they also had an extremely tough one — one who would never again have to wait 19 test innings for another century.

What many people didn't realise, however, was that Williamson was in the midst of an internal struggle, one that crystallised on the tour to Sri Lanka in late 2012 (a tour that would later become infamous for it being the end of Ross Taylor's captaincy reign).

Speaking at the Oxford Union, one of the world's most prestigious private students' societies, Williamson recalled that tour marking a significant point in his journey of self-discovery.

'I had gone through the grades and had some success. All of a sudden I'm in the professional game and my talent is not enough. Everyone was talented and the challenge was so much more about the confidence you had in your own game and trying to execute your own plans, rather than being at school and just turning up and expecting to do well against a team that was less talented,' he told the gathered audience. 'I was sitting in my room in Sri Lanka and everything in my mind, my idea of success, was that I had to score a hundred . . . that was what was drilled into you. I remember sitting there and [realising] that I was judging myself purely on these outcomes and these lofty goals. [If I continued like that] I knew I was going to be constantly suffering and probably not enjoying my experiences as much as I should be.'

In many ways, Williamson said, it was a 'sad' revelation — the idea he wasn't enjoying the thing that had not long ago brought him massive joy.

'From that point there was a conscious decision around trying to treat the game in a way that was true to me. In cricket, and everything really, there is so much failure and so many things we can't control. Learning to accept this and take it in your stride [is so important]. Treat everything as a learning experience rather than trying to ride the highs and avoid the lows.'

It is a credo that Williamson has lived by and, well, the results have been pretty good.

The highlights started to come thick and fast. There was a scintillating 145 not out in an ODI against South Africa at Kimberley, and another against Pakistan in Abu Dhabi that helped

New Zealand to a 3–2 ODI series victory, which was especially gratifying for Williamson as he led the side in Brendon McCullum's absence. That followed 192 in the test series, batting in partnership with double centurion McCullum on the day after they had learned young Australian opener Phillip Hughes had died. In a five-match ODI series against India in 2014 he rattled off scores of 71, 77, 65, 60 and 88.

In 2015, in his last test innings before the World Cup, he scored an unbeaten 242, his first double, in a record unbeaten 365-run sixth-wicket partnership with BJ Watling, turning a huge deficit into a match-winning position. While his World Cup could only be described as solid, he did add spectacular to the mix when he hit Pat Cummins for a straight six at Eden Park to guide New Zealand to a thrilling one-wicket win in pool play.

In his first test innings after the World Cup, he scored a fluent 132 to etch his name into permanence at Lord's.

At the start of the 2015–16 summer, New Zealand toured Australia, the graveyard of visiting batters, but Williamson made it a personal triumph. At the Gabba, not-so-fondly known as the 'Gabbatoir' as it puts those of feeble mind or technique through the grinder, Williamson was on 30 when James Neesham was dismissed to leave New Zealand a deathly 118 for 5, chasing Australia's massive first innings of 556 for 4 declared.

'What follows is the best century I've seen from a New Zealand batsman,' wrote his captain McCullum in *Declared*. 'Kane is magnificent in the face of the pace and hostility of the two Mitchells, Starc and Johnson.'

He was dismissed for 140 and followed that in Perth with 166, playing second fiddle to Taylor, who returned to form emphatically with 290, a record score for a visiting batter.

A month later he made light work of a Seddon Park wicket that was giving everyone else kittens, scoring an unbeaten 108 to guide

New Zealand to a five-wicket win in a tricky fourth-innings chase of 189 against Sri Lanka.

Six months later, Williamson was skipper, with McCullum having bowed out after a home series loss to Australia. Any fears that the burden of captaincy might have a negative effect on his batting were soon allayed. In one of the busiest periods of test cricket in New Zealand history, Williamson scored a century in Zimbabwe, then scored consistently without cracking three figures away to South Africa and India, and home to Pakistan. He scored a match-winning unbeaten century at the Basin Reserve against Bangladesh, then added two more tons in a three-match home series New Zealand were desperately unlucky to lose to South Africa 0–1, with two tests badly affected by weather with the hosts in strong positions. (New Zealand lost the only test of the three that Williamson failed with the bat, which was indicative of the pressure now upon his shoulders.)

He capped a monumental summer by becoming the first player to score a day–night test century in New Zealand. His 102 helped to set up a victory after England had been bowled out for 58 on the first afternoon, with Williamson's diving left-handed catch in the gully to dismiss a slack-jawed Stuart Broad the pick of the dismissals.

A double of 89 and 139 set up a test series win against Pakistan in Abu Dhabi, and an unbeaten double century against Bangladesh in Hamilton highlighted the home summer before the team started preparing for the World Cup in England.

* * * * * * *

Phrases like 'moral victory' and 'honour in defeat' get bandied around all the time in the coverage of sport. Often it is nothing more than a glib acknowledgement of bad luck and circumstance.

The way New Zealand, and in particular Kane Williamson, dealt with the pain of that extraordinary World Cup final, where England were awarded the trophy on a boundary countback rule after the scores were tied at the end of the normal 50 overs and the Super Over, was so profoundly decent that it was being cited as a demonstration in the art of leadership.

An invitation to speak at the Oxford Union — where former prime minister David Lange once famously quipped that he 'could smell the uranium' on a debater's breath — followed and Williamson quickly had the assembled in the palm of his hand when he joked that he would skip over his cricket journey quickly because 'people just want to hear about the World Cup'.

'We walked away from that final, despite so many things that were out of our control deciding that match, and I thought, "What gives me the right to neglect the things that we deem important to us?"'

'We're proud of the way we went about our business that day and proud of that performance.'

Williamson said the mechanism of how the game was decided — if it was still tied after the Super Over the team who had hit the most boundaries in the 50-over game wins — had never entered calculations before the game. In some ways that made the situation easier to deal with because it's not something they would have ever planned for, so there was no failure of execution or oversight. As he said, there will never be another game of cricket decided this way.

'That was kind of the space we were in, so when it happened we had two choices: laugh or cry. I'm glad I didn't choose to cry. It was a pretty crazy experience. The thing we could control was how we wanted to behave, how we wanted to play our cricket and the performance we wanted to put on the board and we felt we ticked those boxes.'

What Williamson has never lingered on is the sense of injustice many New Zealanders felt as they were not just the victim of an arcane ruling, but also on the end of both outrageously bad luck and poor umpiring. Taylor fell victim to a poor leg-before decision, amplified when England opener Jason Roy was given not out despite looking very plumb to the first ball he faced — the DRS view confirming it was crashing into the top of the stump but not by enough to overturn Marais Erasmus's decision. Ben Stokes, whose brilliance ended up being the difference, benefited from Trent Boult standing on the rope after catching him cleanly in the outfield and, more gallingly, was credited with six runs when he inadvertently deflected a Martin Guptill throw to the boundary when coming back for a tightly run two in the game's final over in regulation. It was later revealed that under the laws, he should only have been awarded a five. Anything that could have gone against New Zealand did, and yet they still somehow tied the match.

'It was an amazing game to be part of, [although] that was a hard thing to appreciate at the time,' Williamson told the Oxford Union.

What is also hard to appreciate is just how brilliantly Williamson performed at the World Cup. It has become lost in the praise for his leadership in the most trying of circumstances, but Williamson's batting across the tournament in what were generally difficult conditions was first-rate.

He did not bat at Cardiff as New Zealand steamrolled their way to a 10-wicket victory in their opening match against Sri Lanka, then scored 40 as they continued their winning form against Bangladesh at The Oval. At Taunton he scored an unbeaten 79 as they continued their winning start and that was followed by his *pièce de rèsistance*, 106 not out against South Africa at Edgbaston, when he engineered an unlikely last-over victory which included a six to bring the scores level. 'There cannot be a batsman in the world less liable to panic than Kane Williamson,' wrote former England seam bowler Mike Selvey.

The next game he added 148 as the Black Caps survived a Carlos Brathwaite assault to beat the West Indies by five runs.

New Zealand's form dipped as they lost successive games to

Pakistan, Australia and England, although Williamson remained consistent with 41, 40 and 27, before he showed his acute match awareness with 67 against India in tricky conditions in their Old Trafford semi-final. In the final, he scored a middling 30, but leadership comes in many forms, and his marshalling of his resources that day was first-class, as was his ability to keep his equilibrium.

Across the World Cup, despite playing several matches in tricky batting conditions, Williamson scored 578 runs at an average of 82.6. That, combined with his leadership, saw him awarded player of the tournament.

The day did leave scars. New Zealand toured Australia to start the 2019–20 summer, for the first time since 1987 being 'awarded' a Boxing Day test at the Melbourne Cricket Ground. It was a highly anticipated match-up, but the tour could not have gone any worse for New Zealand. They inexplicably agreed to an itinerary that had them start, without any preparation, with a day–night test in Perth, where they were dutifully thumped after twice being asked to start their innings under lights — one of modern cricket's more perilous assignments. In front of a large crowd of Kiwi tourists and expats, they offered scant resistance at the G, falling to a 247-run defeat. Williamson in particular looked out of sorts, scoring 9 and 0, and it was almost a relief when he missed the final test through illness.

That 0–3 series reverse was an inauspicious start to New Zealand's bid for the World Test Championship, an ICC initiative designed to give context to the bilateral and often lopsided world of test cricket.

(To give an idea of how lopsided, Williamson debuted a full two years before England's star player Joe Root, and by March 2023, Root had played 129 tests to Williamson's 94.)

It was the last real misstep made by New Zealand as they swept India, the West Indies and Pakistan at home. Williamson notched his highest test score of 251 in his only bat against the Windies, missing the second test for the birth of his first child, before reeling off 129, 21 and 238 against Pakistan.

The final, against India at the neutral venue of Southampton's Rose Bowl, was a weather-affected, low-scoring grind through six days. It was a match for bowlers, with India's first-innings 217 met by New Zealand's 249, including a painstaking 177-ball knock from the skipper that ended a run short of a half-century. India tumbled on the final day for 170, leaving Williamson's team an eminently gettable but bum-squeaking 139 to win.

When Williamson was given out leg before to Ravichandran Ashwin for 1 to make New Zealand 39 for 2, all the familiar anxieties bubbled to the surface. The skipper threw his head back in disappointment, but made the right call to review, as ball-tracking showed the ball would have passed harmlessly by leg stump. It was the last time India had a sniff as Williamson got his nose over the ball.

The double of 49 and 52 not out wasn't Williamson's finest moment at the crease, but it was one of his most important in terms of the heavy lifting it did. Gone, finally, was the baggage of the MCG 2015 and Lord's 2019.

The image of him leaving The Rose Bowl arm in arm with Taylor, his partner in so many partnerships throughout the years, cemented his place in New Zealand sporting folklore.

* * * * * * * *

Even in Twenty20 cricket, a game not tailormade for his repertoire of flicks and check drives, Williamson has carved out an impressive and ultimately lucrative record. In the World T20 in 2021, held over due to Covid, he led New Zealand to the final where he scored a stunning 85, but New Zealand struggled, bowling second in the dewy conditions, and lost to Australia.

A year later he was his country's most consistent batter, but they dipped out in the semi-finals to Pakistan, and Williamson was criticised for not being able to accelerate quickly. By that stage he was coming under pressure at his long-time Sunrisers Hyderabad franchise for the same reasons. Once a million-dollar-per-year IPL player for the Sunrisers, two below-par campaigns in 2021 and 2022 saw him let go by the franchise, though he was picked up immediately by Gujarat Titans for the not-insignificant sum of 2 crore, or slightly more than $384,000.

In the first game for his new franchise, he tore ligaments in his knee while fielding, invaliding him out of the game for an extended period and putting his involvement in the 2023 World Cup in peril.

* * * * * * *.

Martin Crowe's large frame, his commanding presence at the crease and his ultra-classical strokeplay mean he will always retain a special place in the hearts of many cricket fans, but there can be no doubt that Williamson has surpassed him and then some as the country's greatest batter. It was something Crowe himself acknowledged in his final years. In 2015, long before Williamson had 'peaked', Crowe wrote a beautiful column getting to the heart and soul of Williamson's brilliance; brilliance that can seem, at times, a little bloodless but is anything but.

'Batting suited him from the minute he picked up his first bat; he had the perfect height, balance, fast-twitch muscles, electric feet, an inquisitive mind. Then he began to grow. Around him was an environment of support and knowledge. He appreciated both and never forgot his origins and roots.

'They were humble and wise people who saw in Williamson an opportunity to light the flame, to fulfil precious potential, and to help a kid embark on a dream. In this space, Williamson's imagination took off. He didn't just score runs, he created masterpieces. Huge centuries, on a regular basis, came from a young mind that could see what no other around him could see. He was very normal, yet in his mental playground he saw way beyond the pale . . .

'A few years back, I met him on a couple of occasions, and offered some insights. He had just started to play first-class cricket when we had a one-on-one net session indoors in Hamilton. I left our session marvelling at what I had learned. He was a sponge, and he was also a giver. He kept the conversation alive, and you felt you could talk and share for yonks, that it needn't end. He sought a new way, a different option, another route to scoring big. Since then, he has climbed into the list of top 10 batsmen in the world. Since then he has smashed down every milestone as he gets better and better, becoming more assured in his method against the very best bowlers.'

There is a strong argument to be made that he has surpassed Sir Richard Hadlee as the finest cricketer this country has produced.

While that's a bar-leaner debate that cannot provide a definitive winner, one person that wouldn't consider entertaining the argument is Williamson himself. Modest to the point of parody, Williamson has won plaudits from journalists around the globe for his class, calmness and humility, but few for his ability to provide 'good copy'.

Williamson has totted up some astonishing numbers but he rarely, if ever, keeps track of them. If he has said it once he has said it 1000 times: he doesn't play cricket for the individual accolades but with the explicit aim of helping his team win games.

During the 2023 home series against England, he passed Taylor to become New Zealand's highest test run-scorer, having long ago set the record for the most test centuries. He has been prolific in the short formats, though his unselfish approach at the crease has seen him score fewer ODI centuries (13 at the time of writing) than you might expect for a player of his undoubted class. To emphasise that point, Williamson has eight scores between 90 and 97, explaining his approach in his coaching book, *Kane Williamson on Cricket*:

'Landmark batting scores like 50s and 100s might seem really important, and they have become statistical benchmarks down through the ages, but don't get consumed by them.

'I've been out a few times when my score has been in the 90s in one-day cricket, playing big shots, and my reasoning is simple. When we're into the back of the innings and I've got guys like Corey Anderson and Luke Ronchi waiting to bat, if I'm not scoring at the same rate they would be, then I'm actually hurting the team.

'If I knuckled down in those situations and made sure I got my three figures, I'd be doing my teammates a disservice. You're there to contribute to the team. You do see it a lot — guys ticking off the runs until they can raise their bat — and that's fine, but it's not why I enjoy the game. It's nice to enjoy other people's successes as well and to play for a common cause, which is to win. If you've got someone that is putting personal achievements ahead of that goal, the environment isn't as healthy as it should be.'

The only holes you could find in his game are an orthodox off-spin action that had enough of a kink in it for him to be banned from the bowling crease, fairly unsympathetic treatment of spinners under his captaincy in test cricket and, as he's got older, difficulty moving through the gears in T20.

You have to dig fairly deep to find a shred of off-field criticism. Having rarely played with the threat of being dropped, perhaps Williamson found it difficult to understand those who played on a knife-edge and thus didn't find it as easy to regulate their emotions following a failure as he did. However, if being slightly oblivious to the inherent weaknesses of the human condition, weaknesses he doesn't possess himself, is the only glove you can lay on him, he's not doing too badly.

Williamson remains on track to one day pass Martin Guptill as the leading scorer in T20Is for New Zealand, and at the time of writing he was only 1000 runs and loose change away from overhauling Ross Taylor's 18,199 runs in all formats, but there is no question that it is test cricket for which he will be most remembered.

If that wasn't already written in the stars, the first months of 2023 ensured it.

Williamson is not only in the very top tier of cricketers ever produced, he has also joined the select club of being one of those athletes New Zealanders like to best think represents our male ideal: strong, humble and quietly brilliant.

Whether he likes it or not, Williamson will be remembered alongside the likes of Richie McCaw and Sir Edmund Hillary as one of the greatest, most humble men's sporting figures New Zealand has produced.

CHAPTER 14
TRENT BOULT

Debut: 2011   Last match: 2022

	Matches	Wickets	Ave	5w (10w)	Economy	S/R
Test:	78	317	27.49	10 (1)	3.00	54.9
ODI:	99	187	23.97	5	4.93	29.1
T20I:	55	74	22.25	-	7.86	16.9

Also: 759 test runs with one 50 and 43 catches

Trent Boult, the baby-faced, fast-bowling assassin, caused something of a stir in 2022 when he announced he was handing back his New Zealand Cricket central contract in order to pursue opportunities in global franchise T20 tournaments.

Coinciding as it did with the Black Caps' wobbling form in test cricket, it was seen not only as a sign that the Establishment could not keep pace with cricket's nouveau riche, but that the good times were over for this iteration of the Black Caps, such has been the importance of the left-arm paceman to the country's fortunes.

'This has been a really tough decision for me, and I'd like to thank NZC for their support in getting to this point,' Boult said in the press release that accompanied his announcement. 'Playing cricket for my country was a childhood dream and I'm so proud of everything I've been able to achieve with the Black Caps over the past 12 years. Ultimately this decision is about my wife Gert and our three young boys. Family has always been the biggest motivator for me, and I feel comfortable with putting it first and preparing ourselves for life after cricket.'

There was a sense of finality to the words, although Boult's playing future with the national side was still opaque at the time of writing. However, New Zealand played the 2022–23 test season without him, and it took some getting used to. For years, one of the sights of the summer was watching Boult's sublimely natural approach to the wicket, his apparently effortless delivery stride and smooth action, and the accompanying grin on his face when he took a wicket or, when his mood was especially light, beat the bat.

It might have run counter to the fast-bowlers' club, but anger never suited Boult. He bowled at his best when he had a smile on his dial, which, thankfully, was often. With the sun shining, a bit of green in the wicket, a new Kookaburra four-piece in his hands and 10 mates waiting for a catch, Boult usually had a look on his face that let you know that life was good.

If he were never to play another test match, he would go down as one of the all-time greats. Couple that with his work in the white-ball arena — work that has seen him become one of the most sought-after T20 bowlers in the world — and his place in the pantheon is secure.

With 317 wickets he occupies a scalene corner of the triangle of New Zealand's most prolific test-bowling pace trio along with Tim Southee (370) and Neil Wagner (258). In particular, the new-ball partnership with Southee will ensure that one name is never far from the other when mentioning the feats of this team.

The left-arm, right-arm, out-swing, in-swing combination was tremendously effective, with New Zealand's greatest bowler, Sir Richard Hadlee, as long ago as 2015 describing them as the 'best ever new-ball combination in our history'.

They have done a bit since then.

* * * * * * *

Of Māori descent, Boult, who has connections to Ngāi Tahu, Ngāti Porou and Ngāi Te Rangi iwi, was never earmarked for stardom as a kid coming through the grades — certainly not to the same extent as two near contemporaries of his, Kane Williamson and Doug Bracewell. There's a brilliant photo of a Tauranga team at one of the famous Riverbend cricket camps, with a snow-haired Williamson and Bracewell in the back row, with Boult in the front holding the bat. Williamson's dad, Brett, is the coach.

A hard-hitting all-rounder in his primary school days, Boult was neither sound enough as a batter nor startling enough as a bowler to raise the eyebrows of youth selectors and at one point missed selection for the Bay of Plenty under-17s.

According to Llorne Howell, who played 12 ODIs for New Zealand, it was his dad John, a former first-class cricketer and long-time administrator who ran an academy at Te Puna, who talked Boult out of quitting the game.

'When Trent was about 16 or 17, he couldn't make the Bay of Plenty under-17 side so he came out to the academy to see my father,' Llorne Howell told *Hawke's Bay Today*. 'Trent said, "Should I give up cricket because I'm not very good?" John said, "No, you're going to be very good so just keep going, mate."'

John Howell might have seen the mechanics of a future great, but others missed it. There was never any sense among teammates and teenage opposition alike that the greatest left-arm seamer in New Zealand cricket history was in their midst, although they might have had an inkling they had the best left-arm seam-bowling guitarist among them as Boult was rarely far from an 'axe', working on riffs and songs.

Guitar would remain a hobby, but everything in his cricket career went into warp speed after he won a national speed-gun competition as a sixth-former at Ōtūmoetai College.

Before then he was a decent cricketer but was more or less the guy who bowled to his brother, Jonathan or Jono as he has always been known, in the backyard of their home or at the nets. Although he made his way into the first-class game as an off-spinner who could bat a bit, Jono was a top-order batter in his youth, and it was during a net session to help him prepare for a tournament that Trent was spotted by an impressed and enthusiastic Dayle Hadlee who was in the midst of a long stint as director of NZC's National Academy. Suddenly the kid who couldn't get a game for Bay of Plenty, who was talked down from quitting, was on the radar of the most important developer of talent in the country.

There were not many teams he missed out on from that point on, including a spot in the New Zealand Under-19 team that went to the World Cup in Malaysia, captained by Williamson and including player of the tournament Tim Southee.

Boult hadn't played a game for Northern Districts when he made the New Zealand A team to tour India. Even more stunning was his selection for the New Zealand squad to tour Australia for the one-day Chappell–Hadlee series. It was a cliffhanger 2–2 series with a washout in the decider and contains a couple of interesting side notes in New Zealand's cricket history — Brendon Diamanti, anybody? — but Boult didn't play, used wisely instead as a net bowler.

He would make his international debut in Australia, but it was not until more than two years later. In between he had broken the L3 vertebra in his back and remodelled his action under the tutelage of Damien Wright, a coach that he didn't immediately hit it off with.

There was a telling passage in a profile on Boult from *The Cricket Monthly*, which detailed his sensitivity to criticism. It concerned the first session he attended with newly appointed Black Caps bowling coach Wright, in which the Australian pointed out that there were eight specific shortcomings in Boult's action and the bowler replied with an 'eff you' and exited stage left.

According to the article, he rang Jono and told him that the new coach was a 'muppet' and he wouldn't be able to work with him. In one of the better older-brother interventions in New Zealand cricket history, right up there with Jeff Crowe convincing Martin not to quit on the eve of the 1992 World Cup, Jono made Trent go back to Wright and ask for the specific faults. An embarrassed Boult collected the information, which included arm positioning and length of delivery stride, and rang back his brother, still seething and believing Wright to be the devil in disguise.

'He is right,' Boult the elder said, at once popping Trent's rage-filled balloon and bringing him back to earth.

He might not necessarily look like a fast bowler, but he has plenty of the bowler's attitude, which could occasionally be trying for coaches and captains alike.

Brendon McCullum once told this author about cricketers having two kinds of confidence: there were those who had quiet, deep-seated confidence in their methodology and needed little outside affirmation, and those who had a more outward confidence and who liked to be told they were doing the right things and on the right path. The latter type was often not a show of confidence at all, but a blanket to hide insecurities. He recognised it because that was who he was until he stopped worrying about what others thought of him, and he recognised it, too, in the early iterations of Boult.

So at 22 but still looking 16, Boult made his test debut in Hobart in 2011, playing his part in one of the stranger test matches between the two sides. New Zealand batted first and as Boult took guard for the first time at a parlous 146 for 8, Brad Haddin, a wicketkeeper who has never bought into the idea that silence is golden, enquired dismissively: 'Mate, does your mother know you are here?' Right at the moment Boult was thankful for the decision to have his braces removed before the tour and while he remained undefeated as first Dean Brownlie (56) and Chris Martin (first-ball duck) were dismissed, he didn't get off the mark as New Zealand crashed to 150 all out.

Boult took three wickets in Australia's first innings of 136, the first, Mr Cricket Mike Hussey himself, who didn't quite withdraw his bat in time while attempting to leave the ball.

New Zealand fared slightly better in the second innings, Boult's tail-end 21 assisting them through to 226. At 122 for 1 chasing 241, Australia had another trans-Tasman test in the bag until Boult lured Usman Khawaja (23) into flashing at a wide ball and from then took on a watching brief as Bracewell (6 for 40) ran through the order to complete an inexplicable seven-run win — the eighth and last time New Zealand have beaten their neighbours in a test.

If Boult thought test cricket was easy, he was soon to be disabused of the notion.

In just his third test, at Dunedin's University Oval, he ran into the broad bats of Graeme Smith and Jacques Kallis, who looked particularly untaxed in playing him. Smith in particular attacked Boult as if on a personal mission to end his career before it had really started, and if that was his wish, it nearly worked, with the selectors promptly dumping Boult after his return of 2 for 151 across the test.

It was a chastening experience for Boult, who still hadn't played a high volume of multi-day cricket at that stage of his career. He learned that it wasn't enough to run in and bowl and hope to take wickets. At test-match level you didn't just need plans but you had to have the skills and accuracy to execute the plans — miracle balls of the kind Boult envisaged, late swing to beat the right-hander on the inside edge and to catch the outside edge of the left-hander, only tended to happen if they could be backed up by over after over of well-directed, more prosaic deliveries.

He knew he had to work smarter and harder. Boult hadn't initially been noted for an unstinting work ethic — which may have been an unfair portrayal because Boult was almost cursed by making bowling look so natural — but by the time Neil Wagner joined him in Mount

Maunganui, it was the first thing the former Otagoite noticed.

'Trent is ultra-positive and confident but extremely hard working. I mean, I thought I worked really hard, but if you could see the work that he put in it was like, "Oh gosh, I need to lift up another level."'

Boult's increasing effort and efficiency returned quick results, including a 6 for 68 haul in a dramatic draw against England at Eden Park, a test New Zealand came one wicket shy of winning, and a five-wicket bag at Headingley on the return visit.

By the time the West Indies arrived in the summer of 2013– 14, the Black Caps were still looking for an uplift in fortunes in test cricket under the captaincy of Brendon McCullum. They had dominated the first test in Dunedin — a test overshadowed by news that broke on the third morning that three New Zealanders were being investigated by the ICC's anti-corruption unit, including Lou Vincent who would later receive a life ban — but rain had interrupted a simple chase. In Wellington, Boult made sure they left nothing to chance, taking 6 for 40 — including three clean bowled in four deliveries — as the Windies crashed to 193 in reply to New Zealand's 441, and 4 for 40 when they followed on. Nine of Boult's 10 wickets came in a single day.

Boult has never taken another 10-wicket haul in tests, but he was a consistent performer with a penchant for taking bags in the loveliest of surrounds, like the 5 for 85 at Lord's and 5 for 60 with a pink ball in Adelaide.

Preceding those two hauls in 2015 was the small matter of the World Cup. It's easy to remember the sharp edge Boult brought to the attack in that tournament, especially the 5 for 27 against mighty Australia at Eden Park, but what is less easily recalled was that Boult was seen as a squad player at best leading into the World Cup but not a first-choice option.

In fact, before the lead-in twin-series against Sri Lanka and Pakistan, Boult had played just 10 one-day internationals and just three at home as concerns were raised about his ability to swing the white ball.

In the seven-match series against Sri Lanka, Boult played the first two matches with a conspicuous absence of success and did not come back into the side until the fifth ODI at Dunedin, where his 4 for 44 showed he retained wicket-taking potential in the short formats. This aligned with McCullum's desire to show a more attacking mindset and less paint-by-numbers approach in the field during the World Cup.

Boult got the nod for the opener, also against Sri Lanka, took two relatively expensive wickets and was a locked-down part of the attack therein. Two more wickets followed against Scotland and one against England in Wellington where he watched as Southee cut a seven-wicket swathe through Eoin Morgan's shell-shocked team.

In the next match, against Australia at Eden Park, it was Boult's time to shine, taking 5 for 27 in front of an enraptured crowd. That should have been the last thing he was required to do but another handy left-armer, Mitchell Starc, replied with six wickets and No. 11 Boult found himself coming to the crease with the speedster on a hat-trick and six runs still required for the win.

He told *Cricket Monthly*: 'I remember swearing and doing a few other things when [Adam Milne] got bowled. And then Tim got bowled . . . I went out there, my heart was moving, definitely, and then to have Kane at the other end . . . I've known him since I was eight years old. If anyone is going to calm me down, it's him. And he tried to. It didn't calm me down.'

A jumpy Boult, having seen his fellow tailenders fail to defend Starc's full and fast deliveries, thought about trying to attack, but in the end he did enough to survive the two balls and left it for his old age-group buddy to swat Pat Cummins over the short long-on boundary to win the match.

Boult followed the five-for with three against Afghanistan, two against Bangladesh, four in the quarter-final against the West Indies and two in the sensational semi-final against South Africa. His early wicket in the final — Aaron Finch caught and bowled for 0 — gave the Black Caps a glimmer of hope, but 183 was well short of a defendable total.

With 22 wickets at an average of 16.9, there was never again any question as to Boult's effectiveness with the white ball, and four years later he would be right in the middle of the most dramatic ODI ever played.

Coming into the final at Lord's, Boult was enjoying another fine tournament, having taken 17 wickets in nine matches, including four-wicket hauls against the West Indies and Australia. His 2 for 42 in a tight semi-final against India included the key wickets of Virat Kohli, leg before for 1, and Ravindra Jadeja (77), who was induced into skying a catch to long-off from a slower ball just when he and MS Dhoni looked to be leading India to victory.

The final, however, did not go Boult's way. So much so that he doesn't like talking about it and has said it's something he might never get over. To sum up his day in four short acts: he appears to have Jason Roy plumb lbw from the first ball of England's chase, but Marais Erasmus gives it not out, and although the ball would have clattered into leg stump, he survives on 'umpire's call'; with England needing 22 off nine balls he catches Ben Stokes near the boundary but stands back onto the rope before relaying it to Guptill; he can't defend 15 off the last over, thanks in large part to four overthrows deflected from Stokes' bat, finishing with 0 for 67 off his 10; he concedes 15 in the Super Over, one too many as it turned out.

There's dumb luck, bad luck and something else entirely to describe Boult's day out at Lord's. No wonder he finds it tough to talk about it.

* * * * * * *

The Boult and Southee partnership is brilliant and long-standing and while it is Southee who has been elevated to leadership positions, there has never been an obvious Batman and Robin relationship. At times Boult is the leader of the attack, at others Southee. Both have endured periods when they were not considered frontline options for the one-day team.

Both are, it has to be noted, brilliant fielders; and while Southee has more range, being equally adept at fielding in the deep, the circle or in the cordon, Boult's athleticism sees him patrolling the deep as a rule. He has taken some of the most incredible boundary-riding catches — one catch off Kieron Pollard in a T20I in Dominica has to be seen to be believed — and he has taken two full-length, one-handed specials while fielding at point, one to dismiss Kumar Sangakkara for 203 at the Basin Reserve.

Boult, despite being an expensive toy in T20 franchise tournaments around the world, has played just 55 T20Is since his debut in the format in 2013, whereas Southee has played 95.

They work so well together because they don't consider one to be more senior to the other. When they added Neil Wagner (and more latterly, Kyle Jamieson) to their club, they got even better.

Said Wagner about the relationship the trio share: 'It got to a point where we started knowing each other really well and trusting each other; we know what our roles are and we've got each other's best interests at heart.

'You know it's going to be swings and roundabouts and seeing how happy they are for you when you take a wicket does go a long way. The extra mile we go for each other is the sort of stuff that we're going to remember for the rest of our lives, not the five-wicket bags.'

There'll be another reason we remember Boult long past his playing days, and while it might seem perverse given all he's done for the ball, there is something about his batting that embodies the fun of cricket.

Boult is a better batter than a No. 11, but somewhere along the line he decided either out of fear (quite possible), laziness (less probable) or a sense of fun that he was going to turn his batting into one of the game's more unique art forms.

His idiosyncrasies at the crease can make Steve Smith's feel almost prudish by comparison. It is not uncommon to see Boult playing a back-foot defensive shot standing on one leg at least two feet outside off stump. In his later years, he started hitting what could only be described as straight forehands down the line. He could hit long, long sixes and could go out in some fairly curious means but escaped the opprobrium Southee received because he never had any pretensions about batting at Nos 8 or 9.

He took huge pride in going past Muttiah Muralitharan's record for the most test runs at No. 11 and if there's one thing that might coax Boult back into full-time test status in his final couple of years in the game, it's the fact that England's Jimmy Anderson has subsequently passed the both of them.

If it takes the lure of some bespoke innings at the bottom of the order to get Boult back, most fans would take it.

It's not easy to finish a piece on Boult without a definitive finish, so to speak, on his international career. He says he wants to play more marquee games for his country, but he has also talked about his desire to travel less and spend more time with his family, as well as set them up for life. Sometimes there are competing forces in sport, and life, that don't allow you to do everything you want.

There's another thing about Boult that is talked about less but is always there. He was desperate to be the best at what he did. He got near enough, too. In 2015, he was ranked as the third-best test bowler in the world. A year later he was the highest-ranked ODI bowler in the game, and in 2022 he climbed to ninth in the world for T20Is. Those are significant achievements.

In recent years he has slipped out of the top 10 in tests.

Some players might say that rankings mean nothing to them; that they're a set of numbers that don't have any material effect on how you will play in your next test, which is the only thing that matters. Boult might not be one of those players, though. He knew what it was like not to be rated when he was a kid. It hurt.

If he thought for a minute that his standards were slipping, that he had no improvement, only regression, left in the test game, he might walk quietly away. He might already have done so.

CHAPTER 15
NEIL WAGNER

Debut: 2012   Last match: 2023

	Matches	Wickets	Ave	5w (10w)	Economy	S/R
Test:	63	258	27.5	9 (-)	3.13	52.6

Also: 842 test runs with one 50 and 17 catches

While an all-time great, Neil Wagner may never have a statue outside one of the country's test grounds. From a purely artistic point of view that's a great pity, because the indefatigable paceman is a sculptor's dream.

Cricket fans would be able to see the bronzed form in their minds: there's Wagner, having just taken another wicket, probably from a bumper gloved down the leg side, on the charge, his knees pumping high and his fist clenched, while his face, contorted into a rictus, manages to capture those competing emotions of rage and pure joy.

Wagner, the cricketer, could never do anything but play with his heart pumping wildly on his sleeve.

There is something about him that represents the best qualities of New Zealand, though of course his story is not that simple. The very fact he has made himself such an integral part of this country's cricket story is all the more admirable when you consider that Wagner's mother Doreen was against Wagner going to an English-speaking school when he was a teenager because the language 'was not my forte'.

He is a hell of a bowler with a hell of a story.

* * * * * * *

'I was born in Pretoria, grew up in Pretoria. It's quite a big place but I was in a smaller town, Pretoria North, which is on the other side of the Magaliesberg mountain that stretches across and splits Pretoria,' Wagner says.

Pretoria is regarded by many as the beating heart of Afrikanerdom. It was founded by Marthinus Pretorius and named for his father Andries, a voortrekker who led the Dutch-speaking settlers of the Cape Colony north and into the South African interior to free themselves from British rule. The elder Pretorius led 464 voortrekkers into the Battle of Blood River against a force of 10,000-plus Zulus. By the end of the battle, it is estimated that 3000 Zulus had perished while three voortrekkers had minor wounds. They established settlements in Natal and reached further up into the highveld, where the financial and administrative capitals of Johannesburg and Pretoria respectively sit.

The people of Pretoria, which has the largest white population in Sub-Saharan Africa, like to see themselves as cut from Pretorius's cloth: tough, pious and extremely resourceful.

The Wagners were no different. As the youngest of three brothers and the runt of the family, Neil quickly learned there were no tears in cricket. David was a left-handed top-order bat and Mark, the middle brother, was a lightning-quick bowler who would go on to play rugby at a high level.

'I always admired what he was capable of in sport,' Wagner said of Mark. 'Both of my brothers were way bigger than me. When I'm standing next to them it's like I'm standing next to Tim [Southee] and KJ [Kyle Jamieson]. I wish I had their size. I'm the odd one out.

'My competitiveness comes from being a younger brother trying to prove myself, 100 per cent. Our backyard games always had a lot riding on them and were fiery. We had the taped tennis balls and they stung a bit. I got bounced on my ear one day by Mark and wanted to cry to my parents but he told me in no uncertain terms that I had to get harder. I had to grow up pretty quickly. It definitely helped mould me into the player I became.'

One of the most prominent emblems of the city is the Voortrekker Monument, another is Loftus Versfeld, the city's rugby ground that has been a Springbok and Northern Transvaal (the Blue Bulls) fortress. Across the road from Loftus is Afrikaanse Hoër Seunskool, or Afrikaans School for Boys, known by its more colloquial and manageable nickname of Affies.

'It's a pretty prestigious, good-quality school that I was pretty fortunate to go to,' Wagner said. 'This is not a well-known thing, but my family struggled financially when I was younger. I was going to go to school at Pretoria North High School where my two brothers went, then an English-speaking private school, St Alban's, came in and offered me a bursary to go there and play cricket.

'My mother was strongly against it because English wasn't really my forte. I wasn't a strong English speaker and she thought I would struggle to adapt at a boarding school where I had to speak the language. When I think about it now, it might have come in quite handy.'

Wagner had shown enough talent as a bustling left-arm quick and top-order bat to get some attention in age-group cricket, but advancing in the South African system was quite dependent on going to the right school and the Wagners were not in a financial position to pick and choose.

'Northern Transvaal and Northerns Cricket said they would help me and that if I was going to make something out of cricket I needed to go to one of the bigger, stronger schools. They helped out financially, which enabled me to go to Affies, which was appreciated, obviously.'

One of the appealing factors about Affies was that Faf du Plessis, 16 months older than Wagner, was already at the school.

'I went to primary school with Faf, we grew up together and played cricket together.'

It was a school that churned out Proteas and Springboks — and Black Caps. While Wagner was at the school, legendary halfback Fourie du Preez was there, as was Pierre Spies and Wynand Olivier, while AB de Villiers, du Plessis, Heino Kuhn, Kruger van Wyk and Wagner would all play test cricket, just not all for South Africa.

Wagner admitted that sometimes the family's straitened circumstances played on his mind.

'There was a time when there was a cricket trip coming up that I knew I wouldn't be going on because it cost a bit of money, but people would step up to sponsor you and help the parents out. There were a few in the team in the same boat. We were extremely grateful for the assistance we got, but I did feel bad in a way, too, because there were all these people helping you to reach my dream. A lot of those people I still have contact with. If it wasn't for those people, I wouldn't be where I am today. My family started finding its feet towards the back end of my school years and that took the pressure off.'

Wagner left school to play for Tuks, the club associated with the University of Pretoria, and made his way into the Northerns first-class set-up, but he was becoming frustrated by his lack of progress and remuneration. He didn't feel any burning desire to get rich off cricket, but he did want a contract that would at least cover the costs of his travel to and from training and matches.

'It was pretty hard to knock the door down and get noticed,' Wagner said. 'I was promised a contract for a few years, but it just didn't happen. I wasn't getting a cent out of first-class cricket, yet I was putting a lot of time and effort into it. I started picking up my studies, doing sports psychology papers on a scholarship.

'I went on a South African Academy tour to Bangladesh and did really well and again was promised a contract but when I came back, they said they couldn't give me a playing contract but could only offer a working one, which was nothing really. I had to coach to earn money.

'I had to make a decision as to whether I was going to pursue this cricketing dream.'

Wagner left to play league cricket in the north of England. His pace and fire made an impression; and as the season was starting to wind down, he had a couple of county contracts to contemplate, contracts he could take up under the Kolpak Rule that meant citizens of countries that are part of European Union Association Agreements, which are free-trade treaties between the EU and other countries, had the right to work in EU countries. South Africa is part of a deal called the Cotonou Agreement with the EU, which meant their players, until the rules were tweaked in 2009, could play county cricket without being considered an overseas player.

Just as he was about to make the call, probably to take an offer from Hove-based Sussex, his agent called with an interesting proposition.

'He said he'd spoken to Mike Hesson who told him they were after a bowler for Otago and would I be interested. There was no discussion about qualifying for New Zealand, but straight away I said, "Yeah, I'd be very interested."'

That's not quite the full story. Hesson wasn't interested in just any old bowler. He specifically wanted Wagner. He'd been scouring tapes but knew that with Otago Cricket's limited budget, there would be a very specific type of player he needed. One who had the sort of intrinsic motivation and a desire to prove himself to the world. One that came without a big price tag.

He kept coming back to a tape from South Africa, where a young left-armer kept steaming in, over after wicketless over. Nothing was in his favour; not the conditions or the physical attributes one normally associates with quicks. He wasn't especially tall and he wasn't even lightning-quick, though he carried himself like he was. He was relentless, though, and that sort of thing brings its own rewards.

For his part, Wagner wasn't bothered that the money would not be as good as in England. He'd had New Zealand on his mind since a cheeky first five-eighth with a bad haircut had made a big impression on him in 2001.

'Every kid in South Africa had a lot of respect and admiration for the All Blacks so there was a lot of excitement when the New Zealand teams came to play in Super Rugby. Affies was right across the road from Loftus Versfeld, the Bulls' home ground, and the Crusaders were training on the school grounds. Andrew Mehrtens was running a kicking clinic and a couple of practice sessions. The following night a few of us from school went and watched the game and as we were walking out the back of the stadium, he straight away recognised us and came over for a chat.

'It was something I will never forget; just how generous and nice he was, and the time he made for the kids, which the Bulls players never did. Instantly I became a Crusaders fan. That was it. I started loving the All Blacks. That lodged the idea of New Zealand in my head, even if the idea of playing cricket there wasn't even a pipe dream at that stage.'

Playing in England, he bumped into James Marshall and compatriot Grant Elliott, who were playing league cricket, and got the chance to bowl to both England and the Black Caps in the nets before the Old Trafford test in 2008 — the test where Ross Taylor scored 154 after taking guard in a pool of Daniel Flynn's blood.

'I went to the test with Faf du Plessis, who was playing for Lancashire and had tickets, and I couldn't stop thinking about the New Zealanders and how good they'd been to me, how much time Jacob Oram gave me. Funnily enough I can't remember Tim [Southee] on that trip, although I'm sure he wouldn't have made any effort towards me,' Wagner said with tongue firmly in cheek.

'A bit later Hess rang me up personally and reiterated that they were after a bowler, and would like to know if I was interested. He said they couldn't promise me a domestic contract beyond a year because it was all performance-based, but they would try to look after me until I got residency and qualified as a local to play for New Zealand.

'I just said, "Where do I sign?"

'I rang my parents up and I was in tears. It was a tough one, emotional. I knew I would get back from the UK and have five days with my family, to pack my bags and emigrate to New Zealand. It was tough knowing I was going to be saying goodbye, but it was an easy decision, especially after bowling to England and New Zealand in the nets. After that, there was no real inspiration for me to try to qualify to play for England. There was nothing about that day that made me walk away and say, "Geez, I want to play for them", but with the New Zealand guys, there was something about them.

'It wasn't the same money, not even close, that it would have been to stay in England — it was only a six-month contract — but it was never a decision about money. I wanted the opportunity to try to play international cricket and I decided if I was going to do it for a team that wasn't South Africa, then I wanted it to be New Zealand because of the similarities in our countries and because of their rugby teams when I was growing up.'

Thanks, Mehrts. And Jake.

The internal feelings might have been warm towards New Zealand, but the extremities were not when he arrived in Dunedin with just one suitcase and one warm jacket. He was picked up from the airport in Momona by Mark Bracewell, brother of John and Brendon, uncle of Doug and father of Michael, and noticed immediately how green it was and, yes, how cold it was.

The mercury levels in the thermometer were not the only issue. He'd ordered a bunch of kit and a kit bag which hadn't arrived from Australia and when it did, a day before his club debut, it was all right-handed equipment, so he had to borrow until some left-handed pads and gloves arrived.

The club was a new one, Pelichet Bay, and only lasted for a couple of seasons, but they played on an artificial wicket and arriving early one morning, Wagner noticed part of it was an unusual colour — it was ice.

'I was thinking to myself, "What have I got myself into here?" But I adapted and ended up loving it. The people I met were so welcoming and made me feel a part of it, but I quickly learned that it didn't pay to say you're supporting the Crusaders. A few of the Otago boys told me straight off the bat that I was never to say that again.'

It didn't take long for Wagner to make an impact. Not all of it was positive. Word got around the traps pretty quickly that there was a young Saffa down south with a big motor, yes, but also a big mouth. He wasn't universally popular.

'I was aware of it,' Wagner said. 'I came over and just started playing the brand of cricket I was taught to play. There was no two ways about it, at that time when you played club cricket in South Africa it felt like first-class cricket over here. When I left, club cricket at home was highly competitive, playing on grass wickets that were better than what University Oval was at the time. I would be facing guys coming in and bowling 140 kph and abusing you — everything was in your face and do or die. It was a completely different brand of cricket.

'Going into my first couple of games in Dunedin I quickly realised no one was like that here. It was a bit strange. Some of the guys I played with at Otago loved it and fed off it. Ian Butler, who arrived in Otago from ND the same year I did, Warren McSkimming, James

McMillan — these guys jumped on the horse with me and went with it. They talked about how aggressive I was and how they liked it, but then other people were coming to me and saying, "Hey, you've got to rein it in a little bit."

'Craig Cumming was the captain and is someone I have got a lot to be thankful for. He felt like an older brother to me and was a role model I could look up to. We butted heads a few times early, but I had huge respect for him because he just wanted the best for me and out of me. There were times when he told me to pull back on the talk and I realised, "Hey, this is just not the New Zealand way, the Kiwi way and if I want to play for New Zealand I'm going to have to adapt."

'It took me a long time to do that, to be honest. Slowly but surely I got better at controlling myself and felt I had to do that to buy into the cricket culture here, to earn respect.'

Sometimes reputations can be hard to shake. A couple of ND bowlers had heard a few reports and weren't going to go out of their way to make life easy for the interloper. Wagner had been giving it large when ND batted, but when it was his turn to get to the crease, Trent Boult had the ball in his hand.

'He gave me a bit of stick,' Wagner recalled. 'He got into me for throwing my hands up in the air and being loud. He ended up nicking me off in that game and to this day he still gives me grief about it.'

There was no guarantee that Wagner was going to play for New Zealand. While he was a consistent wicket-taker in domestic cricket, there were still doubts as to whether his bustling style would translate to test wickets, particularly without raw, top-end pace. It wasn't just that, either; qualifying for residency was proving more tortuous than had been advertised.

He and now wife Lana had just scrimped together enough money to buy their first house in 2012, a two-bedroom townhouse in Dunedin, when the domestic season ended and Wagner had to leave the country because his visa had expired. He went home to South Africa to see his family and apply for a new one, but he did so with a sense of foreboding. Initially he thought he might qualify in time to be eligible for selection to the 2011 World Cup, but that had been pushed out a year because trips out of New Zealand for his brother's wedding and to play in the Champions League meant he hadn't spent the requisite amount of days in New Zealand.

'There was talk about it not happening again in 2012, which was a bit upsetting. Then Otago Cricket CEO Ross Dykes, another guy I owe a lot to, rang me at 3 am in the morning to tell me I had now qualified to play. I was speaking to him in my room and it was quite loud. My parents' room was next door, and they obviously could hear the conversation. They walked into my room and my dad was in tears, very happy and grateful, telling me that my hard work and sacrifice had paid off and meant something — and that was just qualification; I hadn't been picked for anything yet.

'Two days later I was out having a beer with a few of my mates to celebrate my residency and just to chew the fat and yarn. I was three or four beers deep and got another phone call, this one was from [national selection manager] Kim Littlejohn who said, "Hey, you've just been selected to play in the test series in the West Indies." Gosh. I had to get back to my parents' pretty quickly.

'I knew what the goal was, but I never knew if I was going to be able to achieve it or not. There's a lot of stuff you have to sacrifice to get there and even talking about it now I get a bit overwhelmed if I'm being honest.'

* * * * * * * *

After such a long wait to play for his adopted country, Wagner didn't exactly blow the doors down once he got there.

His first series in the Caribbean was a poor one on and off the pitch, with coach John Wright signalling his intention to leave and captain Ross Taylor struggling to get everybody on the same page. Wagner had no interest whatsoever in the internal politics of the day; he just wanted to play cricket and take wickets.

Wagner took four wickets across the series, a modest return, but his first, Kieran Powell, was caught behind by Affies' alumnus van Wyk for 134, which was at the very least a unique happening and, potentially, an extremely difficult pub-quiz question.

He continued his slow start in his one test on the disastrous tour to South Africa in early 2013, taking 1 for 135 at Port Elizabeth, his only scalp Graeme Smith who gloved one down leg side.

When they played England in reciprocal home-and-away series in 2013, Wagner started to show more potential, taking 19 wickets across five tests. In Bangladesh he took his first five-wicket bag, at Mirpur, showing an ability to provide an edge even on unresponsive surfaces.

It wasn't until India arrived for two tests that Wagner really started to show how he could become a key part of future attacks. At Eden Park he took four first-innings wickets but saved his best work for the second, taking another four, including a snorting bouncer from around the wicket to left-handed century-maker Shikhar Dhawan.

This is how ESPNcricinfo's ball-by-ball coverage described the key moment in the victory: 'Wagner has produced this wicket out of nowhere. What a luxury to have such a player on call. What heart, what spirit shown by Wagner. Goes round the wicket, produces a bouncer that is too difficult for Dhawan to leave. It is going across him, but has started just outside leg, and there is no room. As he weaves away, he fails to get his glove out of the harm's way. It kisses the glove. Wagner, what a beaut.'

Wagner took a six-wicket haul in the first innings against Australia in Christchurch in 2016, McCullum's final test, despite a fractured knuckle and split webbing on his bowling hand, another one in his next test in Bulawayo, and finished the tour to Africa with an emotional five-wicket bag on his old home ground of Centurion.

'I had a lot of goosebumps when I walked out,' Wagner told reporters. 'I remember sitting on that bank and watching Allan Donald and Shaun Pollock bowl and really feeling love for this game. To walk out today and represent the Black Caps in a test against South Africa was an amazing feeling. I loved every moment of it.'

A year later he returned his best figures in tests, 7 for 39 against the West Indies in Wellington.

He doesn't really keep track of these numbers and specific figures, he reckoned. When he first got to New Zealand, he said that was all he did — 'it was all about taking wickets, taking as many as I could and trying to be the best at everything' — but he soon came to realise it 'wasn't the Kiwi way'; his Otago colleagues wanted a teammate, not an accountant.

Somehow, despite never playing for numbers, he's stacked them up, taking 258 wickets in 63 tests at the same average as Boult, a better average than Southee and a better strike rate than both of them. For a period there in 2019, he was ranked the second-best bowler in the world, and from 2016 through to 2022, aside from one little dip in 2018, he has been a consistent presence in the world's top 10-ranked test bowlers.

He says the only time he's been worried about numbers is when it hasn't worked for him, like trying to make the one-day team or play T20 cricket.

'Seeing your name up there in wicket lists with some of the greats with Trent and Tim, Sir Richard and Dan, it's pretty special. It's something I would never have believed possible. Once my career comes to an end I'll sit back and look at it and reflect and be pretty proud of what I've been able to achieve. At the moment, though, it's about just keeping on doing what I do for the team and find a way of contributing.'

Anyway, trying to tell the Wagner story with numbers would be crass. It would be like trying to explain why AC/DC are so great live by looking at the sheet music.

Watching Wagner operate with his tail up — and, really, when isn't it up? — is more of a sensation because there wasn't really anybody like him.

In a YouTube video made about Wagner, cricket journalist and analyst Jarrod Kimber described him as cricket's ultramodernist.

'There is no other bowler in the history of cricket like Neil Wagner,' he began. 'He was averaging high-30s after 12 tests and had no obvious skills that would change that . . . there was no reason to think he'd be anything different than a fringe player with a lot of ticker.'

The things working against Wagner were myriad. By international standards, he was not fast. By fast-bowling physique standards, he was not big. He could swing the new ball, but not a heck of a lot and, anyway, he seldom worked with the new ball. He didn't jag it off the seam. Sometimes, in fact, he didn't even hit the seam, which, in their earlier days before they became besties, used to frustrate his more illustrious teammates who were trying to keep the Kookaburra in tip-top condition.

What did he have in his favour, then? A big engine and a relentless range of short-pitched deliveries. He bowled an astonishing number of deliveries between nipple and neck height. He bowled them from all angles. Left-arm seam bowlers do not bowl around the wicket to left-handed batters. It's just not a thing . . . until Wagner made it a thing. He helped win the aforementioned test against India by doing it and he also played a massive role in getting New Zealand to the World Test Championship by doing it, too.

Okay, so we all remember Mitchell Santner's one-handed over-his-head catch with the overs slipping away to beat Pakistan at Mount Maunganui in 2020, but that test was an etched-in-stone draw until

Wagner came around the wicket to Fawad Alam, a man who had showed awesome restraint and had batted more than six and a half hours for his 102, and had him gloving a pull to BJ Watling.

Heck, even on the last day of that final at Southampton, he had the outrageously talented Ravi Jadeja succumbing to that angle, edging behind to Watling with a look of horror on his face.

As Ross Taylor noted in *Black & White*, Wagner has developed imitators — Ben Stokes has become an almost exclusively short-ball bowler, and Mark Wood, who has genuinely frightening pace, has bowled searing short-ball spells — which is the sincerest form of flattery.

It's unlikely, however, that any will do it with quite the chutzpah Wagner displayed.

'He's a force of nature,' Taylor wrote. 'He has been criticised for bowling what is basically bodyline, the implication being that the umpires shouldn't allow him to bowl so much short stuff. When the wicket is flat, bowlers have to find a way, and Waggy has done that better than anyone . . .

'All quicks bowl short balls, but most of them can't keep it up for overs on end. Wags bangs in three or four an over for over after over. And there's an art to consistently bowling short deliveries that the umpires don't regard as bouncers: if the umpires start designating them as bouncers, the Wagner-style relentless short-pitched attack becomes unsustainable because of the two bouncers an over rule.'

Perhaps his most staggering spell, in terms of the sheer physical effort involved, was the one on the final day against Pakistan at Mount Maunganui. Wagner thought he was bowling on one broken toe, but it was later discovered it was actually two, having taken a yorker on the foot by the imposing Shaheen Shah Afridi while batting on day two.

'It hurts every time I walk,' he told reporters at the ground. 'Walking to fine leg, doing anything, twisting, turning, as soon as you bend your toe a little bit, it hurts.

'You just try to put it out of your mind and get on with it. I take a lot of pride in [playing hurt] . . . I wouldn't want to sit on the side with my foot up and watch the boys do the hard work out there. I'd have a bit of FOMO [fear of missing out]. Test matches don't come easy. Playing for your country is something you can never take for granted. I know how bloody hard I had to work to get where I am now so I'm sure as hell not going to sit on the side watching other people do it.'

It didn't help that he had a deep-seated fear of needles and the only way to operate was on a painkilling injection.

'I thought damn it, I can't bear the pain. I'll get a jab. That took the pain away for a little bit and that helped, but at five o'clock it started wearing off again pretty quickly.

'It's going to be damn sore, no doubt about it, but bowling is always sore. I've never bowled a game when something doesn't hurt. It's part of it. I'm just going to have to find a way to contribute to the team.'

That just might be the essence of Wagner there. Or maybe it was more recently, when England, and in particular exciting young talent Harry Brook and brilliant veteran Joe Root, took him apart for three-quarters of the test series. Wagner looked spent, his effectiveness blunted to the point where England's batters were reverse-scooping him over the slips cordon and flat-batting him down the ground for six.

Somehow, reaching deep into his 36-year-old reserves, Wagner engineered a victory on the final day of the second test, his wickets including Root and Stokes to the short ball, before enticing James Anderson to, you probably guessed by now, glove one down the leg side, this time to a diving Tom Blundell, to end the test.

It was a bit different, that series. Boult was no longer there alongside him and Southee was not just his mate but his skipper. Without a central contract, Boult's test future is murky. Wagner, too, is not getting any younger. The most prolific wicket-taking trio in New Zealand cricket history might be in its final throes, but the mateship will endure. All the angst about his early days in the country are long gone.

Southee spoke to the *Herald* with admiration about Wagner's decision to uproot his life to come here, and a bit of regret about how he was received when he came into the Black Caps: 'He came here and was sledging our domestic cricketers. For us New Zealanders it was a bit different. It's foreign to us. We're not used to it. He was in your face.'

'Then he came into the New Zealand side with myself, Trent, Doug Bracewell. And we were all good mates. Suddenly we've got this guy from South Africa — he didn't quite gel straight away. It took time — he broke us down. We got to know him.'

Wagner was once described to me by a teammate as like a Labrador: always keen for a pat on the head and loyal to a fault.

He's the guy who provides the nasty, sometimes even cynical, edge to the New Zealand attack and somehow makes them more . . . likeable?

He's the guy who came over as a bullish South African, served a long apprenticeship and ended up '100 per cent Kiwi'. New Zealand cricket has been all the more fortunate for his perseverance.

As he'd say: 'I'm not the best or most talented. I just have to work really hard.'

CHAPTER 16
TOM LATHAM
(13TH MAN)

Debit: 2012   Last match: 2023

	Matches	Runs	Ave	S/R	100s	50s	Dismissals*
Test:	74	5150	41.53	47.15	13	27	86
ODI:	130	3762	35.49	85.24	7	21	126
T20I:	26	516	25.80	108.86	-	3	19

Wins as captain: Tests 4 (win % 44.4), ODIs 22 (win % 71), T20Is 6 (win % 46)

*Includes catches as a keeper and a fielder, and stumpings

During the process of writing this book, it became clear I was in the midst of committing a sin of omission.

In this case, the omission was southpaw opener, white-ball keeper and occasional captain, Thomas William Maxwell Latham.

He had come very, very close to making the final cut of 12, but missed out not through any major shortcomings on his part — though when you burrow into his career he does have some weirdly anomalous numbers — but because for the majority of his time in the Black Caps he has batted in the considerable shadow of Kane Williamson and Ross Taylor. The others selected for these pages all appeared to be either slightly better or slightly more influential than him across the various formats.

Even accounting for the tendency towards recency bias, over the summer of 2022–23 it became increasingly difficult to support that argument, so here he is, a late inclusion but no less important for it — a travelling reserve if you like.

Latham bats with an understated excellence. His record creeps up on you until you can't ignore it. Just seven New Zealanders have scored 5000 test runs and he is one of them. If John Wright was the benchmark for gritty New Zealand southpaw openers then consider this: Latham will pass Wright's 5334 tally in 185 runs' time and unless he has a cataclysmic drop in form he will have done so in fewer tests, fewer innings and with a higher average; he would have done so scoring more centuries and more 50s. He is a great player, one whose charms might occasionally slip under the radar with outsiders but never do inside the changing rooms.

While his compact technique and unflappability make him perfectly suited to tests, his one-day international record is also superb. In fact, his versatility probably doesn't get talked about often enough. He opens the batting in tests, while in ODIs he keeps wicket and usually bats at No. 5, roles so far apart in their requirements they would seem incompatible.

When Kane Williamson has been unavailable, which in the past ODI World Cup cycle has been often, Latham has stood in effectively as skipper in tests and quite brilliantly in one-day cricket. His win record in ODIs stands at an impressive 71 per cent and while the sample size is not enormous, it is not trifling either. Many expected him to be the natural successor to Williamson when he stood down from captaincy of the test side in 2022, but management opted for the slightly bolder strategy of Tim Southee. Not surprisingly for a man who has never courted controversy, there was not a peep of dissent from Latham.

* * * * * * *

Latham's ability was recognised early in Canterbury cricket circles, his run-scoring exploits already in evidence at Cobham Intermediate. It helped that he had a famous father: Rod Latham was a former test opener who rose to some form of notoriety during the 1992 World Cup when his part-time slow-medium bowling saw him join Willie Watson, Gavin Larsen and Chris Harris in a quartet known as Dibbly, Dobbly, Wibbly and Wobbly.

'I remember going down and watching Dad at the end of his career. It was cool being around a cricket environment,' Latham told the *Otago Daily Times* in 2022.

Rod was also a fullback for some powerful Canterbury rugby sides, which afforded him near royal status in Christchurch. It also meant his son's progress through Christchurch Boys' High School — a school noted for producing Black Caps and All Blacks — was closely monitored. It wasn't obvious which of his son's sporting loves was going to take root more firmly, either.

'Rugby was my passion growing up,' Tom recalled. 'I enjoyed that a little bit more than cricket, then cricket started to take over and rugby took a backward step. I played hooker . . . I was a little bit rounder back in the day. I played for school and also Christchurch [Football Club, the oldest rugby club in New Zealand] and Burnside. I think it was Year 11 when I stopped playing rugby to focus on cricket.'

Latham progressed in the time-honoured fashion, playing for Canterbury through the age groups and making the New Zealand Under-19s, who were given a big shot of winning the 2010 World Cup. It was being hosted in New Zealand and largely in Christchurch. The team was full of future internationals including Latham, Corey Anderson, the Bracewells Michael and Doug, Ben Wheeler, Tom Blundell and Dane Cleaver, the latter two barely getting a game.

(Also time-honoured was New Zealand's propensity to pick multiple wicketkeepers, with Latham, Cleaver, Blundell and Michael

Bracewell all glovemen.)

They cruised through pool play but were tipped up by eventual winners Australia, who had Mitchell Marsh and Josh Hazlewood among relative no-names, in the quarter-finals. They then lost to South Africa, before beating an England team containing Joe Root, Ben Stokes, James Vince and Jos Buttler. The team was captained by Azeem Rafiq, who has found himself at the centre of a racism scandal at Yorkshire Cricket Club.

Latham didn't stand out at the tournament, scoring one unbeaten half-century and averaging 27.4 for the tournament, but it nevertheless provided a springboard into the Canterbury senior set-up and he made a mark early, scoring 65 on his first-class debut.

His elevation to the New Zealand side seemed preordained, but it didn't come in the longer form, which he seemed more suited to, rather in about as low-key settings as you can imagine: a 2012 home ODI series against a non-competitive Zimbabwe side. Latham strung together 24, 48 and 7 not out in limited opportunities, which was enough to get him on the plane to the West Indies. He made his T20I debut on the mainland United States of America, however, as New Zealand played the West Indies in Lauderhill, Florida, before the one-dayers and tests — Latham was not in the squad for the latter — moved to the Caribbean.

It is fair to say Latham's game did not appear to be a natural fit for T20 and it remained a curiosity that he only played his first T20I on New Zealand soil in 2023 in a series against Sri Lanka, 11 years after his first, when the bulk of New Zealand's first-choice players were already at the Indian Premier League, including usual keeper-batter Devon Conway.

Latham made his test debut against India at the Basin Reserve, in 2014, a test that would later belong to Brendon McCullum. Batting at No. 4, Latham was nicked off for an eight-ball duck, leaving him with the butt-clenching prospect of coming into bat on a pair when

New Zealand were desperately trying to save the test. His 29 is not going to make it onto any plaques, but he was under way and, having been dismissed off the final ball before lunch on the third day, got to put his feet up and watch McCullum, BJ Watling and his Under-19s teammate Neesham bat the team to safety.

Latham's role across the formats was not defined. That could be seen as a disadvantage. Often young cricketers struggle to adjust between formats and the different modes of batting and bowling required for different times of the match. In Latham's case it was a boon.

'I was sort of a utility guy; I wasn't necessarily first choice in the team, but managed to fill a lot of spots, whether it was at the top of the order, the middle or with the gloves,' he said.

After one test at No. 4, the selectors saw enough in him to decide he was the answer to a problem that had been plaguing New Zealand for what seemed an eternity — the opening batting slot. In his second test against the West Indies at historic Sabina Park, Kingston, he went out to face the new ball, scored a match double of 83 and 73 in a crushing New Zealand win and hasn't batted anywhere else in the test team since. In the following test he added 82 and 36 and it was clear New Zealand had found not just the answer to a long-standing problem but a player with the potential to dominate at the highest level. That feeling was confirmed when he scored centuries in back-to-back tests against Pakistan in the United Arab Emirates.

The path of a young test batter is never linear and it is rarely smooth. Latham's upwards trajectory halted, and it would be 17 innings before he reached three figures again, though he did add half-centuries at Lord's and Headingley against England, and an even 50 against Australia at the Adelaide Oval.

It was back home against Sri Lanka in 2015 that he cracked the century mark again, scoring an unbeaten 109. The following year he added two more centuries, again in back-to-back tests, this time against a weak Zimbabwe attack in Bulawayo. It set in store a pattern that perhaps prevented Latham from achieving that amorphous 'great' status sooner. He tended to monster weaker sides, particularly at home, but struggled against, for want of a better term, the 'Anglo' nations and India.

This can be an unfair charge. After all, most players struggle against better sides — that's why they're 'better sides' — but Latham's numbers veer towards the extreme. He averages 92, 69 and 85 against Bangladesh, Sri Lanka and Zimbabwe respectively, the last off a small sample size, and 27, 32, 32 and a brutal 10 against, in order, Australia, England, India and South Africa.

Latham is too good for his struggles against those teams to continue, surely, but it has been an impediment to universal appreciation.

In the two years between December 2016 and '18, Latham endured another fallow period that this time extended to 18 completed innings without a ton. He was never terribly out of form, scoring four half-centuries in the period, but he made up for a lack of three-figure scores in some style, embarking on the most prolific red-ball period of his career. He scored five centuries in his next 10 innings, most of them of the big variety, with 264 not out against Sri Lanka, 176 against the same opposition, 161 against Bangladesh in Hamilton and a match-altering 154 in gruelling conditions in Colombo, again against Sri Lanka. He capped this golden period with 105 against England at Seddon Park.

The century against England took Latham's tally to 11, one short of John Wright's record for an opener and record for a left-hander, but he would have to wait a long time to match it — 28 innings, 26 of them completed. He came close, reaching 50 seven times and being agonisingly stumped for 95 against India at Kanpur when he lost track of the ball after getting an inside edge while defending Axar Patel.

When he did equal Wright's record, he made sure it was another big one, racking up 252 against Bangladesh in Christchurch. He didn't have to wait too long to pass him, scoring his 13th test century in Karachi against Pakistan in late 2022. Since then he has added four more 50s to underline his consistent output. At the end of the 2022–23 summer he had amassed 40 scores of 50-plus for New Zealand in tests, putting him ahead of such luminaries as Wright, Nathan Astle and Martin Crowe (all 35), and behind only Brendon McCullum (43), Ross Taylor (54), Stephen Fleming (55) and Williamson (61), all of whom have played considerably more than his 74 tests.

He might not be New Zealand's greatest test opener — with the likes of Stewie Dempster, Bert Sutcliffe, Glenn Turner, Wright and Mark Richardson all spanning markedly different eras, that is an argument that can never be settled — but he will be the most prolific, and that counts for something.

If anything, Latham's record in one-day cricket might be more impressive.

While he might not be the slickest gloveman New Zealand has produced, he is far better than merely competent.

After being used up and down the order, anywhere from opening to No. 9, Latham has settled into the No. 5 slot, one of the trickiest positions where you can be asked to rebuild an innings if things have got off to a poor start, or to hit boundaries from ball one if you're coming in late to apply finishing flourishes.

Latham is not a natural six hitter, but he can clear the ropes when called upon. It is his unflappable nature, however, that remains his biggest asset. He has seen most scenarios the 50-over game can throw at him and adjusts accordingly. His skill against spin — he is a rare bird for a New Zealander in that he is as comfortable in using his feet to get down the wicket as he is in sweeping — means he can push the pace in turning conditions more effectively than others.

Middle-order centuries are not easy to come by in ODI cricket, but Latham has four and another three as an opener, which again puts him among New Zealand's finest. Only Taylor (21), Martin Guptill (18), Nathan Astle (16), Williamson (13) and Fleming (8), have scored more than Latham, and of those men, only Williamson has scored one batting No. 5 or lower.

His ODI prowess was never better illustrated than in November 2022. Latham came to the crease at Eden Park with New Zealand struggling mightily at 88 for 3 in the 20th over, chasing India's imposing 306 for 7. Williamson was at the other end undefeated on 29. After one ball of the 48th over the same two players walked from the ground undefeated, with Williamson 94 and Latham 145.

'Incredible innings from Tom Latham,' Williamson gushed in the aftermath. 'On these drop-in pitches, you bowl full and straight, and it can be difficult. It was one of the most special ODI knocks I have seen.'

If there's a gap on Latham's ODI CV, it's the lack of a signature World Cup performance. He was a non-playing member of the 2015 squad and didn't have a great tournament in England in 2019, though his scrappy and well-paced 47 in the final was oh-so-close to being the pivotal knock. He will have further chances to fill that gap.

While he has the advantage of big gloves in ODI cricket, it is worth noting that Latham is a brilliant barehanded catcher, particularly in the slips. While his double of 30 and 9 might not have set the world alight in the World Test Championship final in Southampton, his five catches — three in the slips, one at square leg and one at fly slip — were crucial. He has 86 catches in tests, 78 as a fielder.

He is a great slip fielder; that's never been in doubt.

He's a great player, too, though that might have taken a little longer to realise than it should have.

ABOUT THE AUTHOR

Dylan Cleaver has been obsessed with the summer sport since his earliest days on this planet. The first Black Caps test he covered as a journalist was Stephen Fleming's first as skipper, a four-wicket loss to England at the old Lancaster Park. Long before then, Cleaver had sat on the terraces of his hometown Pukekura Park watching his beloved CD and dreaming of a cricket career himself. It was only a lack of talent and application that quashed that. Instead, he has spent the better part of three decades covering the sport for mastheads such as the *New Zealand Herald, Herald on Sunday, Sunday Star-Times* and *Sunday News*, alongside contributing to overseas publications like *The Cricket Monthly* and *The Nightwatchman*. Cleaver has won close to 40 national journalism awards, including Best Investigation at the Canon Media Awards in 2015 for his work on match-fixing allegations involving former New Zealand cricketers. He has been named Sports Journalist of the Year on multiple occasions, including for his ground-breaking work linking the high rates of dementia in former rugby players with head injuries suffered in their playing days. He lives on the North Shore with his wife Michelle and two teenage children Liam and Olivia.

SOURCES/BIBLIOGRAPHY

Brendon McCullum, *Declared*, Mower (2016).

Brendon McCullum, *Inside Twenty20*, Hodder Moa (2010).

'The McCullum Effect: How a blue-collar urchin rekindled New Zealand's love of cricket', *New Zealand Herald* (2016).

'A Touch of Baz', *The Cricket Monthly* (2015).

'2014 New Zealander of the Year: Brendon McCullum', *New Zealand Herald* (2014).

'Martin Crowe: How McCullum helped me let go', *ESPNcricinfo* (2014).

'Kane is Able', *The Cricket Monthly* (2015).

'How Kane Williamson looks at big moments and takes their power away', *Cricinfo* (2023).

Cricket with Kane Williamson, Penguin Random House New Zealand (2016).

'Kane Williamson | Full Q&A at The Oxford Union', Oxford Union via YouTube (2019).

'Martin Crowe: The serenity of Kane Williamson', *Cricinfo* (2015).

Ross Taylor: Black & White, with Paul Thomas, Mower (2022).

'In Search of Ross Taylor', *The Cricket Monthly* (2017).

'Martin Crowe: The story of Ross Taylor', *Cricinfo* (2013).

'This is Ross Taylor: The end of a long, thrilling innings', *Stuff* (2022).

Daniel Vettori: Turning Point, with Richard Boock, Hodder Moa (2008).

'Vettori's steady rise from gangly to googly', *New Zealand Herald* (2010).

'I had two cups of tea in my hands and they were shaking', *ESPNcricinfo* (2010).

'Time for Andy Moles to do the right thing', *Stuff* (2009).

'Latham strikes right balance between family life and international cricket', *Otago Daily Times* (2022).

'The Soggy Series Is Finally Over' [featuring Tom Latham], *The BYC* podcast (2002).

Out of the Park: The Craig McMillan Story, with Neil Reid, Hodder Moa (2008).

Shane Bond, Looking Back, with Dylan Cleaver, Hodder Moa (2010).

'Live and Let Fly: Shane Bond's unforgettable club season in Cumbria', *Cricbuzz* (2022).

Nathan Astle, with Phil Gifford, Hodder Moa (2007).

'It was the best I'd hit it. I never repeated it', *The Cricket Monthly* (2018).

'Seven ways to stay alive', *The Cricket Monthly* (2017).

ICC World Test Championship, Wikipedia.

'Yes, the Black Caps are the world champions, let that sink in', *New Zealand Herald* (2021).

'Move over WTC, the World Bad Behaviour Championship has a winner', *ESPNcricinfo* (2021).

'Kiwis do fly, to the top of the world', *Sydney Morning Herald* (2021).

'Martin's all geared up', *Western Leader* (2009).

'Martin Guptill released from NZC contract "effective immediately"', tvnz.co.nz (2022).

'Total recall', Dylan Cleaver, *Nightwatchman* Issue 26 (2019).

'Marty Two-Toes has his foot in the door', *New Zealand Herald* (2009).

Stephen Fleming: Balance of Power, with Richard Boock, Hodder Moa Beckett (2004).

New Zealand Test Cricket Captains, Matthew Appleby, Reed (2002).

Glenn Turner: Lifting the Covers, with Brian Turner, Longacre (1998).

'Should the Black Caps return to Pakistan? I survived the 2002 bombing — I wouldn't go back', *Stuff* (2018).

'An in-depth interview with Black Caps star Tim Southee', *New Zealand Herald* (2020).

'"I'd like to continue to play" — Tim Southee turns to James Anderson and Ross Taylor for inspiration', *ESPNcricinfo* (2020).

'Tim Southee, the support act who is front and centre of New Zealand's best-ever attack', *ESPNcricinfo* (2020).

'Southee opts for mid-air leg before cricket', *New Zealand Herald* (2011).

'Noticing Tim Southee', *Jarrod Kimber's Sports Almanac* (2021).

'Southee gets top marks from his cricket teacher', *Northern Advocate* (2008).

'Tim Southee's Secret' | Chatting Cricket with Laura McGoldrick, Sky Sport via YouTube (2021).

Tim Southee Feature, Spark Sport via YouTube (2022).

'Taniwha Tim', *New Zealand Rugby World* (2021).

'Homecoming for "fully converted Kiwi" Neil Wagner', *ESPNcricinfo* (2016).

'"Serious pain": How Black Cap Neil Wagner battled through pain to "bowl for mates"', *New Zealand Herald* (2020).

'Neil Wagner's in tune with New Zealand fans', *New Zealand Herald* (2018).

'Neil Wagner: The Ultramodernist' | Cricket Video Essay, Jarrod Kimber via YouTube (2020).

'Neil Wagner: From Pretoria to Mosgiel' | SKY TV, via YouTube (2017).

'BJ Watling: The "perfect test career"', *Between Two Beers* podcast (2021).

'Brendon McCullum — Touching Greatness', *Reel Tails with Sweens* podcast (2021).

'The Guy In The Glass', Peter Dale Wimbrow Sr (1934).

'BJ Watling's Final Test' | Tribute From Family & Teammates, NZC via YouTube (2021).

'Our BJ opens up', *Stuff* (2009).

'Black Caps wicket keeper BJ Watling calls time on career', *New Zealand Herald* (2021).

'Day to remember 378', *New Zealand Herald* (2008).

'Sir Richard Hadlee: Trent Boult, Tim Southee NZ's best bowling combo', *Stuff* (2015).

'Why isn't BJ Watling a bigger deal than he is?', *ESPNcricinfo* (2019).

'Not your typical macho fast bowler', *New Zealand Herald* (2015).

'How Packer's revolution changed cricket', *Inside the Games* (2017).

'Swing, smile, repeat: the secrets of Trent Boult's success', *The Cricket Monthly* (2021).

Ken Rutherford: A Hell of a Way to Make a Living, with Chris Mirams, Hodder Moa Beckett (1995).

'Howell family factor had influenced the likes of teenage Kane Williamson, Trent Boult', *Hawke's Bay Today* (2018).

'Atherton slams Vettori for late arrival', *Otago Daily Times* (2008).

'Notes from the Basin #2', *The Bounce* (2023).